MIND

A HISTORICAL AND PHILOSOPHICAL INTRODUCTION TO THE MAJOR THEORIES

MIND

A HISTORICAL AND PHILOSOPHICAL
INTRODUCTION TO THE MAJOR THEORIES

André Kukla

and

Joel Walmsley

Hackett Publishing Company, Inc.
Indianapolis/Cambridge

09 08 07 06   1 2 3 4 5 6 7

For further information, please address

Hackett Publishing Company, Inc.
P.O. Box 44937
Indianapolis, IN 46244-0937

www.hackettpublishing.com

Cover design by Brian Rak and Abigail Coyle
Text design by Elizabeth Wilson
Composition by Brighid Willson
Printed at Edwards Brothers, Inc.

Library of Congress Cataloging-in-Publication Data

Kukla, André, 1942–
   Mind : a historical and philosophical introduction to the major theories /
André Kukla and Joel Walmsley.
      p. cm.
   Includes bibliographical references and index.
   ISBN-13: 978-0-87220-832-2 (pbk.)
   ISBN-10: 0-87220-832-X (pbk.)
   ISBN-13: 978-0-87220-833-9 (cloth)
   ISBN-10: 0-87220-833-8 (cloth)
   1. Psychology—Philosophy—History. I. Walmsley, Joel. II. Title.
   BF38.K843 2006
   150—dc22
                                       2006007293

Contents

Preface

This book is intended to be an introduction to the science of psychology for the nonspecialist who isn't afraid to do a little thinking. Readers with a prior introduction to psychology will note substantial differences between our book and the usual introductory volume. The differences have mostly to do with the roles played by empirical research and theoretical development. The usual introductory books mainly focus on accounts of experiments and the data they generate. Theories also get some attention; but the resolution of theoretical issues is treated as ancillary to the main business of science, which is gathering data. The ancillary functions most often mentioned are (1) providing succinct and convenient summaries of established data, and (2) instigating further empirical research. In fact, the authors of the usual introductions must regard theoretical engagement as wholly dispensable, for their books include generous servings of data that have no bearing on any theoretical issues. An experiment need only be cleverly designed or make for an entertaining narrative in order to qualify for inclusion. The view that theories are merely ancillary or perhaps altogether dispensable also explains the usual introductions' blandly ecumenical "theory-appreciation" approach to theoretical disagreements: it's an indication of the low regard in which theories are held that their differences don't even need to be resolved.

In contrast, we think that arriving at good theories is what science is all about. Theories aren't merely summaries of data or instigators of further research—they're our best guesses, all things considered, as to the underlying principles according to which the world runs. It seems obvious to us that the best way to introduce psychology to the novice is to evaluate psychologists' most influential guesses as to the underlying principles of the mind. Consequently, our introductory book concerns itself mainly with theoretical ideas. Data also get some play, but only insofar as they help to resolve a theoretical issue. We believe that data-gathering activities that have no bearing on any theoretical issues are of little or no scientific value.

In brief, we put ourselves forward as the *rationalist* counterbalance to the hegemony of *empiricism* among authors of introductions to psychology. If there's one thing that empiricists want the nonspecialist to know about psychology, it's something of the data that have been uncovered by empirical research. If there's one thing *we* think the nonspecialist should know about psychology, it's the answers, however tentative they might be, to the deepest theoretical questions that have been asked. The different books resulting from these divergent predilections are snapshots of the same scene taken from different angles. Whichever angle is ultimately judged to be the best one from which to introduce psychology, it's nice to have samples of both.

As mentioned above, we wrote this book for the intelligent nonspecialist. We think it would also be suitable as a primary text for courses in Systems and Theories of Psychology, Personality Theory, Theories of Human Nature, or Philosophical Psychology, when the instructor wants a short treatise that can be supplemented by lots of readings from primary sources. Ultimately, we'd like to see the book adopted as a primary text for Introduction to Psychology courses, but that would require more of a sea change than we can reasonably expect.

1. Cartesianism

1.1. Dualism and Materialism

The word "psychology" is derived from the Greek for mind (*psyche*) and speech or reason (*logos*). An introduction to the major theories of mind therefore qualifies as a theoretically based introduction to psychology. It isn't so easy, however, to say what is meant by "mind." As we will see, different theoretical traditions in psychology have operated with different conceptions of the mental. These differences have sometimes been profound. The definition that we're about to give is the one with which psychology—or at least the part of psychology that's covered in this book—begins.

Our story begins with the seventeenth-century philosopher René Descartes. (*Cartesianism*—the title of this chapter—refers to Descartes' system of philosophy and psychology.) For Descartes, the mind is an immaterial entity that functions as the repository of a person's conscious experiences. Conscious experiences, in turn, are best defined by enumeration: they include, but are not necessarily restricted to, one's thoughts, perceptions, feelings, mental images, desires, and intentions. The mind's immateriality entails that it can't be identified with the physical body or any portion thereof. Cartesians regard persons as amalgams of two substances: material bodies and immaterial minds. For this reason, their view is said to be a type of *dualism*. According to dualists, the mind isn't the same thing as the brain. The latter is undoubtedly a material object. You can weigh the brain, measure its length, and kick it around like a football; but you can't weigh or measure or give somebody a kick in the mind.

Let's clarify the relationship between dualism and Cartesianism. Dualism is one of the tenets of Cartesianism, but it isn't the only one.

Moreover, there are dualists who aren't Cartesians. For instance, most of the major religions of the world are dualistic, at least in their popular forms. This is evidenced in some cases by the belief in an afterlife in Heaven or Hell, in other cases by the belief in reincarnation. Both these beliefs are based on the assumption that there's some portion of the person—enough of a portion, in fact, to carry one's personal identity—that manages to survive the dissolution of all the physical parts. Such a portion would ipso facto be immaterial. Thus, orthodox Muslims are dualists, but they certainly aren't Cartesians. Among religious dualists, the immaterial portion of a person is often called that person's soul. In essence, a mind is the same thing as a soul, without the added implication of immortality. Secular dualists sometimes believe that the mind is *produced* by the brain. Unlike the soul, it can't exist independently of this material object. But it isn't *identical* to the brain. The mind still belongs to a separate, immaterial realm.

The main philosophical opponent of dualism is *materialism*. In the present context, a materialist is not someone who values material goods over immaterial rewards. When we speak of materialism, we mean the view that the only things that exist are material goods. The most important consequence of this philosophical doctrine is that we human beings, like everything else, are physical objects; no different in essence from stones or puddles of water. Persons differ from puddles and stones only in the complexity of their structure: we're made up an enormous number of tiny parts that are connected in bafflingly complicated ways. In principle, we could predict a person's behavior from the laws of physics, just as we can calculate the path that a stone will follow if thrown with a particular force. This isn't possible in practice only because the greater complexity of living organisms makes the required calculations too laborious to complete, even with the aid of our best computers. So we need the rough-and-ready laws of psychology as a stopgap measure to make up our current inability to calculate the exact behavioral "path" a person will follow from the laws of physics.

Most (although not all) dualists take a very different view of the genesis of human behavior. Believing that human beings are not entirely physical, they conclude that human activity is not fully determined by the laws of physics. Their view is that people have *free will*: within limits, the path that humans take is determined by what they freely choose to do. The laws of physics still apply to people: if you drop a person out of an airplane without a parachute, he'll fall at exactly the rate prescribed by physics. There are limits to freedom of the will! But at least the laws of physics can't prescribe what a person will do down to the last detail—because a person, unlike a stone, can freely choose to do any of a number of things.

It's our impression that some people are naturally inclined toward the dualist philosophy, and others toward materialism: as soon as they understand the options, either materialism or dualism strikes them as obviously true; the other as absurd. It's important for both sides to remember that these questions have been debated for literally thousands of years, and that there have been rational and intelligent people on both sides. So, although the "right" answer may seem obvious at first glance, the issue is actually very complex.

The cases for dualism and materialism will be assessed in due course. It might be useful, however, to say a few words now to render each view at least minimally plausible to partisans of the other perspective. If you are against materialism, you claim that human beings don't fit into the broad and unified picture of the world that is painted by contemporary scientific research. According to this picture, everything in the universe is made out of the swarm of fundamental particles precipitated by the Big Bang. There's no known way to integrate the appearance of immaterial minds with this account. This may not count for much among the conventionally religious, but it's an embarrassment for those whose primary cognitive allegiance is to modern science.

The hope for immortality is sufficient to account for the lure of dualism among the conventionally religious, but secular dualists who deny that the mind can exist without the brain must base their opinion on more coldly rational considerations. What is it that impels them to posit immaterial minds, even though this forces them to the uncongenial conclusion that our scientific picture of the world is drastically off base? Well, consider the following thought experiment. Suppose that somebody is looking up at a cloudless sky and all she sees is blue. Now, without disturbing her experience, open up her skull and examine her brain. You'll find nothing anywhere in the brain that's blue. So where is the blue experience located? Dualists say that the fact that there is no blue region in space that corresponds to the blue experience shows that the experience isn't in space at all. Material entities, however, all have locations in space. Therefore the blue experience is immaterial. Materialists think that they can deal

with this question as well (usually by arguing that the question is illegitimate in some way) but at least materialists ought to be able to see
where secular dualists might be coming from.

Actually, we've been discussing two different issues as though they
were one and the same. One issue concerns the *composition* of a person—whether a person is just an intricate type of physical object, or
something more. These compositional hypotheses are what the terms
"materialism" and "dualism" strictly refer to. The problem of deciding
between materialism and dualism (as well as some other, more exotic
compositional hypotheses) is the *mind-body problem*. The second issue
has to do with the laws governing the sequence of events in the world.
Here the contrast is between *determinism* and *voluntarism*. Determinism
is the view that scientific laws can, in principle, predict everything that
happens in the world, human behavior included. Voluntarism is the
view that people—and perhaps some other organisms—have free will,
so that some aspects of their behavior are unpredictable, even in principle. Later on, we'll see that some theorists maintain that determinism and voluntarism are not incompatible but most of the discussion
of this topic presupposes that it's an either–or choice.

Dualism and voluntarism were welded together in the history of
ideas by Descartes (1641/1984). They're the chief features (but not the
only features) of the doctrine that goes by the name of Cartesianism.
Descartes gave the definitive formulation of a view of human nature
that was so influential that it became the common sense of the next
few hundred years. It's still the view of most people today. It's the picture of people as immaterial minds inhabiting a material body (that's
the dualism part), and driving the body around like a car (that's the
voluntarism part). Interestingly, Descartes believed that this picture
applied only to human beings. Other living organisms were entirely
material and their actions were totally determined by physical law.
Their behavior was due to the pressure of physical stimuli causing various levers and springs and pipes filled with fluids to activate the muscles in ways that were in principle predictable from the laws of
physics. Here's how he put it:

> I know that animals do many things better than we do, but
> this does not surprise me. It can even be used to prove that
> they act naturally and mechanically, like a clock which tells
> the time better than our judgment does. Doubtless when the

swallows come in the spring, they operate like clocks. The actions of honeybees are of the same nature; so also is the discipline of cranes in flight, and of apes in fighting, if it is true that they keep discipline. Their instinct to bury their dead is no stranger than that of dogs and cats which scratch the earth for the purpose of burying their excrement; they hardly ever actually bury it, which shows that they act only by instinct and without thinking. The most one say is that though the animals do not perform any action which shows us that they think, still, since the organs of their bodies are not very different from ours, it may be conjectured that there is attached to these organs some thought such as we experience in ourselves, but of a very much less perfect kind. To this I have nothing to reply except that if they thought as we do, they would have an immortal soul like us. This is unlikely, because there is no reason to believe it of some animals without believing it of all, and many of them such as oysters and sponges are too imperfect for this to be credible. (Cottingham, Stoothoff, Murdoch, and Kenny 1991, 302–4)

The reader might find some amusement in the game of locating weak spots in this argument. We'll mention one just to get the game started: Descartes has his facts on animal behavior wrong. Cats don't usually fail in their attempts to bury their excrement, and dogs don't even try to bury their excrement. These factual mistakes alone don't greatly alter the persuasiveness of the argument, but they do suggest that Descartes' opinion on this subject wasn't based on a close observation of nature.

The opposite of Cartesianism would be a theory that espouses materialism as opposed to dualism, and determinism as opposed to voluntarism. There is no shortage of psychological theories of this type in the twentieth century. Among those to be discussed, the clearest example is the behavioral psychology of B. F. Skinner. Skinnerians extend Descartes' theory of animal nature to human nature: people, like animals, are conceived to be predictable physical mechanisms. A corollary of this view is that animals differ from us only in degree, not in kind. It isn't surprising, then, that it's behavioral psychologists who introduced and largely relied on the notorious rat-in-a-maze technique for advancing our understanding of human nature.

Descartes was a voluntaristic dualist, and Skinner was a deterministic materialist. What about the other two possibilities—deterministic dualism and voluntaristic materialism? Well, another theory we're going to discuss is Freud's psychoanalytic theory. Freud is an example of a deterministic dualist. His view was that mental states are not identical to physical states, but that they're still entirely predictable on the basis of nonphysical laws of the mind. He called his position *psychic determinism*. (A word of warning about the term "psychic": you'll encounter this word again and again if you read Freud in English translation. In Freud's writings, this word is always used as a synonym for "mental" or "psychological." It never has anything to do with the occult. In fact, Freud had an extreme aversion to occultism.)

So we have examples of three of the four possible combinations of materialism/dualism and determinism/voluntarism. There are no important psychologists of the fourth, voluntarist-materialist type. However, some have speculated that the laws of quantum mechanics allow for free will in a purely material world. This proposal will be discussed in section 1.3.

This is as good a place as any to make the point that dualism isn't the only alternative to materialism. We mentioned that dualism gets its name by virtue of the fact that it posits the existence of two kinds of substances—the physical and the mental. Materialism is said to be a type of *monism* by virtue of the fact that it posits the existence of only one of the dualist's two substances—the physical. There is, of course, another possible type of monism—the one that posits the existence of only the mental. This alternative monism goes by the name of "idealism," and its most eminent proponent is the eighteenth-century philosopher, Bishop George Berkeley (pronounced "Barkley"). Berkeley argued that the only information that's available to us is through certain sensory (as well as other sorts of) experiences. Thus when we speak of tables and chairs, we can only be referring to bundles of sensations—certain looks and feels that tend to come together. What Berkeley and other idealists deny is that our sensations are caused by independently existing physical objects. Samuel Johnson, a contemporary of Berkeley's, reacted to the latter's philosophy by kicking a stone and saying "I refute it thus!" This was an ineffectual refutation. Berkeley could simply have said that the sensation of solidity that Johnson experienced was an ingredient in the bundle of sensations that we call a "stone."

There's a third type of monism—*neutral monism*—according to which the one and only type of substance in the world is neither physical nor mental. It's something more basic than either. According to neutral monists, the physical and the mental are merely two aspects of this fundamental stuff, or perhaps two different ways of talking about it. The late-nineteenth-century American philosopher and psychologist William James was a neutral monist.

Idealism and neutral monism are interesting compositional hypotheses. Both have their problems; but, as we will see, so do dualism and materialism. Some of the traditional psychological systems of Asia are probably best interpreted as idealistic. In the history of scientific psychology, however, idealistic and neutral-monistic themes have rarely come into play. The contest has been almost entirely between materialists and dualists. This may have been a mistake, but there it is.

1.2. Three Arguments Against Dualism

There are several standard arguments that purport to show that dualism is false. The first is that dualism conflicts with the most fundamental laws of science. In section 1.1, we mentioned that a major motivation for materialism comes from the fact that immaterial substances don't fit into the modern scientific picture of the world. From the perspective of modern science, the assumption that immaterial substances exist would be a tacked-on hypothesis that had no organic connection to any well-established theories. The argument in *this* section makes the stronger claim that dualism is actually *incompatible* with modern science. It claims to show that if you accept modern science, then you can't also endorse dualism without contradicting yourself.

The scientific principles at issue are the conservation laws of physics. According to the law of the conservation of energy, the total quantity of motion in the universe can neither be diminished nor increased. If something slows down, something else has to speed up by a corresponding amount, and vice versa (think of colliding billiard balls). Getting up from the chair in which you've been sitting constitutes an increase in the motion of your body. The law of the conservation of energy stipulates that this increase must be accompanied by a decrease in energy somewhere in the universe. For example, you might be knocked out of your chair by a collision with a flying condor. In this case, the increase in your motion would be matched by the decrease in the condor's motion. In the case where you simply get up of your own accord, the compensatory decrease in motion is presumably suffered by microevents within your body. But dualists tell us that getting up can be caused by an act of immaterial will. If they're right, then the increase in your body's motion sometimes represents a net increase in the total quantity of motion in the world. If this were ever to take place, we would have to conclude that the law of the conservation of energy is false.

Actually, Descartes was aware of this problem and offered a solution. He conceded that our immaterial minds couldn't cause an increase or a decrease in total motion. However, we could—by an act of will—alter the direction of preexisting motion. On this account, you manage to will yourself out of your chair by converting the energy of selected microevents within your body into the requisite gross bodily movement. Your act of will produces both the increase in bodily movement and the compensatory decrease in the energy of the microevents. The result is new motion without violating energy conservation. What was not clearly understood in Descartes' time, however, was that there's another fundamental law of physics—the law of the conservation of momentum—according to which the total quantity of motion in any *direction* must also remain constant. So no matter how you slice it, there's no room in modern physics for immaterial causes of material events.

This argument is something for dualists to worry about, but it isn't conclusive for two reasons. First, the incompatibility of dualism and the conservation laws entails that they can't both be true. We must repudiate at least one of them, on pain of contradicting ourselves, but the argument doesn't dictate which one we have to give up. It's logically feasible for a dualist to accept the foregoing argument, and to conclude that the conservation laws are false. This would be an extreme measure, however, as the conservation laws are probably the most firmly believed principles in all of science.

The second escape route for dualists is the one that most historical dualists have taken. Even if we continue to accept the conservation laws, the conclusion of the incompatibility argument isn't that there is no immaterial mind—it's just that you can't have an immaterial mind causing behavior. Actually, there are several dualist points of view on the causal relations between mind and body. *Interactionism* is the dualist view that mental events can cause physical events, and that physical events can cause mental events. An example of a mental event causing a physical event is you willing yourself to get up from your chair causing your getting up from your chair. An example of a physical event causing a mental event is your retina being bombarded by electromagnetic radiation of a certain frequency causing you to have the visual experience of blue. Interactionism is Descartes' brand of dualism. It's also the doctrine that gets into trouble with physics.

But consider the alternative form for dualism that goes by the name of *epiphenomenalism*. Epiphenomenalists agree with interactionists that physical events can cause mental events but they deny that mental events can cause physical events. In this view, your impression that you will yourself out of your chair is an illusion. In reality, both your act of will and your physical movement are simultaneously caused by another physical event (perhaps a neural event). According to epiphenomenalists, our consciousness is a bystander in the spectacle of life, a witness to events that it's powerless to affect. The renowned nineteenth-century biologist T. H. Huxley was an epiphenomenalist:

> The consciousness of brutes would appear to be related to the mechanism of their body simply as a collateral product of its working, and to be completely without any power of modifying that working, as the steam-whistle which accompanies the work of a locomotive engine is without influence upon its machinery. Their volition, if they have any, is an emotion *indicative* of physical changes, not a *cause* of such changes. . . . to the best of my judgment, the argumentation which applies to brutes holds equally good of men. . . . We are conscious automata. (Quoted in James 1890, 131)

To revert to an earlier metaphor, we're not the drivers of the car—we're just passengers. Why would anybody adopt such a peculiar view? To avoid the conflict with physics! Since this type of dualism denies that mental events can cause behavior, the conservation laws aren't violated by it.

The second argument against dualism is based on the idea that there can't be a causal connection between material and immaterial events. The paradigmatic case of one event causing another is to be found, once again, in the interplay of billiard balls. Billiard ball 1 causes the previously stationary billiard ball 2 to move by coming into contact with it and imparting some of its own (ball 1's) motion. It's been argued that this contact between two surfaces is a universally necessary feature of all cause-and-effect relations. When an event appears to have an effect at a distance from itself, closer analysis and observation reveals that the effect is transmitted through the intervening space by a chain of contacting elements that happen to be difficult or perhaps impossible for human beings to observe directly. This is presumably what happens when you hear the sound of a drum. To the naked eye, it looks as though the striking of the drum has an effect at a distance from itself: the drum is struck *there,* and the auditory experience that occurs as a result of this striking takes place *here.* However, it's well verified that this effect is carried by a succession of intermediate events, each of which involves a contact between surfaces. The vibration of the drum causes the molecules of air that come into contact with the drum to vibrate; these vibrating molecules impinge on slightly more distant molecules and causes them to vibrate; and so on. The gap from *there* to *here* is bridged when the air molecules inside your ear come into contact with your eardrum, causing it to start vibrating. You can easily confirm this phenomenon by placing a ringing alarm clock in a bell jar and pumping the air out of the jar: the alarm clock becomes inaudible. If the clock is the old-fashioned kind with a bell on top, you can see that the bell is still vibrating; but now that there are no air molecules in contact with it, there is nothing to carry the movement from there to here. Contrary to the vast majority of science fiction movies, spaceships that explode in the vacuum of outer space don't make a peep.

What does all this have to do with dualism? Well, if it's true that causality always involves a contact between two surfaces, then the only thing that can be causally related to a physical state of affairs is another physical state of affairs. This is because immaterial mental states have no surfaces. The very concept of a surface applies only to material objects. This is an argument against both epiphenomenalism and interactionism. It's true that epiphenomenalists deny that mental events can cause physical events, but they still posit a causal connection between the physical and the mental. According to epiphenomenalism, physical causes can have mental effects. If causality requires contact, however, then there can be no causal relationship between physical events and mental events in either direction.

Let's look at this argument more closely. Consider once again what happens when you hear a drumbeat. In the previous paragraph, we traced a series of effects that were carried from drum head to eardrum by successive contacts between surfaces. Of course, the vibration of your eardrum doesn't yet constitute your hearing the drum (most deaf people have intact, properly vibrating eardrums). The motion of the eardrum is further transmitted to various physical structures inside the head, eventually issuing in complex and poorly understood neurological events in the brain. Though it may be poorly understood, this part of the story poses no difficulty in principle to the thesis that causal effects are transmitted by contact. However, the effect on the brain isn't the end of the story, at least not for dualists. According to dualism, the experience of hearing the drum is a nonphysical event. Thus it can't be equated with any state of the brain. There has to be one more step in the account of what happens when you hear a drum: the last neurological event in the chain has to be converted into an immaterial auditory experience. Interactionists and epiphenomenalists both want to say that the last neurological event *causes* the immaterial auditory experience to take place. But if causality always involves contact, this is impossible.

Interactionists and epiphenomenalists have two replies. First, they may deny that causality requires contact. Even if it's true that causality in our *physical* theories always involves contact, it isn't obvious why this universal feature of physical theories should be turned into a requirement for all causal theories of any kind. In fact, the assumption that causality requires contact comes very close to simply assuming that epiphenomenalism and interactionism are wrong. It's supposed to be an argument *showing* that epiphenomenalism and interactionism are wrong. To assume the truth of what you purport to prove is to commit the logical sin of begging the question. (What's wrong with begging the question is, obviously, that you can prove *anything* if you're allowed to assume it.) Thus the assumption that causality requires contact is illegitimate in the debate between materialists and interactionists/epiphenomenalists.

Moreover, it isn't even true that causality has involved contact in all respectable physical theories. Some scientists and philosophers have promulgated the "no causation without contact" principle but by no means has it commanded universal assent. There have been scientific theories that posit "action to a distance," which is another term for causation without contact. The most famous case is Newton's gravitational theory. According to Newton's theory, the moon's gravitational force causes the tides on the earth. But the surfaces of the moon and the earth don't touch, nor does Newton postulate any intermediate physical events that carry the gravitational influence from the moon to the earth. If physicists can dispense with the principle that causality requires contact, then so can dualists.

The second dualist reply to the argument from causality is that there's a third type of dualism—*parallelism*—for which the issue doesn't even arise. Like all dualists, parallelists suppose that mental events can't be identified with any physical events. But unlike interactionists and epiphenomenalists, they claim that there are no causal connections in either direction between physical and mental events: your acts of will don't cause your body to move, and none of your brain states is responsible for your hearing the sound of a drum. Physical events can only cause or be caused by other physical events, and mental events can only cause or be caused by other mental events. The two types of events thus comprise two sequences of happenings that run alongside each other, without ever influencing each other.

Parallelism is immune to the problems of both the argument from the conservation laws of physics and the no-surfaces argument. But it's heir to a difficulty of a new kind. The problem for parallelism is to account for the frequent *harmony* that's exhibited by the two supposedly causally unrelated sequences of events. If there are no causal connections between the two chains, how do we explain the fact that our mental decisions to have a cup of coffee are so often followed by the physical behavior of having a cup of coffee? Interactionists have a simple explanation: other things being equal, the decision to have a cup of coffee *causes* the having of a cup of coffee. Epiphenomenalists can't avail themselves of this straightforward account, but they still have a coherent story to tell. They can say that the decision to have a cup of coffee and the having of a cup of coffee are both the effects of another physical event. Neither of these explanations is available to parallelists, since they deny that there can be any causal connection between the physical and the mental. Then what keeps the two series of events—our mental decisions and our behavior—coordinated, or parallel? The same question can be asked of the coordination between sensory experiences, such as hearing a drumbeat, and their putative physical causes, such as the beating of a drum. The only answer ever proposed is that God maintains the parallelism between the two independent sequences. Even among theists, this answer stands accused of merely trading one mystery for another of equal proportion. The new mystery is this: why does God choose to play this peculiar game?

The third argument against dualism applies to all three forms—interactionism, epiphenomenalism, and parallelism—equally. It's that materialism is a *simpler* theory than dualism. Before presenting the argument, we need to say a few general words about theoretical simplicity. It's a basic principle of scientific method that when choosing between two rival theories that are otherwise equally good, we should prefer the simpler one. This methodological rule goes back at least to the Middle Ages, when William of Ockham formulated what came to be known as *Ockham's razor:* in trying to explain a phenomenon, we should not multiply entities beyond necessity. Suppose, for example that a theory—call it T1—explains a set of data by postulating the existence of six different kinds of subatomic particles, and that a rival theory—T2—explains the same data just as well by positing three kind of particles. Then, according to Ockham's razor, we should prefer T2. Similar considerations apply to the number of laws that comprise the competing theories: all other factors being equal, a theory that explains the data with two laws is better than a theory that explains the same data with twelve laws.

What if T1 posits fewer entities but more laws than T2? In that case, it isn't immediately obvious which is the simpler theory. There have been many attempts to formulate rules of simplicity that are more precise than Ockham's very general advice. None of these has as yet been successful. In practice, the simplicity judgments of scientists who work in the same field usually agree. But their judgments are purely intuitive. To call them "intuitive" is to say that they're not obtained by the conscious application of any explicit rules. It doesn't rule out the possibility that simplicity judgments are obtained by the *un*conscious application of *implicit* rules, in which case we may hope that these rules will be discovered by future researchers. For the time being, however, there is no substitute available for the exercise of scientific intuition. This may come as a surprise to those who suppose that the scientific method is a collection of explicit procedures that tell us precisely what conclusion to draw in any circumstance. Judging the relative simplicity of competing theories is only one of many essential scientific tasks that are based on scientific intuition.

The preference for simplicity has directed scientists' theoretical choices for centuries. Indeed, the most important episode in the history of science—the Copernican revolution—is mainly a story about simplicity considerations. Until the sixteenth century, it was almost universally believed that the sun, as well as the planets, revolves about the earth. This hypothesis seemed to be corroborated by direct observation: we can actually see the sun rising in the east, traveling across the sky, and setting in the west. In the first major conflict between science and the received views of common sense, Copernicus proposed that the earth, as well as the other planets, revolves and rotates about the sun. This hypothesis accounts for the apparent motion of the sun as well as the received view does. Why did Copernicus' view prevail? It might be supposed that the Copernican hypothesis provided more correct predictions of the positions of the other planets but in fact, the pre-Copernican system provided about as good a fit with astronomical observation as the Copernican system. The Copernican hypothesis didn't improve the accuracy of astronomical predictions because Copernicus erroneously assumed that the orbits of the planets around the sun are circular (a century after Copernicus, Johannes Kepler discovered that the orbits are elliptical). But in order to perform as well empirically as the Copernican theory, the pre-Copernican theory had to postulate that the planets revolve about the earth in complex orbits called "epicycles"—essentially circles within circles within circles. The fact remained, however, that Copernicus' system offered no empirical advantage over its predecessor. So why did it win? Because circles are simpler than epicycles.

In psychology, we'll see that the preference for simple theories accounts for much of the attraction of behavioral psychology. Psychoanalysis, its main rival in the early decades of the twentieth century, was one of the most complex psychological theories ever devised. In contrast, behavioral psychology promised to explain all behavior with just three concepts—stimulus, response, and reinforcement—and two laws—the laws of classical and instrumental conditioning.

Why should we prefer simple theories over complicated ones? This methodological rule seems to be based on the presupposition that the universe is a simple place that operates on simple principles. But why should we believe that? Might it not be the case that the universe operates on enormously complex principles? Perhaps there are no universal principles at all, but only approximately true laws that are riddled with exceptions. The status of simplicity considerations is a deep and difficult issue in the philosophy of science. For the purposes of this discussion, we'll take it as a given that that's how scientists make theoretical choices.

Back to dualism and materialism. The argument from simplicity is that Ockham's razor tells us to prefer materialism. Materialism posits the existence of one kind of stuff in the universe, whereas dualism posits the existence of two kinds of stuff. Therefore, if the two theories are otherwise equally good, we should be materialists. Of course, the two theories may not otherwise be equally good but the burden is on dualists to specify an advantage that's purchased by the greater complexity of their hypothesis. If it's a tie—if, for example, neither side can point to an advantage—then Ockham's razor declares materialism to be the winner.

In light of all these arguments, the final word on dualism is that it suffers from severe problems, but that none of its ills is terminal. Dualists might even be able to save their thesis from the simplicity argument by showing that dualist theories are in other ways better than materialist theories, so that you get something in return for the extra complexity. This hasn't happened yet, however. In fact, we'll see that the most recent theories of psychology tend to be agnostic with respect to the dualism-versus-materialism issue—they work just as well with either assumption. The result is that most contemporary psychologists have opted for materialism on the grounds of simplicity. But dualism is by no means dead. In fact, it made a bit of a comeback in the 1990s (Chalmers 1996; Foster 1991).

Finally, it shouldn't be forgotten that a refutation of dualism isn't automatically a proof of materialism. Materialism has other rivals, such as idealism and neutral monism, the plausibility of which is unaffected by the rejection of dualism.

1.3. Voluntarism and Determinism

The other major limb of Cartesianism is *voluntarism*. You won't be surprised to learn that there's no universally acknowledged winner in the free-will-versus-determinism debate either. Nevertheless, it's instructive to go over the main arguments in the field. The fact that they don't provide us with a definitive answer doesn't mean that their study has no intellectual value. Knowing where a particular consideration falls short in proving its point is itself a species of knowledge.

The main argument against determinism is that it seems to be incompatible with some of our most basic beliefs about morality and rationality. Let's talk about morality first. Suppose that someone ties strings to various locations on your arms and legs, and controls your movements like a puppeteer. Suppose then that, by pulling on the appropriate strings, he causes you to pick up a loaded gun and shoot someone. Under these circumstances, no one would say that you've committed a blameworthy or criminal act. The reason, of course, is that your movements were compelled by causal necessity—you couldn't have done otherwise. But determinism is the doctrine that *every* movement is compelled by causal necessity—that no one can *ever* behave otherwise than how she in fact behaves. If this doctrine is true, it seems that we can never hold anyone responsible, whether morally or legally, for any of her actions. One might as well heap blame (or praise) on the moon for illuminating the night sky.

There are two traditional determinist responses to this problem, both of which are problematic. The first is to affirm that every action is caused, but also to maintain that some caused actions may nevertheless qualify as voluntary. It all depends on the nature of the cause. In the case where someone literally pulls your strings, the movements produced aren't necessarily the ones you *want* to produce. In fact, you may be horrified to observe yourself picking up the gun, aiming it, and pulling the trigger. Compare the very different case in which the cause of the same movements is your intention to kill the target person. There's no reason why a determinist shouldn't concede that a person's own intentions and preferences can be the cause of that person's actions. But isn't doing what we intend to do the essence of acting freely? The proposal is that actions that are caused by the actor's own intentions qualify as being voluntary, and therefore as candidates for praise or blame. Actions that are caused by anything else are involuntary. This view is called *compatibilism,* since it maintains that a thoroughgoing determinism is compatible with voluntarism.

The weakness of compatibilism is easy to see. If determinism is true, then our intentions also have causes. Perhaps intentions are best thought of as caused by neurophysiological events, perhaps by sociocultural factors. Either way, our intentions are caused by something other than further intentions. Therefore, by the compatibilist's own principle, people aren't responsible for having the intentions that they have. Our intentions are foisted on us "from the outside" just as surely as the movements produced by tugging strings. But if people aren't responsible for their intentions, it seems exceedingly strange to hold them responsible for the behavioral effects of these intentions. Imagine that a pill is developed, the ingestion of which invariably causes the person to shoot someone. This pill in effect plays the same causal role as the tugging of strings in our earlier example. Imagine also that a *second* pill is developed, the ingestion of which invariably causes the person to *intend* to shoot someone. Compatibilists are committed to saying that someone who ingests the second pill is responsible for firing the gun, while someone who ingests the first pill isn't. However, it seems compelling to say that people who take either pill are in the same moral and legal boat.

The second determinist response to the incompatibility of determinism and our ideas about morality is to jettison our ideas about morality. B. F. Skinner exemplifies this position in his transparently titled book, *Beyond Freedom and Dignity* (1971). Skinner regards such concepts as freedom and responsibility as relics of a prescientific mode of thinking that should be abandoned completely. This is more easily said than done. For example, what can a Skinnerian mean by saying that our ideas about freedom "should" be abandoned? Doesn't the claim that something should be done entail that we have a choice in the matter—we choose rightly if we do it and wrongly if we don't— and that we're therefore responsible for getting it right? We don't, after all, complain that a planet should have been some place other than it was. If there's no freedom, then either we will be caused to give up the concept of freedom or we won't. There's no "should" about it.

Skinner tacitly and illegitimately relies on the notion of free will on more than one occasion. A prime example can be found in his views on the efficacy of behavioral engineering (1971, 142–43). Skinner maintains that behavior is fully determined by the organism's "reinforcement history"; i.e., the pattern of rewards and punishments that's been experienced in conjunction with past behaviors. He notes that the reinforcement contingencies that shape behavior are largely haphazard and uncontrolled. So it's largely a matter of luck whether one is rewarded for prosocial and constructive behavior, or for antisocial and destructive behavior. The situation could be greatly improved, Skinner says, if society were organized by behavioral scientists who understood the principles of reinforcement theory—they could set things up to assure that only desirable behavior is rewarded.

How can this work? The behavioral engineers' setting up of reinforcement contingencies is itself a species of behavior. Thus, according to Skinner's own theory, the way that the behavioral engineers will set things up will depend on *their* reinforcement histories. Now there are two possibilities: either (1) the engineers' reinforcement histories were guided by a prior generation of behavioral engineers, or (2) they were shaped by the haphazard contingencies of the unengineered world. If (2) is the case, then there's no reason to expect any benefit from behavioral engineering: the haphazard contingencies of the unengineered world still determine the course of behavior at one remove. If (1) is the case, then we must ask what determines the behavior of the prior generation of engineers—a still earlier generation of engineers, or haphazard contingencies. Eventually we must arrive at the first generation of engineers, and their behavior must by default be shaped by haphazard contingencies. This haphazardness of reinforcement history would then be inherited by each successive generation of engineers, and from the current generation to the population at large. Therefore there's no reason to expect that behavioral engineering can be of any benefit. The initial plausibility of the proposal depends on thinking of the engineers as making free and judicious choices of how to set up the reinforcement contingencies.

In fact, isn't the whole enterprise of rationality undone by determinism? Very roughly, to be rational is to hold the beliefs that we *should* hold, given the evidence that's available to us. But if everything is determined, then so are our beliefs. We'll believe that the earth is round if a sufficient cause of believing that the earth is round acts on us; and if the cause is absent, we *won't* believe it. As in the case of morality, there's no place for "shoulds" in this account. Skinner tries to bite the bullet on this point, confessing that his belief that all behavior is caused by the organism's reinforcement history is itself caused by *his own* reinforcement history (Skinner 1964, 99). But if this is so, then there's no reason to heed his opinion.

Determinists have sometimes tried to overcome this difficulty by claiming that a belief can be both caused and rational at the same time (this is another sort of compatibilism). The reason given is that the *cause* of believing a particular proposition may be identical to the *rational grounds* for believing it. For example, the cause of your believing that the earth is round may be the event of encountering good evidence that the earth is round, such as photographs of the planet taken from outer space. When this happens, let's say that a proposition is *rationally caused*. When a proposition is rationally caused, we have the good fortune of being caused to believe what we *should*, on rational grounds, believe anyway. But this confluence could only be a stroke of luck. In principle, the belief that the earth is round could be caused by the ingestion of cranberries, or by encountering evidence that would warrant believing that the earth is flat. Moreover, if determinism is true, then there seems to be no way that we could be rationally persuaded that there are rationally caused beliefs. Coming to believe that there are rationally caused beliefs is itself going to be the result of a causal process. So we would need to assume that *that* belief—the belief that there are rationally caused beliefs—is rationally caused. But this is to assume precisely what we set out to show. Determinism seems to entail that there can be no rational grounds for adopting any beliefs, including the belief in determinism that got us into this mess in the first place.

So, does voluntarism win? Unfortunately, voluntarism faces difficulties of the same proportions. Voluntarists say that there are some events in the world that are irremediably unpredictable. Modern physics says the same thing. According to quantum mechanics, there are events in the physical world that cannot be predicted. Moreover, this unpredictability can't be remedied by any amount of additional information or computational power. Quantum indeterminacy is built into the very fabric of the universe. For example, there are pairs of subatomic events, A and B, such that each occurs with a probability of 50%; but the sequence in which they occur (e.g., BABBBAA . . .) is entirely random.

Quantum mechanics shows that determinism isn't a necessary presupposition of science. On the face of it, it also seems to be a powerful argument for the plausibility of voluntarism. Indeed, as mentioned in section 1.1, some have speculated that the laws of quantum mechanics allow for free will even in a purely material world. But quantum randomness doesn't seem to capture our idea of free will any better than determinism does. A random process can be thought of as governed by the flip of a coin: if it's heads A happens, and if it's tails B happens. But it makes no sense to hold people responsible for their actions if these actions are governed by the flip of a coin! By the same token, our beliefs can't be rational if they're adopted in accordance to the dictates of a coin flip. What's missing from randomness is the connection between the choices made by a freely willing agent and the personal characteristics of the agent—e.g., her interests or her prior beliefs. However, if there is a discoverable connection between choices and personal characteristics, then the personal characteristics can be thought of as causes of the choices, and then the choices are no longer free. The problem for voluntarism is that neither determinism nor randomness provides an adequate model of freely willed behavior. Until voluntarists are able to construct a third type of pattern among events that does the job, it won't have been shown that the term "free will" has any coherent meaning.

So, our ideas about morality and rationality face a dilemma. On the one hand, there seems to be no place for them in either a deterministic or a quantum-style probabilistic world. On the other hand, there's no other potential interpretation of what counts as "voluntarism" on the table. We can't live with voluntarism, and we can't live without it. What's a moral, rational person to do? In particular, since this very book is intended to be a contribution to the rational enterprise of science, what's a scientist to do? In practice, scientists exhibit a curious sort of methodological dualism with respect to the voluntarism-determinism issue. They assume that the phenomena under investigation are either determined or probabilistic, but they use the voluntaristic language of rationality to discuss their own and their colleagues' scientific activities. They "hypothesize," "accept," and "reject" hypotheses on the basis of evidence, draw "inferences," and so on. It's never claimed in a scientific paper that a view contrary to the author's was caused by the opponent's cultural milieu or by indigestion. This modus operandi is evidently based on the presupposition that there is a space in the universe for rationality, although nobody can provide a description of how that space differs from the rest of the world.

The scientist's methodological dualism is especially problematic in the case of psychology. In psychology, the phenomena being investigated belong to the same class as the investigators: they're both human beings! This makes the ascription of fundamentally different properties to investigators and investigatees particularly dubious. The dualism is reflected in psychological reports by the conventional use of different symbols to refer to the two parties: S and E. Ss are subjects, Es are experimenters. S's decisions are caused, E's are free. But today's S can become tomorrow's E, and today's E can become tomorrow's S. How does one deal with the fact that S = E? It was noted in the previous paragraph that the methodological dualism of science is based on the presupposition that there is a space for rationality. The methodological dualism of psychology is evidently based on the even stronger assumption that the space of rationality is contained within the space of causality—that one and the same event can be both caused and free. This is an enormous leap of faith.

2. The Rise and Fall of Introspective Psychology

2.1. Introspectionism

Psychology became a scientific discipline in the 1870s. Descartes, among many others, had written about psychological issues centuries before that. But these protopsychologists didn't conceive of psychology as a discrete enterprise with its own methods and goals. The first fully self-conscious psychologist was arguably Wilhelm Wundt (1874). Wundt founded the first psychological laboratory. He also laid down the fundamental theoretical and methodological principles that dominated psychology during the first half-century of its existence. At a later time, when rival approaches to psychology had developed, Wundt's way of doing psychology came to be known as *introspectionism* or *introspective psychology*. In the closing decades of the nineteenth century, however, it was simply "psychology." Except for the work of a few isolated mavericks, there was no other kind.

Introspectionism adopted the Cartesian assumption of dualism: the world is a combination of physical objects and immaterial minds. The physical portion is the province of physics and the derivative "natural sciences," such as chemistry or physiology. Psychology is the science that deals with the mental portion. It's worth noting that the dominant psychological theory of the mid-twentieth century, *behaviorism,* had a completely different account of the subject matter of psychology. Behaviorists made a point of denying that there can *be* a science of the mind. Behaviorism gets its name from the doctrine that the only feasible subject matter for a science of psychology is the behavior of organisms—that is to say, the purely physical movements exhibited by living beings. According to the behaviorists, psychology is the science that tries to explain and predict behavior.

The research methods of introspectionism and behaviorism were also drastically different. The behaviorists introduced into psychology the method of "running subjects": the experimenter (E) puts *others* (Ss) into various situations, and observes and records how they behave in that situation. Wundt's introspective methodology couldn't be more different. First there's no distinction between Es and Ss: the E puts *himself* in various situations. Moreover, what's observed and recorded isn't behavior—it's what is *experienced* in the mental realm—E's sensations, thoughts, feelings, and so on. That's what "introspection" means: looking within.

Sometimes introspective psychologists used assistants to do the observing for them. When they did, the activities of the two individuals involved—experimenter and assistant—might be indistinguishable from the activities of an E and his S in a subject-running behavioristic experiment. But the *interpretation* of what had taken place would be different. For example, suppose that E puts another person in some situation and the other person reports seeing a white flash. If E is a behaviorist, then the other person is an S, and the information obtained from this investigation is:

(A) S said "I see a white flash."

This is, of course, a fact about the behavior of S in the experimental situation—namely, the fact that S's vocal chords vibrated in such a way as to produce the sound "I see a white flash." However, if E is an introspective psychologist, then the other person isn't a subject but an assistant, and the assistant's report has same status as E's own. If E had put himself in the situation, he wouldn't report, "I say 'I see a white flash'"—he'd say "I see a white flash!" By the same token, when his assistant reports a white flash, E doesn't suppose that the information obtained is merely that his assistant *said*, "I see a white flash." It's:

(B) My assistant saw a white flash.

So, we have two different accounts of the result of E's investigation—two descriptions of one and the same little song and dance between E and his partner. Viewed behavioristically, E acquires a datum about the other's verbal behavior; viewed introspectively, E acquires a datum about the other's visual experience.

Which account is the best? Obviously we're not going to answer that question by doing an experiment. We just saw that the same experiment is interpreted in different ways by behaviorists and introspectionists. If we do another experiment, we're just going to get divergent interpretations again. Not all scientific issues can be settled by experimentation, or indeed by any other form of observation. Some issues can only be dealt with by *argumentation*. The mind-body and voluntarism-determinism issues are probably of that type. The behaviorism-versus-introspectionism issue has also generated its share of arguments. We'll get a taste of these arguments later in this chapter and a full dose of them in Chapter 6.

Introspection has a weird history. In the nineteenth century, mainstream psychologists relied almost entirely on introspective data. During the mid-twentieth-century hegemony of behaviorism, introspection all but disappeared from psychology. Nowadays, in the postbehavioristic era of cognitive science, psychologists are split about 50-50 on the legitimacy of the introspective method—it's more controversial than ever. (We distinguish here between "introspection" and "introspectionism." The former refers to the method of looking within and reporting our mental states. It's the legitimacy of this research method that's currently controversial. Introspection*ism* is the name of a general theory of psychology, called so because it relies on introspection.) But, as the rest of this chapter will demonstrate, there's a lot more to the psychology of introspectionism than the method of introspection. Nobody is an introspectionist any more—i.e., nobody believes in the whole package of nineteenth-century psychological assumptions. But some people still think there's a place for introspection in psychology.

If introspectionism is extinct, why is it discussed at length in an introductory book? Because all the major twentieth-century theories of psychology were *reactions* to introspective psychology. They were different diagnoses of what was wrong with introspectionism, and they made different suggestions for how to fix its deficiencies. We have to start with introspectionism because one can't understand the twentieth-century theories unless one knows what problems they were trying to fix.

Let's look at introspectionism more closely. As we know, it relied on the method of introspection after which it was named. This involved: (1) inducing experiences in oneself by various experimental arrangements, (2) trying to describe the resulting mental state as precisely as possible, and (3) looking for recurring patterns in the data—experiences that always go together, or that always succeed one another, and so on.

Introspection was conceived to be a difficult skill to master, requiring special training. Untrained observers were prone to making various systematic errors. The most famous of these is the *stimulus error:* when asked to describe their experience, naïve observers routinely describe the physical event that *causes* their experience instead. For example, suppose you look at a coin that is held at a 45-degree angle from your face. If asked to describe your visual experience, you're apt to say something like, "I see a silvery circle." According to introspectionist orthodoxy, you would be commiting the stimulus error. It's true that there's a silvery circle in front of your eyes (the coin) and that this circular object is the cause of your visual experience. But none of this answers the question you were asked. You were asked to describe your visual *experience,* not the object that caused it, and when a circular object is viewed at an angle, you don't see a circle, you see an ellipse.

Introspectionism was also strongly influenced by the then-recent development of the atomic theory of matter by the chemist John Dalton. Chemistry is the science that aims to discover the properties of the substances that comprise the physical world. At first glance, this seems to be a thoroughly daunting task, for the number of different substances is astronomically large. There's gold and water and grass and milk and cloud-stuff and hair and spiderweb-stuff and jello, to name only a few. The atomic theory postulates that all physical substances are combinations of a relatively small number of material elements that are themselves irreducible to any other substances. Already in Wundt's day, the atomic theory was able to explain the chemical properties of literally thousands of different types of materials on the basis of this combinatorial hypothesis. This was a highly prized achievement because it greatly simplified the account of physical matter.

The introspectionists thought that the task of psychology was to do the same in the realm of mental states—to reduce the apparently endless complexity and variety of our mental states to a few types of *experiential* atoms. The psychologist's task was to find the fundamental constituents of experience and their laws of composition, such that you could explain the varieties of experiences as combinations of these elements. This task gave introspectionism its second name: *structuralism*. Both names refer to one and the same school of psychology. Introspectionism refers to its method of research; structuralism refers to its goal, which was to find the structure of complex experiences by working out how they're built up out of experiential atoms.

Let's pause to appreciate the magnitude of the proposed task. Our experiential states exhibit roughly the same degree of variation as the substances of the physical world. There are the experiences of surprise, nostalgia, nausea, déjà vu, afterimages, dreams; the feeling of inebriation; the sensation of a full bladder; the creepy feeling up and down your back that someone is watching you—the list goes on and on. All these were thought to be analyzable as combinations of a small number of experiential elements by a kind of "mental chemistry" (the term was actually used). So nostalgia might be decomposed into a mental image of a remembered pleasant experience, accompanied by the feeling of sadness at the thought that it's now past.

An introspectionist research topic: is the taste of lemonade a compound of the taste of sweetness combined with the taste of sourness? Perhaps our inclination to assent to this compositional hypothesis is due to the fact that we know that lemonade is made out of sugar, which tastes sweet when eaten by itself, and lemon, which tastes sour. But to think this way is to commit the stimulus error. The question isn't about the composition of lemonade—it's about the composition of its *taste*. The fact that lemonade is made up of something that tastes sweet plus something that tastes sour doesn't tell us whether the taste of lemonade is the sum of the two tastes. It may be that when you combine something that tastes sweet with something that tastes sour, you get a brand-new, undecomposable taste—an experiential atom. The way to find out is to sip lemonade and introspect—to see if you can detect sweetness and sourness side by side.

This way of practicing psychology was completely abandoned by the 1920s. The main reason for the demise of introspectionism was that introspective psychologists could never *agree* about the data acquired by introspection. In the other sciences there was an ever-growing body of agreed-upon facts; but in psychology, every introspectionist seemed to have his own list of experiential atoms. The last blow was what is known as the *imageless-thought controversy*. The most basic introspectionist principle, due to Wundt the founder, was that all experiential elements can be grouped into three families: *sensations, feelings,* and *images.* Experiences can be made up of combinations of elements from more than one category but when you get down to the *elementary* experiences, they're always a sensation or an image or a feeling—or so it was widely believed.

During the 1890s, at the University of Würzburg in Germany, Oswald Külpe undertook a series of introspective investigations of *thinking*. The orthodox line on this subject was that to think is to experience a series of visual or auditory or perhaps kinesthetic *images*. Thus, thinking was already accounted for in the basic threefold taxonomy. But Külpe's trained associates reported that in thinking about some topic, they could, if they tried, *suppress* all imagery and still continue to think. When asked to solve a problem, a certain amount of time would go by during which they introspected no images of any kind—and then the answer would come. Suppressing thought-related imagery completely was reported to be very difficult—but it occurred now and then. Even if it occurred only once in the history of the world, it meant that Wundt's identification of thoughts with images had to be rejected. In fact, Külpe claimed that he had discovered a fourth family of mental states: *thoughts.*

In the context of introspective psychology, this was a major discovery, akin to the discovery of a new element in chemistry. But the discovery met with resistance. At Cornell University, the leading American introspectionist E. B. Titchener took up the defense of Wundtian orthodoxy. He argued that the Würzburg investigators had simply made an observational error. According to Titchener, there is no imageless thought, but the patterns of images that constitute thoughts are so subtle, elusive, and faint that the Würzburgers had overlooked them. In other words, Külpe's associates were inadequately trained. Titchener reported that when his own, presumably more qualified associates introspected on thinking, they were always able to detect an image associated with every thought. The Würzburgers' rejoinder, in a nutshell, was that the disagreement was due to the inadequate training of the Cornell investigators. Evidently they were all unable to suppress their mental images; but if they could, they'd find that they could still continue to think.

This argument went back and forth for about twenty years. Then psychology turned behavioristic. From the 1920s to the 1970s, psychologists turned their backs on issues relating to mental states, and the imageless-thought controversy was dropped without achieving a resolution. The subject of imagery has only recently been reexamined. In the present discussion, it isn't important what the current opinion of the old controversy is; what's important is that introspectionists couldn't even agree on a basic taxonomy of experiential atoms. Having been told this much about imageless thought, the reader might be curious to know where things stand today. The current mainstream opinion sides with Külpe—not because of introspective evidence of imageless thought, but because of a theoretical argument. Suppose that thinking of George Washington is a matter of having an image—a little mental picture of George—in one's head. Now, any picture of George Washington is also a picture of a man. So why isn't this mental picture the equivalent of entertaining the general idea of a man? Well, if we concede that the image *is* identical to the idea of a man, we get the absurdity that the idea of George Washington is identical to the general idea of a man (since both are identical to the same image). Therefore the image *isn't* identical to the idea of a man. But to say this is tacitly to admit that there's more to entertaining the idea of a man than forming a picture of a man.

In fact, an image of George Washington is also an image of a human being, a mammal, a living thing, a thing that's found on planet earth, and indefinitely many other types of entities; but the corresponding thoughts are certainly not the same. Also, if you form an image of George Washington, you have to imagine him with a particular facial expression. Suppose you picture him looking wistful. Then why isn't having this image equal to entertaining the idea of wistfulness? In sum, thinking can't *just* be a matter of having images, because the image by itself doesn't tell you which of its features is being used as a vehicle for the thought. These considerations leave it open that having images may be an essential *part* of every thought. Thus, strictly speaking, it doesn't establish the existence of imageless thought. But the conclusion that it does come to is strong enough to show that Wundt's tripartite system is incomplete: there's no place in it for the part of thought that isn't imagistic. Back to the main story.

2.2. The Behaviorist Critique

The lack of agreement exemplified by the imageless-thought controversy was endemic throughout introspective psychology. It eventually led to its universal abandonment. It's out of the rejection of introspectionism that the three major psychological theories of the first half of the twentieth century arose: *behaviorism, psychoanalysis,* and *phenomenology.* Historically, what differentiated these three schools of psychology was that each of them had a different diagnosis of what had gone wrong with introspectionism, and a different suggestion for how to fix it. Each diagnosis and cure became the orthodoxy of a different group of psychologists.

The diagnosis and cure that gained the most favor among English-speaking academic psychologists was given its most influential formulation by John B. Watson (1913). He called the cure "behaviorism." Watson argued that introspectionism had gone astray at the very first step—its choice of subject matter. According to Watson, it wasn't surprising that introspective psychologists could never agree about the facts because the facts they were dealing with were about so insubstantial and elusive a thing as inner experience. If psychology was to develop an agreed-upon body of facts, it should make its subject matter the same as that of all the successful sciences. Without exception, the successful sciences studied some aspect of the physical world. The astronomer studied the planets and stars, the physiologist looked at the internal structure of living organisms, the geologist studied the earth, and so on. What aspect of the physical world could appropriately be assigned to psychology? Watson's answer was *behavior:* the physical movements through space and time of living organisms under various environmental conditions—or, in the language that the behaviorists came to favor, the responses elicited by various stimuli. Watson wrote:

> . . . behavioristic psychology has as its goal *to be able, given the stimulus, to predict the response*—or, *seeing the reaction take place, to state what the stimulus is that has called out the reaction.* (1930/1970, 17–18)

Watson's claim was that that's the *totality* of psychology. The only work there is for psychologists to do is to find lawful relations between stimuli and responses. Psychology had lost its soul when it became a scientific discipline. With the advent of behaviorism, it lost its mind.

Watson believed that if—and only if—psychologists followed this prescription, they would make the same kind of rapid progress as had been the hallmark of the physical sciences. He didn't give any clear reasons why the study of mental states was doomed to failure. He just noted that as a matter of historical fact, the science of mental life had been tried, and it had failed. Later behaviorists constructed various arguments for why the study of mental states must always fail. These will be discussed in Chapter 6. For now, we wish only to note that these arguments fall into two general families, which go by the name of *methodological behaviorism* and *metaphysical behaviorism*.

Methodological behaviorists argue that there's something about mental states that makes them unsuitable for scientific study. This approach doesn't necessarily deny that there is a dualism of the mental and the physical. The claim is that even if immaterial mental states do exist, there can't be a science of them. Metaphysical behaviorists are materialists who argue that there can be no science of the mind because mental states, being immaterial entities, don't exist. The claim is that the nineteenth-century science of the mind was akin to a science of demons and witches, which also was practiced at one time. Both enterprises were based on a ghastly mistake: their subject matter didn't exist!

Viewed from the lofty perch of the mind-body problem, the difference between the two types of behaviorism is greater than the difference between introspectionism and methodological behaviorism. Introspectionism and methodological behaviorism stand together on the same side of the great metaphysical divide between dualism and materialism, whereas metaphysical behaviorism stands alone on the other side. However, both behaviorisms lead to the same nonintrospective modes of research and nonmentalistic theoretical principles. They merely provide different rationales for these methods and principles.

As mentioned above, behaviorism became the orthodox view among English-speaking academic psychologists. Psychologists from France and Germany, as well as clinical psychologists the world over, went in other directions. The fact that academic psychologists and clinical psychologists made different theoretical choices is understandable, at least in a general way. These two groups have different missions. The clinicians want to be able to produce a beneficial effect on their suffering patients; the academic psychologists are concerned with discovering the truth, whether that truth has beneficial consequences or not. It's at least reasonable to conjecture that clinicians and academicians might find their respective ends best served by different theories. Suppose, for example, that the scientific evidence favors theory T1 over theory T2. One would straightforwardly expect academic psychologists to prefer the better-confirmed T1. But suppose further that T1 has nothing to say about clinical practice, while T2 provides ample guidance for clinical practice. In that case, adopting T1 would be an empty gesture for clinicians. Unless they wish to forego theoretical guidance completely, they would have to adopt T2 by default, even though T2 is less likely to be true.

The geographical differences in theory choice between the English-speaking world and the continent of Europe are more difficult to rationalize. It's worth noting that a similar bifurcation occurred in the twentieth century in the discipline of philosophy; the contemporary philosophical literature routinely distinguishes between "Anglo-American" and "Continental" philosophy. These geographical differences strongly suggest that theoretical and philosophical choices are determined at least in part by sociocultural factors rather than by objective evidence and rational argument.

2.3. The Psychoanalytic Critique

The second reaction to introspectionism was Sigmund Freud's psychoanalytic theory (1917/1966). According to psychoanalysis, the problem with introspectionism wasn't that it studied mental states, but that it assumed that all mental states are *conscious*. Indeed, nineteenth-century psychologists tended to treat "mental" and "conscious" as synonymous expressions. Freud made the distinction, and maintained that much of our mental life proceeds without the benefit of consciousness. By restricting their attention to conscious mental states, introspectionists ended up studying only the tip of the iceberg of the mind. As most of the iceberg is under water, so is most of mental life unconscious. Moreover, the properties of the above-water conscious portion can't be understood in isolation from its submerged unconscious base. Introspectionism failed because most of what happens to us, including the nature of our conscious experience, is determined by unconscious forces that are *not available to introspection*. That's what "unconscious" means; a present mental state is unconscious if you can't observe its presence, no matter how carefully and thoroughly you search within.

On this account, the method of introspection still has a role to play:

it provides us with information about consciousness. But this method needs to be *supplemented* by indirect techniques that permit us to make inferences about the nature of our unconscious mental states. For this purpose, Freud developed a variety of new investigative techniques, including dream analysis and free association, the latter being a procedure wherein one says whatever comes into one's head without consciously controlling the content. (For a brief period of time, he also employed hypnosis but he later abandoned it, having come to believe that the hypnotic subject would say anything the hypnotist wanted him to say.) These nonintrospective procedures were supposed to contain clues from which one could infer the nonintrospectable events going on at the unconscious level. The general strategy is well known in science when dealing with unobservable events. Electrons and other subatomic particles are too small to be observed directly, but physicists are able to infer their properties from the tracks they leave on photographic plates. In the same way, dreams and the content of free association are supposed to contain the tracks of unconscious mental states.

Dream analysis and free association are widely presumed to be techniques of psychoanalytical *therapy*. And so they are. But they're also the sources of data upon which psychoanalysts base their theories of human nature. They're the psychoanalytic supplement to the method of introspection. They're also the psychoanalytic alternative to running subjects. Freud didn't run subjects himself. He knew about the subject-running methodology being developed at the same time as his methods. However, he regarded it as a defective source of psychological data. His reasons will be discussed in Chapter 4.

Psychoanalysis became the orthodox view among clinical psychologists the world over. In the middle portions of the twentieth century in North America, psychology was in a most peculiar state. In the universities, psychologists were almost exclusively behaviorists who talked the language of stimulus and response. At the same time, in mental hospitals and in private clinical practice, psychologists were almost exclusively psychoanalysts who spoke the radically different language of id, ego, and superego. The two groups had little to do with each other. Each had their own journals and went to their own conferences. If you wanted to study psychoanalysis, you had to attend one of a number of freestanding psychoanalytical institutes, most of which were unaffiliated with any university.

2.4. The Phenomenological Critique

The third main stream of psychological thought in the twentieth century was phenomenology. The word "phenomenology" is unfamiliar to many otherwise well-educated people in North America. The psychoanalytical therapist is a Hollywood cliché: he's the bearded gentleman sitting behind the couch, scribbling notes on a tiny pad as his patient recounts a dream. The image of the lab-coated behavioral psychologist running rats in a maze is only slightly less familiar. But what's a phenomenologist? This third type of psychologist is virtually unknown to lay audiences in the English-speaking world. Anglo-American psychologists don't know much about phenomenology either. But phenomenology became the orthodox view of psychology among academic psychologists on the continent of Europe. Every well-educated person knows about phenomenology in France and Germany. Thus did the three main theories carve up the world of psychology among them.

The three theoretical approaches aren't so much single theories as they are *families* of theories sharing common assumptions. While Freud's was the first and historically the most important psychoanalytical theory, it soon had to contend with rival formulations by Carl Jung, Alfred Adler, and others. All of these theories share the sine qua non of psychoanalysis: an emphasis on unconscious mental processes. In Chapter 5, we'll see that there are also several competing behavioral theories, all of which employ the language of stimulus and response. There are several phenomenological theories as well. In our discussion, we'll follow the variety that's most readily accessible to the English-speaking reader: *Gestalt psychology*. The relative comprehensibility of Gestalt psychology is due to the fact that the founder, Max Wertheimer (1925/1938), and his two chief disciples, Wolfgang Köhler (1930) and Kurt Koffka (1935), all emigrated from their native Germany to the United States, where they found themselves beset on all sides by behaviorists. Academic survival required them to address their American colleagues in terms that they could understand. Hence the writings of the Gestaltists form a useful bridge between the Anglo-American and Continental psychological traditions.

Of the three twentieth-century schools, phenomenology is the most similar to the preceding psychology of introspectionism. The subject matter is the same: conscious experience (phenomenologists tend to be very wary of the concept of the unconscious). The investigative method is also the same: introspection. What phenomenologists object to, and what they think led to the demise of introspective psychology, is its *structuralism*—the assumption that all experiences can be analyzed into elementary experiential atoms. Let's see how this objection plays itself out in one realm of experience: the visual field.

According to introspectionist orthodoxy, the atoms of visual experience are colored dots, each one being the smallest size that can be perceived. There's a different type of atom for each discriminable color. Expanses of a single color, like the sight of the blue sky, are analyzed into a mass of identically colored dots with no spaces between them. In sum, the visual field is thought to be a collection of little, experiential tiles. This is called, appropriately enough, the *mosaic hypothesis.*

If the mosaic hypothesis is right, you would in principle be able to give a complete description of your visual experience by providing a sort of bit map of your visual field, specifying the color of the dot at each location. In order to keep track of the dots already accounted for, you'd have to follow a systematic procedure. For example, you might start at the top left of your visual field, go across to the top right, then go back to the left and do the second line (like a typewriter), and so on. To make it easier to describe portions of their visual field, introspective psychologists used to look at the target stimulus through a peephole that was moved around the scene. That way they could see each colored dot in isolation, and describe it accurately.

The Gestalt psychologists objected as follows: if you examine your visual field by using a moving peephole, then of course your total experience is going to turn out to be a sum of colored dots. But that result is imposed by your method of observation. Looking through a peephole one dot at a time ensures that you'll never get anything but a sum of colored dots. However, experience as it occurs in daily life *isn't* usually analyzable into elementary parts in this way. Usually, the complete experience has properties that are lost when you observe and describe your experience one little part at a time. This critique was summarized in the Gestalt slogan "the whole is greater than the sum of its parts." This is a catchy way of saying that the mosaic hypothesis, as well as every other manifestation of structuralism, is false.

The Gestaltists developed various experiential demonstrations of the inadequacy of structuralism. True to the method of introspection, they didn't run subjects. They reported their own experiences and gave directions for how others could observe the same phenomena in *their* own experience. In our view, the most persuasive and direct way to make the Gestaltists' point is to contemplate the nature of reversible figures. We've all seen reversible figures. The most famous is the one that can be seen either as a vase or as two faces in profile. Another one is either a young woman or an old hag. The experiential datum required for the demonstration—the part that has to be provided by introspection—is only that the event of seeing one aspect of the figure (say, the young woman) is a different visual experience from the event of seeing the other aspect (the old hag). The rest is all argumentation. What else could the young woman and the old hag be, if not different visual experiences? Well, you might be entertaining two different descriptions of one and the same experience. Consider this figure: l. What you see when you look at it could qualify either as the letter ell or as the numeral one. But your visual experience doesn't change when you stop taking it to be an ell and start taking it to be a one. The claim is that this isn't all that's going on when you switch from one aspect of the reversible figure to the other. "Young woman" and "old hag" aren't just two different descriptions of the same visual experiences—they're two different experiences. If your introspection is uncertain on this point, consider the fact that it sometimes takes a certain amount of mental effort to see one of the aspects of the figure. This happens even after you've already seen both aspects before. You've seen both the young woman and the old hag, but right now you can't make the young woman shift over to the hag. Yet you still know that the hag is there to be seen. If "seeing the young woman" and "seeing the old hag" were merely a matter of having two equally good descriptions of one and the same experience, you wouldn't be experiencing any difficulty in seeing the hag—just knowing that the "old hag" description fits would already be equivalent to seeing the hag. In fact, you could see the young woman and the old hag simultaneously. But this isn't what happens.

Now suppose an introspective psychologist wanted to give a complete description of each of the two visual experiences. Believing in the mosaic hypothesis, this is how she would proceed. First she gets the young woman aspect into view. Then, without letting the aspect switch, she sweeps her visual field with a peephole and constructs a dot-by-dot description of what she sees in each location. Then she switches over to the old hag aspect and does the same thing. If the mosaic hypothesis is correct, she has constructed complete descriptions of her two visual experiences. Now compare the two descriptions. Suppose that at location X of the young-woman experience, the peephole revealed a chartreuse-colored dot. Then the old-hag experience will also have a chartreuse-colored dot at the same location. This is so because the physical object being observed (the tiny bit of paper that shows through the peephole) is the same, and the mode of observing it (through the peephole) is the same. The same argument can be run on any and all locations in the visual field. It follows that the descriptions of the two experiences are identical, dot for dot. But if the descriptions of two *different* things are identical, it's clear that these descriptions must be incomplete. Evidently, the experiential differences between seeing the figure as a young woman and seeing it as an old hag are lost in the analysis into elementary parts. Therefore, the mosaic hypothesis fails.

Gestaltists argued that the same kind of failure could be demonstrated with any and all elemental analyses of experience. No matter how you break up experiences into parts, there are always properties of the whole experiences that get lost in the analysis. So what's the remedy? Simply to do the same thing as the introspective psychologists did, but without presupposing that the resulting data must always take the form of a decomposition of the experience into elementary parts. To do this is still to introspect; but "introspection" has such a strong connotation of structuralism that most phenomenologists prefer to avoid it, speaking instead of "phenomenological observation."

In the final analysis, phenomenologists agree with introspectionists on both the subject matter of psychology (consciousness) and the appropriate method for its investigation (introspection). They merely reject one of its theoretical postulates. In contrast, psychoanalysts want to *supplement* both the introspectionists' subject matter (with unconscious mental states) and methods (with free association and dream analysis). Finally, the behaviorists *reject* the introspectionists' subject matter and method, wishing to substitute the study of behavior for the study of consciousness and the method of running subjects for the method of introspection. Clearly, phenomenology is the twentieth-century school that remains closest to the nineteenth-century tradition, whereas behaviorism is the school that departs most radically from that tradition.

2.5. The Third Generation

Behaviorism, psychoanalysis, and phenomenology developed pretty much independently from one another through the first two-thirds of the twentieth century. From about 1920 to about 1970, their domination of the world of psychology was nearly complete. Virtually every psychologist belonged to one of the three schools. Moreover, one could almost always tell which school any psychologist belonged to by reading a few sentences drawn at random from their writings.

The first major new development was the advent of *humanistic psychology*. This third-generation approach started in the 1950s with Carl Rogers (1951), peaked in the 1960s with Abraham Maslow (1968), and entered a period of rapid decline in the 1970s. There still are some humanistic psychologists, however, especially in California. Like behaviorism, humanistic psychology is a distinctively Anglo-American movement. This is why its proponents called it the "third force" in contemporary psychology, when it was really the fourth force. By the humanistic psychologists' reckoning, the first two forces were behaviorism and psychoanalysis. They didn't count phenomenology, which was scarcely represented in the English-speaking world.

The humanistic agenda was mainly *critical* and *practical*. For a while it was the only available alternative to behaviorism in North American universities; so it attracted people of diverse interests and ideas whose only commonality was a dissatisfaction with the behaviorist exclusion of the mental. On the positive side, its emphasis was heavily on psychotherapeutic techniques. It produced various therapeutic novelties, the most important of which was the idea of therapy for the normal to help them to achieve supernormal levels of functioning. But it never developed a coherent and unified theoretical platform.

The rapid decline of humanistic psychology was precipitated in large part by the development in the 1970s of *cognitive science*. This latest psychological paradigm also has a critique of behaviorism; but it also offers a relatively well-worked-out set of theoretical ideas. So it co-opted a lot of theoretically minded psychologists whose allegiance to humanistic psychology was due mainly to its antibehaviorism.

Computers have played a central and paradoxical role in the development of cognitive science. The story will be told in detail in Chapter 7 but here's a foretaste. It began to be noticed in the 1960s and 1970s that some of the language used by computer scientists to discuss the operation of computers was, or at least appeared to be, *mentalistic*. One might have thought that this similarity between computers and human beings would reinforce the idea that humans are nothing more than deterministic machines. But, at least among American academic psychologists, the idea of humans as machines was already maximally strong. These psychologists were, after all, behaviorists who regarded the mind as irrelevant to the explanation of behavior. In this intellectual climate, the ascription of mental states to computers was a radically liberalizing step—for if material computers can have mental states, then surely it's unreasonable to deny that human beings can have them too, even if one insists that humans are totally material devices.

The main point of cognitive science is that it rejects the behavioristic tenet that mental states don't exist or can't be studied scientifically. There are, however, significant similarities between the two schools. The most important of these is that cognitive scientists continue to rely heavily on the behaviorists' subject-running methodology. There are also similarities between cognitive science and the other two twentieth-century approaches. Like psychoanalysis, cognitive science ascribes an important role to unconscious mental processes. Finally, in recent years, there's been an influx of phenomenological ideas into cognitive science. For example, cognitive scientists have been increasingly willing to use introspection or phenomenological observation as a source of data additional to the results of subject-running experiments. This has led some optimists to speculate that cognitive science may represent a synthesis of the best ideas in each of the older traditions.

In the rest of this book, we'll have a few more things to say in passing about phenomenology and humanistic psychology. The topics we'll deal with in depth are psychoanalysis, behaviorism, and cognitive science.

3. The Background of Psychoanalysis

3.1. Irrational Behavior

The psychologists of the nineteenth century studied mental states. What did they have to say about behavior? The short answer is: not very much. Introspectionists had inherited the Cartesian view that human actions are freely chosen by acts of will. A person surveys the alternatives available to her, weighs her options, and *decides* what to do. The entire process is conscious and rational. A consequence of this is that we should all be able to explain why we did what we did in terms of what we *wanted* to accomplish and what we *believed* were the means available for accomplishing it. When asked to explain our behavior, we need only introspect to come up with the answer—because it's always a conscious act of will and conscious calculations that produce human activity. Thus if you want to know why someone is running down the street, you need only ask her, whereupon you'll receive an explanation in terms of her current desires and beliefs: "I'm running because I *want* to get to the store before it closes, and I *believe* that it's going to close very soon." With that kind of infallible resource at hand, who needs behavioral psychologists?

If this view seems absurdly naïve now, it's largely as a result of Freud's influence. He *demolished* the principle that all behavior is consciously and rationally willed. It's not only psychoanalysts who reject it nowadays—psychologists of every theoretical stripe reject it. Freud wasn't the first person to talk about the unconscious and irrational wellsprings of action. But it's through his writings and lectures that the idea came to be universally accepted. In his medical practice, Freud saw countless examples of psychopathological phenomena that didn't fit into the rationalistic framework. One thinks here of gross mental deviance, such as a psychopathic killer who murders children just for fun. But homicidal psychopathy is *not* a good example of irrational behavior in the sense that's relevant here. "Rational" and "rationality" are defined in many different ways in different contexts. The definition that's appropriate in the context of our discussion of psychoanalysis is this one: your behavior is reckoned to be rational if you're doing what *you* believe will get you what *you* want. So, if a psychopath enjoys killing, and if he thinks he can get away with it, it's not necessarily irrational for him to kill.

Given the above definition of rationality, it's the little neuroses of everyday life that most clearly qualify as irrational. Take phobias for instance—the fear of circumstances that *the actor herself* regards as harmless. Suppose that you're extremely afraid of flying in airplanes. Your fear may or may not be a phobia—you can't tell just by looking at the object of the fear. If you think that flying is more dangerous than riding in a car, you're mistaken—fatality statistics show otherwise—but making a factual error is not the same thing as being irrational. According to the definition, the rationality or irrationality of your behavior is relative to *your beliefs*. So if you think that flying is dangerous, it's rational for you not to fly. But some people know what the statistics say, and they believe them; yet they still avoid flying. When asked why, they say they don't know. They themselves characterize their own behavior as irrational. That's a phobia. It's also a disconfirmation of the Descartes-inspired, nineteenth-century view that we can always explain our own behavior.

The same point can be made with compulsive behavior. By definition, this is behavior that you consciously don't want to engage in, but are driven to engage in by some force other than your conscious will. There are people who wash their hands hundreds of times a day. Some do so out of an exaggerated sense of cleanliness. But many of them— the compulsive neurotics—know that their hands are thoroughly clean, but feel compelled to wash them anyway. If they try to abstain from washing, they experience mounting anxiety. They can't stop washing, but they don't know why. This would never happen if the nineteenth-century view of human action were correct.

Historically the most important anti-Cartesian example—the one that gave Freud the idea—was his observation of *posthypnotic suggestion*. The phenomenon is well known. You tell a hypnotized subject to do something when she awakens, and you instruct her not to remember being told. Very often this works: you give the subject a posthypnotic suggestion to open a window, wake her up, and she gets up and opens the window. Things get interesting when you ask her why she acted as she did. Sometimes she'll simply look mystified and confess that she doesn't know. But often she'll fabricate a reason, claiming that she opened the window because the room was hot and stuffy, or something of the kind. In this case, the hypnotist and everyone else who was present at the implanting of the posthypnotic suggestion are in a position to know with certainty that the subject's explanation of her own behavior is incorrect. *We* know why she did it, but *she* doesn't know. Apparently, the imperative to come up with a rational explanation for everything we do is sometimes so strong that we're impelled to *invent* rational reasons for our irrational behavior. Freud called this phenomenon *rationalization,* and it looms large in his thinking.

3.2. The Concept of the Unconscious

Freud's first and most basic conclusion from these observations was that there are unconscious causes of behavior. To say that the causes of some behavior are unconscious is only to say that they're not available to introspection. The phobic or the compulsive can look within all she wants, but she won't find the beliefs and desires that explain her behavior. In retrospect, the general point seems obvious—the Cartesian view of behavior is demolished simply by noting that a lot of people want to quit smoking and yet continue to smoke. In some cases, the persistence of smoking could be due to the fact that the desire to quit is weaker than other conscious desires that are satisfied by smoking. But this isn't always the case. Some smokers wouldn't hesitate to take a pill that's guaranteed to make them quit, which shows that their desire to quit is prepotent. Yet they don't quit. That's a perfect example of irrational behavior. Whatever it is that keeps these smokers smoking, it isn't any belief or desire that they're aware of; it's something unconscious.

It's important to understand that this conclusion is no longer controversial. It's almost universally accepted by psychologists of nearly all theoretical persuasions that there are unconscious causes of behavior. But psychoanalysis goes further. What makes a theory a *psychoanalytic* theory is mainly that it takes this next step: the unconscious determinants of behavior are nevertheless conceived of as *mental* (Freud says "psychic").

Everybody agrees that the cause of the smoker's behavior is unconscious but only psychoanalysts take the unconscious cause to be an *unconscious desire*. On this view, the smoker consciously wants to quit smoking, but something in him that he's not conscious of *wants to smoke*—and the unconscious desire is stronger than the conscious desire. Psychoanalysts preserve the mentalistic vocabulary that nineteenth-century psychology used to explain behavior—the language of beliefs, desires, intentions, feelings, perceptions, etc.—but allowed that we sometimes harbor beliefs, desires, and so on, that we're not aware of.

The first reaction of Freud's critics was that an unconscious mental state is a contradiction in terms, like a married bachelor. Logically there couldn't be such a thing and thus Freud's theory could be dismissed out of hand—one didn't even have to submit it to experimental or other observational tests. These critics were technically right, but they missed the point. Freud wasn't using mentalistic terms in what was then their current sense. He was proposing that we *change the definitions* of mentalistic terms like "belief" and "desire." In effect, he introduced a new set of concepts. The justification for using the same old mentalistic terms for the new concepts was that the similarities between an old-fashioned, nineteenth-century "desire" and a new-style, psychoanalytic "desire" were far more striking than the differences. A new-style desire is related to behavior and other mental states in exactly the same way as an old-fashioned desire. The only difference is that a new-style desire may or may not be conscious.

This conceptual revision has been fully accepted in everyday language. We're all Freudians now, at least when we're not being professional psychologists. Consider the following unremarkable statement: "I've been friends with him for years, but I just realized that I never *really* liked him." This report doesn't sound odd to us at all; but to the nineteenth-century ear, the reference to an unconscious mental attitude would sound utterly paradoxical, like "I'm married, but I'm still a bachelor."

3.3. The Existence of the Unconscious

It's one thing to make up a new concept; it's another to say that the concept as defined refers to something real. The term "mermaid" has a clear definition—it's a creature with the anatomy of a human being from the waist up and of a fish below the waist. But the clarity of the definition doesn't entail that there are such things as mermaids in the world. Similarly, having introduced the concept of unconscious mental states, Freud now owes us an argument to the effect that there are such things.

Before presenting the psychoanalyst's case, we need to make a distinction between two kinds of concepts or terms. One important difference between "unconscious mental state" and "mermaid" is that the first is a *theoretical term* while the second is an *observation term*. Observation terms refer to entities like tables and mountains and mermaids that can be directly perceived (if they exist); theoretical terms refer to entities like electrons and the force of gravity and the gross national product that are unobservable, even in principle. We can hope to determine whether there are mermaids simply by looking but we will never be able to see electrons, even if they exist. This is what our current theories of physics tell us. Nevertheless, physicists believe that electrons exist. Their belief, however, is based on an inference. They believe in imperceptible electrons because many things that they do perceive in cloud chambers and on photographic plates can be neatly explained by the hypothesis that they're caused by imperceptible electrons. By the same token, it's true that you can't introspectively observe unconscious mental processes—if you could, they wouldn't be unconscious. But Freud thought that the character of what *is* introspected can be explained best by the hypothesis that there are also unconscious mental states.

So what's the evidence for the existence of unconscious mental states? Let's start by doing an introspective experiment. We're going to call your attention to certain sensory experiences. These experiences are subtle, so you may not be able to detect them right away. As was the case with switching aspects of a reversible figure, you'll need to expend a moment of attentional effort before you "get" them. As was the case with reversible figures, the effort plays an essential role in the theoretical analysis that follows. The sensory experiences are all going to be sensations of pressure. Ready?

Note the sensation of your backside pressing down on the seat. Stop reading for a few moments and search for it. Got it? It's an enormously strong sensation. Yet it wasn't there a moment before we called your attention to it—if it had been in your field of consciousness all along, you wouldn't have needed that moment of searching before you found it. Now note the sensation of the book in your hands, the long sleeves against your arms, the soles of your feet pressing against the floor, the place where your crossed legs meet, the glasses on the bridge of your nose, the belt constricting your waist.

Here is a veritable universe of sensations that leap up at you out of nowhere when you cast your attention on them. What are we to say about this phenomenon? We might want to say that the sensations were there all along, but that we were *unconscious* of them, and that they *became* conscious when we attended to them. But we're not logically compelled to say that. An alternative account is that the pressure sensations weren't there when we weren't looking for them, and that the act of looking for them brought them into being. So now we have two competing theoretical explanations of the same phenomenon. How do we choose between them?

Ordinarily, when two theories T1 and T2 conflict, scientists try to find some observational hypothesis about which the theories make divergent predictions. If T1 entails that hypothesis H is true and T2 entails that H is false, then it's clear how we should proceed: simply make the observations that are required to ascertain whether H is true or false. The theory with the prediction that proves to be correct is the winner. But this standard procedure isn't going to help us resolve the conflict between the two theories about our pressure sensations. The problem here is that both theories have identical observational consequences: no matter how stealthily you sneak up on your experience, its observation is going to be compatible with both the theory that it was there beforehand but unconscious, and the theory that it was created ab ovo by your introspective act. Whenever two theories have identical observational consequences, they're said to be *empirically equivalent*. Empirical equivalence sometimes happens in science. Quantum mechanics is a notorious example: there are different quantum-mechanical theories that make identical predictions for all possible experiments. When two rival theories are empirically equivalent, every observation that confirms one of them also confirms the other, and every observation that *dis*confirms one also disconfirms the other. Thus it's obvious that the conflict between them can't be settled by experiment or any other observational procedure. Once again, the only potential path to a resolution is via logical argumentation.

Let's return to our two empirically equivalent theories of the pressure sensations. Note, to begin with, that one can formulate a corresponding pair of theories about the physical world. Maybe the planet Mars ceases to exist when nobody is looking at it. Maybe *everything* ceases to exist when it ceases to be observed. This theory and the theory that physical objects persist when no one is looking are also empirically equivalent. Why do we prefer the continuous existence theory? Because it's *simpler.* If Mars exists continuously whether or not it's being observed, you can write simple and elegant equations that describe its motion. But these equations aren't valid if the planets pop in and out of existence depending on whether they're being observed. Periods during which the planet Mars is under observation are going to be determined by such complex factors as the weather in the vicinity of certain observatories and the state of health of certain astronomers. If Mars exists only when it's observed, its career is going to contain highly irregular gaps. There will be no simple and elegant description of its path. This is a reason to prefer the continuous existence theory.

Psychoanalysts can use the same type of argument to establish the existence of unintrospected mental states. The theory that your headache continues to exist unconsciously during intervals when you're distracted from it is arguably simpler than the theory that your headache pops in and out of existence as you attend or cease to attend to it. It has to be admitted, though, that the greater simplicity of the continuous-existence theory is not as crystal clear in the case of mental states as it is in the case of physical objects. The psychoanalyst has an argument, but it isn't a conclusive argument.

Here's another consideration in favor of the psychoanalytic hypothesis. Think of the times you've driven home without attending to your driving. Sometimes you come out of your reverie to find yourself in front of your house, though you don't remember stopping at red lights, making turns at the right places, or checking the rearview mirror before changing lanes. If you say that you didn't see the red lights, you've got to construct an explanation for how you managed to stop at them anyway. One theory is that you saw them unconsciously—that's what a psychoanalyst would want to say. But there's an obvious competitor here too: maybe you consciously saw each red light, but immediately forgot that you'd seen it.

The best evidence for unconscious mental states is to be found in the experimental research of cognitive scientists. The cognitive-science approach to psychology, like the psychoanalytic approach, relies heavily on the existence of such states. The unconscious states and processes postulated by the two approaches are quite different— the cognitive science states and processes aren't nearly as sexy as their psychoanalytical counterparts. However, both agree on the general hypothesis that there's a lot of mental activity going on without the benefit of consciousness. The many research results that support this hypothesis in cognitive science automatically provide support for the corresponding psychoanalytic hypothesis. We will discuss a single study—an early (for cognitive science) classic by James Lackner and Merrill Garrett (1972) that makes its point very forcefully.

Lackner and Garrett equipped their subjects with earphones and directed a different stream of speech in each ear. The instructions were to listen to one of the streams and ignore the other. Prior research had established that in a situation like this, subjects would be unable to report anything about the content of the unattended channel. In this experiment, all subjects heard a series of ambiguous sentences in the attended channel, such as "The officer put out the lantern." At the same time, half the subjects received a disambiguating sentence through the unattended channel—e.g., "He extinguished the lantern," or "He brought the lantern outside." A second group of subjects received an unrelated sentence through the unattended channel. As in previous studies, subjects in both groups were unable to report the content of the unattended channel. When asked to interpret the ambiguous sentences heard over the attended channel, subjects in the second group were evenly divided between the two interpretations. This is consistent with the hypothesis that they chose their interpretations at random. However, subjects in the first group overwhelmingly selected the interpretations that were in line with the disambiguating sentences fed to the unattended channel. That is to say, subjects who received (but didn't attend to) the sentence "He extinguished the lantern" interpreted "The officer put out the lantern" accordingly, while those who received "He brought the lantern outside" interpreted the ambiguous sentence in accordance with *their* unattended sentence. They did this *even though they were unable to report anything about the content of the unattended sentence.*

In this experiment, it's clear that the unattended sentences had an effect on behavior even though they weren't consciously understood. So there was an unconscious *cause* of the subjects' behavior. Was the unconscious cause an unconscious *mental state?* It certainly seems so.

For it to have produced the effect it had, something in the subjects that's not conscious needed to figure out what the sentences spoken in the unattended channel *meant*. Something *understood* those sounds, and it wasn't consciousness. So there can be unconscious understanding.

3.4. Other Minds

Lackner and Garrett's experiment takes us a big step beyond what can be established on the basis of introspection on our pressure sensations. As a result of the introspective experiment, you may conclude that *you* had experiences of which *you* were unconscious but on the basis of Lackner and Garrett's study, you can conclude that *other people* are unconscious of some of *their* own mental states. If you were to ask one of Lackner and Garrett's subjects whether the unattended message had any influence on her interpretation of the target sentence, she would presumably say that it hadn't. But, as in the case of the fabrications following posthypnotic suggestion, *you* would be in a position to know that *she's* wrong. You know something about her mental life that she doesn't. This conclusion is, once again, totally foreign to the pre-Freudian Cartesian view. It's a central tenet of Cartesianism that each of us is the ultimate and infallible authority on his own mental life. Lackner and Garrett show us that other evidence can *override* one's personal testimony about one's own mental processes.

This point is related to a well-known philosophical problem—the problem of *other minds*. How do you know that other people have mental states like you do? In your own case, you can introspectively observe at least some of your own mental states. But you can't observe *their* mental states—all you can observe is their behavior. For all you know, there's nothing going on inside that *accompanies* their behavior. When they hit their thumb with a hammer and say "yeow!" how can you tell that they're additionally experiencing the sensation of pain? *Solipsism* is the view that you *can't* tell—that as far as you know, you're the only conscious being in the universe. (That's the weak sense of the word "solipsism." There's also a stronger sense according to which a solipsist is someone who claims that as far as she can tell, she's the only thing, conscious or otherwise, that exists.)

The common-sense reply to the solipsist's skeptical doubt is that your belief in other minds is based on a generalization from your own case. Whenever you hit your thumb with a hammer and say "yeow!" this behavior is accompanied by a sensation of pain. Therefore when you see *someone else* exhibit the same behavior, you infer that they have the same accompanying sensation. What turns the question about other minds into a problem is that the foregoing generalization argument is very weak. The weakness isn't that there's something wrong with generalization per se. Having observed a multitude of ravens and found them all to be black, you're justified in accepting the hypothesis that all ravens are black. Of course, this hypothesis isn't logically forced on you by your observations—there's no logical contradiction in supposing that all observed ravens have been black, but that the rest of them are white. The claim is only that the data lend credence to the generalization. Your conclusion that all ravens are black may turn out to be wrong, but it's a good bet, given the evidence at hand.

The problem with the generalization argument for other minds is that in this instance, the generalization is based on only a single case: your behavior is accompanied by mental states, therefore (you conclude), other people's behavior is also accompanied by mental states. This is like generalizing about ravens after having observed only a single one. A single raven is bound to possess numerous properties that can't be projected to the general population of ravens. A single raven will weigh a certain amount and measure a certain length from beak to tail; it will also possess idiosyncratic markings—perhaps a small oblique scratch on its left leg. But this gives us very little reason to suppose that *all* ravens weigh precisely that amount, are precisely that length, and have precisely that type of scratch on their left leg. The inference from your mental states to others' would seem to be just as weak. In fact, it's even worse. In the case of the ravens, there's at least the possibility of finding out whether your hasty generalizations were right or wrong. You need only observe more ravens. This option isn't available in the case of other minds. You can *never* observe another person's mental states; therefore you will *never* have more than a single case on which to base your generalization.

There's a lot more that can be said about the philosophical problem of other minds. Whether or not solipsism can be refuted, however, the fact remains that we *believe* that others have pains and beliefs just like we do. It's important to distinguish here the *philosophical* problem from the *psychological* problem relating to other minds. The former is the problem of how to *justify* our beliefs about other people's mental states; the latter is the problem of how we come to *possess* our beliefs about other minds, regardless of whether these beliefs are justified. Generalization based on our own case isn't a good solution to the philosophical problem, but it does seem to be the answer to the psychological problem. When you see someone hit his thumb with a hammer and hear him say "yeow!" you *do* infer that he's experiencing pain on the basis of the fact that you would be experiencing pain if you were in that situation. You may not know how to justify this inference. But justified or not, that's at least a roughly correct description of how you form your beliefs about other minds. For the rest of this chapter, we'll simply assume that the inference to other minds is justified. However, we'll have to return to this issue when we discuss behaviorism in detail.

Now suppose that you make this inference: you observe someone acting just like you do when you're angry, and so infer that he's angry. Suppose also that you ask him why he's angry, and he screams back at you: "I'm not angry!" What are you to make of this state of affairs? Well, Lackner and Garrett's study showed us that personal testimony about one's own mental states can sometimes be overridden by behavioral evidence. So there are at least some circumstances in which it would be appropriate for you to think that he's wrong about his mental state and to continue to think that he's angry. It seemed to Freud that he encountered this kind of situation over and over again in his clinical practice—patients who acted exactly as though they had a particular mental state, except that they denied having it. In fact, even the patient's *speech* was sometimes consistent with a mental state that the person denied having. For example, while speaking in glowingly laudatory terms about his mother, the patient would unexpectedly say, "I hate her." When confronted with the contradiction, the patient would either deny having said "I hate her," or attribute it to a slip of the tongue (he'd meant to say "I hail her").

Our discussion has arrived at the famous analysis of *Freudian slips*— actions that run counter to the actor's conscious intentions and that are attributed by the actor to mechanical errors of execution. Freud called such slips *parapraxes*. Of course, it's only reasonable to allow that we sometimes simply make mechanical mistakes in the execution of our conscious plans (although Freud seems loath to admit it): we try to say "she sells seashells by the seashore" and get our tongue all tangled up. But Freud cited two features of many parapraxes that can't be explained by the hypothesis of mechanical error. First, he claimed to have observed many cases in which all or most of the errors were in that same direction: the patient always accidentally disparaged his mother and never accidentally complimented her. If the errors were due to mechanical failure, we would expect to get a 50-50 split. Secondly, in most cases the misstatements fit with various non-verbal behaviors. The patient who inadvertently said that he hated his mother had the facial expression and displayed the posture of someone who was proclaiming his hatred.

Both these features are what we would expect to find if the patient harbored the feelings and attitudes that he denies having. Sometimes the patient even knows that he has these feelings, but is simply unwilling to admit it. In that case, the parapraxes are due to a failure in his attempt to hide his conscious feelings. There are circumstances, however, wherein the hypothesis of a hidden conscious attitude is very implausible—e.g., if the patient comes to admit that he hates his mother, but still maintains that he previously wasn't conscious of any such feelings. If the behavior is the same, then so is the accompanying mental state—or so it's been assumed for the purpose of this discussion. The patient who talks and behaves as though he hates his mother *does* hate his mother—and if he isn't conscious of hating her, then his hatred must be unconscious. Freud considered the parapraxes to be particularly strong evidence for the existence of unconscious mental states.

3.5. Resistance

When we instructed you to examine your pressure sensations, we called your attention to a series of unconscious experiences, whereupon they almost immediately became conscious. Freud, however, found that calling his patients' attention to their unconscious feelings didn't always elicit a quick assent. Sometimes, the patient whose face contorted with anger at every mention of his mother continued to deny having any negative feelings toward her. In fact, he denied it with what seemed to Freud to be unaccountable vehemence: "Hate my mother? That's crazy! She's a saint! I worship her!" Freud called this phenomenon *resistance*.

A lot of the details of psychoanalytic theory take the particular form that they do because of the need to account for resistance. Freud's view, which has also become the common-sense view, is that people sometimes don't want to *admit* to themselves that they have certain ignoble thoughts and feelings, so they fool themselves into thinking that they don't have them. But when you try to get precise about this explanation, you find it's very difficult to work out. How exactly do you go about fooling yourself? In order not to let yourself be aware of a particular thought, don't you have to know *what not to let yourself be aware of?* It's like telling yourself: "I must not think of a white horse"—oops, you did it.

Freud struggled with the problem of how to represent resistance throughout his career. He floated several different theoretical explanations. They all had in common the idea that the mind is divided into different portions that work more or less independently of one another. One portion gets fooled, and another portion does the fooling. To this day, there's no general consensus about whether Freud succeeded. Be that as it may, the idea that the mind is divided into relatively independent portions also looms large in contemporary cognitive science, where the portions go by the name of *modules*. The portions aren't the same as Freud's, but in any case, the idea of modularity is Freud's second most important and most lasting contribution to psychology (the first being the idea of unconscious mental states).

In Freud's earliest theories, the psychoanalytic modules were the *conscious mind,* the *preconscious mind,* and the *unconscious mind*—*Cs, Pcs, and Ucs.* Cs was the repository of conscious mental states. Pcs contained unconscious mental elements that could become conscious by just attending to them, like the pressure sensations. Cs was conceived to have free access to the contents of Pcs—Cs could rummage through Pcs, picking up whatever items it encountered and making them its own. Ucs contained material that was inaccessible to consciousness—the stuff that's protected by resistance.

These terms—particularly "conscious mind" and "unconscious mind"—are still often used in popular literature and Hollywood films. But Freud soon abandoned this system, mainly because he couldn't wed it to a coherent explanation of how resistance takes place and is maintained. In his mature theory (which will be presented in the next chapter), the modules are the *id,* the *ego,* and the *superego.* "Conscious" and "unconscious" are no longer the names of mental modules—they're properties of some of the activities of the modules. For example, some of the things that happen in the ego are conscious, but some are unconscious. Hollywood notwithstanding, it's no longer possible to speak of "the conscious mind" or "the unconscious mind" as though these are discrete entities or systems.

We close this chapter with a word on the neural correlates of the Freudian modules. Some people have speculated that the ego and the id can be identified with the cortex and the lower portion of the brain. Others have suggested that that the ego and the id are the left and right cerebral hemisphere, respectively. Freud himself didn't suppose that the id, ego, and superego correspond to *any* localizable physical structures in the brain. He thought they *might* correspond to physical structures, but that it wouldn't make any difference to the truth of his theory if they didn't. The ego might turn out to be rather like the postal system. The postal system is dispersed all over the country. Moreover, we could change the locations of all the post offices and mailboxes, or shut down half the post offices, or add new ones, and it would still be the postal system. What makes the postal system a unitary thing isn't its location or its specific physical parts, but its *function:* it's the system that gets the mail distributed. Freud conceived of the mental modules as also defined by their function. This view later came to be called *functionalism.* We'll have a lot more to say about functionalism when we discuss cognitive science, whose mental modules are also functionally defined. The idea of functionalism is yet another way in which Freud anticipated recent developments.

The next task is to sketch Freud's mature theory. His main theoretical problem is to account for the resistance to allowing oneself to become conscious of certain mental contents.

4. The Theory of Psychoanalysis

4.1. The Pleasure Principle

The fundamental principle of psychoanalytic theory—the one on which everything else in the theory depends—is the *pleasure principle.* According to the pleasure principle, all behavior follows this pattern:

wish → pain → activity → wish fulfillment → pleasure

Take something we all do from infancy onward: eating food. Eating is preceded by a *wish* for food—this is the wish that goes by the name of hunger. The presence of an ungratified wish is experienced as *pain,* which increases in intensity with time (we get hungrier and hungrier). The rising pain of the ungratified wish mobilizes the organism into *activity* (looking for food). The activity continues until it brings about *wish fulfillment* (in the case of hunger, that's the consumption of food). Finally, wish fulfillment produces *pleasure.*

What does the pleasure principle assert? That not having what you want is painful, that pain galvanizes you to action, and that the pain goes away when your action produces what you want. This sounds very much like a truism—how could it fail to be true? Well, there's no doubt that some of our behavior follows this pattern; but it's by no means obvious that *all* behavior does. What about *idealistic* behavior? Don't people sometimes withstand the pain of ungratified desire in order to do what they think is morally right? What about a mother who goes hungry to feed her children, or someone who submits to torture rather than betray his political cause? At least at first glance, these people would not be acting to diminish their pain. By adopting the pleasure principle, Freud commits himself to explaining every apparent instance of idealistic behavior as a way of obtaining pleasure in the end.

Freud's theory belongs to a broader category of *hedonistic* theories. Like materialism, hedonism has a technical meaning that's different from its everyday sense. In its everyday sense, it's a prescription for how one *should* live one's life—it's the advice that one should always strive to maximize pleasure and minimize pain. In its present sense, it doesn't make any suggestions about how one should live. It's an attempt to describe how people *do* live. Hedonism in this sense is the view that people *do* always strive to maximize pleasure and minimize pain, whether it's a good idea to live that way or not.

Moreover, Freud's is a very special type of hedonism. Confronted with the self-sacrificing mother as a counterexample, a (descriptive) hedonist could say something like the following. Idealistic behavior— going hungry to feed her children—gives the mother a glow of self-righteousness that makes her feel good. In fact, it gives her more pleasure than she would obtain if she ate the food herself. So she's still maximizing pleasure. But this theoretical move isn't available to Freud. He claims that the *only* source of pleasure is the gratification of what he calls the *instincts.* These are biological deficits that, if allowed to continue indefinitely, would be detrimental to the survival of the self or the species. The instincts include hunger, thirst, sex, the avoidance of tissue damage, and pretty much nothing else. Thus Freud is committed to the view that altruistic behavior like the mother's has to be explained, not only as pleasure seeking, but as a gratification of a biologically based need. Warm glows of self-righteousness aren't in the game.

The same conclusion applies to cultural pursuits like science, art, religion, sports, and etiquette. These human activities aren't transparently attempts at instinctive gratification—how does the discovery of a new type of galaxy help to secure the survival of the discoverer, or of the species? We'll see that Freud claims that such cultural pursuits are *indirect* means of instinctive gratification. The pleasure principle commits him to saying this (given his view of the causes of pleasure). The production of cultural or idealistic behavior as an offshoot of the attempt to gratify the instincts is called *sublimation.*

There's another way in which Freud's is a special type of hedonism:

he identifies pleasure with a reduction in the intensity of pain. This contrasts sharply with our everyday notions of pleasure and pain. According to our everyday notions, pleasure and pain are two distinct dimensions of experience. One can experience more or less pleasure, as well as more or less pain. Between the pleasure and pain dimensions, there's a zero point that corresponds to the "neutral" state in which there's neither pleasure nor pain. With this conception of pleasure-pain, hedonism becomes the doctrine that people behave as follows: (1) when they're on the pain side of the zero point, they try to move toward the zero (thereby diminishing pain); and (2) when they're on the pleasure side, they strive to move as far *away* from the zero point as possible (thereby increasing pleasure). Freud's hedonism says the same thing about pain-related behavior. What about the pleasure side? In Freud's view, there's pain on one side of the zero point and *nothing* on the other side—pleasure is nothing more than the *movement* from a more-painful to a less-painful state. Therefore the pleasure-seeking component of Freudian hedonism is indistinguishable from the pain-reducing component.

It might appear that the two versions of hedonism are merely two different descriptions of one and the same set of phenomena. But the two views have significantly different behavioral consequences. Consider what happens when you're at the zero point, feeling neither pleasure nor pain. The everyday hedonist's scheme allows that you might still be actively trying to acquire positive pleasures. In the Freudian scheme, however, if you feel no pain, there's no *possibility* for pleasure (pleasure being a diminution of pain). Hence there can be no hedonistic motive for action. The pleasure principle tells us the same thing directly: all behavior begins with the pain of an ungratified wish—you won't do anything unless you're suffering. This curious hypothesis flies in the face of common sense. We'll see that it eventually gets the theory into trouble but we'll also see that this curious view of pleasure-pain has striking similarities to some of the most influential behavioristic theories, and that it gets *those* theories into similar trouble.

Freud's theory has been characterized as very pessimistic. For one thing, it purports to unmask humanity's high and noble pursuits, revealing them to be nothing more than devious strategies for gratifying our biological needs. For another thing, it denies the existence of positively pleasureful states—the best state that an organism can hope to attain is the complete absence of pain. As he grew older, Freud's pessimism only deepened. Late in his career, he conceded that human behavior is sometimes elicited by motives other than the preservation of self and species. These motives had nothing to do with the good, the true, or the beautiful, however. The new instinct was an innate drive toward death and destruction (Freud 1920/1984). Later Freud saw the human condition as a perpetual struggle between the life-affirming instincts ("Eros") and the life-denying instincts ("Thanatos"). Most psychoanalysts chose to stay with the earlier, somewhat less pessimistic theory. It's the more influential early theory that's expounded in this chapter.

Freud adds two subsidiary principles to the pleasure principle. These specify what happens when the *instinct object* isn't forthcoming. (A terminological note: the instinct object is the state of affairs that produces instinctive gratification. The instinct object of the hunger instinct is the consumption of food or, more loosely, food itself.) As time without gratification goes by, the pain of the ungratified instinct gets stronger and stronger. At some point, the pain reaches such a level that it begins to debilitate us, so that it becomes increasingly difficult for us to *find* the instinct object, or to acquire it even if we find it. By a process of evolution, nature has supplied us with two mechanisms that extend the period of time during which we can function in the absence of instinctive gratification. They both work by *partially* and *temporarily* diminishing the pain of ungratified desire.

The first subsidiary principle can be diagrammed as follows:

wish → pain → affective discharge → partial and temporary pain reduction

An "affective discharge" could also be called a temper tantrum. Supposedly we tend to throw a tantrum when we don't get what we want because it makes us feel better, despite our continued deprivation. This raises an interesting question: why do babies cry when they're in a state of need? In part, it's because they've learned that crying hastens the arrival of the bottle. But that's not the whole story, because from the moment of their birth, infants cry when they're uncomfortable—long before they've had an opportunity to learn that it's an effective technique for getting what they want. Freud says that they cry because it gives them temporary relief.

The second subsidiary principle is much more important to the development of psychoanalytic theory:

wish → pain → hallucinatory wish fulfillment → partial and temporary pain reduction

"Hallucinatory wish fulfillment" means having a mental image of the absent instinct object. In common parlance, a hallucination is a subjective image mistaken for an objective perception. In the present context, it doesn't matter whether you have this erroneous belief about your subjective image or not—just having the image is enough to bring relief. So a hungry person who isn't getting any food will indulge in fantasies about food, and these fantasies will help to assuage the hunger. Of course, this is only a temporary effect. Eventually the pain of ungratified hunger overwhelms this mechanism. But the fantasies extend the period of time during which the pain is manageable. For reasons that will be explained shortly, it's not only imagistic pictures of the instinct object itself that have this palliative effect. Images of objects *associated* with the instinct objects, like knives and forks, work just as well.

It's because of this secondary principle that dreams turn out to be so important to psychoanalytic theory. According to Freud, dreams are composed entirely of compensatory subjective images. It follows that the content of dreams can provide information about the dreamer's ungratified needs. Dreams need interpretation, however, because the images aren't necessarily pictures of the instinct object. They can also be associates of the instinct object. A man can be represented by his hat, a woman named "Penny" represented by a penny, and so on.

There's partial experimental confirmation of the second subsidiary mechanism in a study by David McClelland and John Atkinson (1948). The authors ensured that one group of subjects had eaten a meal one hour before the experiment, that another group hadn't eaten for four hours before, and that a third group had fasted for a full sixteen hours. The subjects sat in front of an illuminated blank or smudged screen and were asked to describe what they saw. The experimenters found that the hungrier the group, the more often it reported seeing instrumental objects related to eating, such as knives and forks. This is exactly what Freud would have predicted. Less favorable to psychoanalytic theory was the finding that the groups didn't differ in the frequency with which they reported seeing instances of the instinct object itself, such as bananas or hamburgers. In any case, there's at least some experimental evidence that the continued absence of the instinct object generates "hallucinatory" activity. From the Freudian theory, we would also predict that this activity makes subjects temporarily feel better. To our knowledge, this hypothesis has never been tested. It would be easy enough to do so. We could divide our subjects into a food-deprived group that performs the smudgy-screen task, and an equally food-deprived group that performs an arithmetical task requiring a lot of attention. Since the smudgy-screen task offers more opportunities for hallucinatory wish fulfillment, the prediction would be that the smudgy-screen subjects would report feeling better than the subjects who had to keep their heads filled with numbers.

4.2. The Reality Principle

The psychoanalytic story told so far goes like this: at first, in accordance with the pleasure principle, the organism lies in a heap, totally inert until activated by the pain of an instinctive need; next, the pain instigates behavior, which continues until the instinct object is secured; and finally, the acquisition of the instinct object eliminates the pain, and the organism falls back in a heap, totally inactive once again—until the next instinctive need comes along. We suspect that this will not strike most readers as an apt description of their life. But it is a more plausible description of a *newborn infant's* life—and in fact, Freud does stipulate that it's the organism's state at birth, and that as time goes by, the operation of the pleasure principle is modified in significant ways.

Freud also says that at this early stage of life, when only the pleasure principle rules, *consciousness* has not yet developed. The pain, the activation, and the gratification postulated by the pleasure principle are all unconscious. Does this mean that newborn infants are unconscious all the time? Yes, it does. But how can this be maintained? After all, the infant exhibits intentional, goal-directed behavior when she acts so as to acquire the instinct object. Can there be intentional behavior without consciousness? Intentional behavior without consciousness is what psychoanalysis is all about. Consider what happens when you're walking home by a familiar route while engaged in intense conversation. You can be so absorbed in the conversation that the process of walking becomes completely unconscious. Yet, even though you're not attending to the movements of your legs and arms, you manage to avoid bumping into people, you step up and down curbs, and so on. This is very complex intentional behavior without consciousness. It's true that in this example, you're still conscious—it's just that you're conscious of something other than your walking. It's not at all clear, however, that the concomitant consciousness of something else in any way facilitates the unconscious behavior.

More persuasively, there's a familiar phenomenon wherein intentional behavior seems to take place without being accompanied by consciousness of anything whatsoever: the phenomenon of sleepwalking. Sleepwalkers are routinely capable of complex, goal-directed motor activity. For example, they usually walk through doorways rather than bumping into walls. If the sleepwalker is indeed unconscious, then complex behavior doesn't require consciousness. In any case, Freud regards the behavior of the infant as akin to that of the sleepwalker.

According to Freud, one can even engage in *thinking* without being conscious. However, unconscious thinking suffers from severe limitations. Unconscious thinking does not allow for logical reasoning, cause-and-effect analysis, and distinguishing a real object from either a subjective image of the object or anything that's in any way associated with the object. Freud calls this sort of thinking *primary process* thinking. It's because unconscious thinking is always primary process thinking that hallucinatory wish fulfillment effects a temporary reduction of pain: the unconscious infant is sunk in primary process thought, and so can't distinguish between the real instinct object and a subjective image of it—when the infant gets an image of it, he thinks he's got the real thing and is temporarily satisfied.

Now suppose that you have the infant's mentality, and that you become activated by the hunger instinct. In accordance with the pleasure principle, you'll begin to search for the appropriate instinct object, which in this case is food. When you succeed in securing the instinct object, you'll experience a decrease in the pain due to your ungratified instinctive need. But the acquisition of some instinct objects can cause more pain than they diminish. For example, in your quest for food, you might see a banana lying in the middle of a busy highway. If you try to get the banana, you're going to get hit by a truck. But this is the kind of cause-and-effect reasoning that's beyond the capacity of an unconscious, primary-process-thinking organism. What happens next?

The theoretical apparatus developed so far leads to the prediction that you go for the banana and get hit by a truck. If that were the whole story that psychoanalysis has to tell, we would have to wonder how any of us ever manages to survive to adulthood. We can imagine an ideal environment wherein an individual always receives immediate gratification of all her instinctive needs—as soon as she feels the first twinge of hunger, a cheeseburger magically appears in her hand. If that were the human condition, then the story of psychoanalysis would indeed already be finished: the individual would remain unconscious and immersed in primary process thought. The real world, however, is not a Garden of Eden. Sooner or later in everyone's life, conflicts between instinctive needs and the constraints of reality arise. You want the banana, but you can't get it without being hit by a truck. According to Freud, the only reason you usually survive these conflicts is that you develop a conscious, rational *calculating organ* that can take the constraints of reality into account. This organ is able to calculate that getting the banana in the present circumstances would lead to more pain than it would assuage, and to conclude that you would be better served by foregoing the banana and looking for a less problematic instinct object. The name of the organ that can do this is the *ego.*

The ego is a postnatal addition to the mental apparatus that we're born with. The innate apparatus is now called the *id* and continues, as before, to be unconscious and capable only of primary process thinking. The ego is the structure that can do what the id can't: engage in logical and causal reasoning, and distinguish objective perceptions of reality from subjective images. Freud calls this kind of mental activity *secondary process* thinking.

Once the ego is in place, the pleasure principle is no longer a complete description of the genesis of behavior. It is replaced by the *reality principle:*

> wish → pain → *delay* of wish fulfillment → activity → wish fulfillment → pleasure

Note that the reality principle contains the whole of the pleasure principle as one if its parts. The only difference between the two is that the reality principle adds the possibility of a delay prior to the activity that leads to wish fulfillment. The new behavioral capacity is the ability to desist from jumping on the first instinct object we encounter, because we rationally judge it to be unsafe, and to continue searching until a safer avenue to gratification is found.

Does this return us to the Cartesian conception of behavior as determined by a conscious and rational agent? Far from it. Let's focus on what *doesn't* change in the transition from the pleasure principle to the reality principle. According to the reality principle, behavior *still* starts with an unconscious desire from the id. In normal circumstances, this desire is conveyed to the ego, whose job it is to find a safe method of satisfying the id's demand. What the ego *can't* do is to consciously and rationally choose the *goal* of behavior. The goal is *always* instinctive gratification. All the ego can do is delay gratification when circumstances are inauspicious. This is a far cry from the executive role of the freely willing Cartesian soul.

An interesting note: when we talk about the ego, we're talking about what we usually consider to be our *self*. In fact, "ego" means "I" in Latin. It's easy to see that the first-person pronoun "I" doesn't refer to our total organism. If asked what you've been doing for the past hour or two, you would never seriously say, "I've been digesting my food." Yet your digestion is certainly an activity of your total organism. Presumably, your "I" refers only to the conscious part of your total organism—i.e., to your ego—which is not implicated in your digestive activities. So the postulate that one's ego can't choose the goals of one's behavior may be translated into the following startling proposition: *I* can't choose the goal of my own behavior. All *I* can do is delay gratification. I am a manager, not the CEO.

How does the ego manage to delay the id's drive for gratification? The ego may have come to the rational conclusion that a delay would actually further the id's agenda in the long run. But it's no use trying to explain the argument to the primary-process thinking id. The ego has no choice but to *manipulate* the id into quiescence. Leverage for the manipulation is provided by the ubiquitous mechanism of temporary pain reduction via hallucinatory wish fulfillment. When the id demands gratification and the ego judges that all the currently available instinct objects are inappropriate, the ego will supply the id with a hallucinatory substitute for the instinct object. For example, a man who can find no safe sexual partner may paint a picture of a naked woman. The stupid id, being restricted to primary process thinking, can't tell the difference and thinks it's got the real thing. So it temporarily stops pressing for gratification—and that's how the delay is effected.

Recall the definition of sublimation: the production of culture as a by-product of the quest for instinctive gratification. The example of the sex-starved painter shows us how sublimation is supposed to work: delaying gratification by providing the id with a hallucinatory substitute *inadvertently* results in the production of a work of art. For Freud, *all* cultural activities are produced by this sublimatory delay mechanism. A consequence of this view is that if all our instinctive needs were immediately met from birth—if we lived in the Garden of Eden—then we would never produce culture, since there would be nothing to sublimate. In fact, denizens of Eden would never be propelled into any sort of activity, since action occurs only during intervals of ungratified desire. In fact, they would never become conscious, since the conscious ego develops out of conflict between desire and reality.

Freud tried to work out the details of his sublimation theory in a series of books on such topics as art and religion. In each case, he tried to show that the cultural activity at issue was a sublimation of an ungratified biological need. The need was almost always sexual, which led to the popular opinion that Freud claimed that all behavior is sexually motivated. This is a misapprehension of Freud's view. It isn't all sex for Freud—it's all *pleasure*. It's true that in Freud's case histories, the sublimation is almost always based on an ungratified sexual need but this isn't due to any general psychoanalytical principle. It's due to the historical accident that our culture places numerous constraints on the gratification of sexual desire. There are rules about how you can do it, who you can do it with, when and where you can do it, and so on. Moreover, there are heavy sanctions for rule breakers. The result is that there's a lot of ungratified sexuality available for sublimating. Some anthropologists have claimed that there are societies in which sexual gratification is as casual and unproblematic as eating a sandwich is for us (Mead 1928). Psychoanalytic theory would lead us to expect that the cultural activities of such a society would be based on the sublimation of entirely different needs. If there were a society that made as much trouble about eating as ours does about sex, its painters would paint pictures of cheeseburgers instead of naked women, its adolescents would tell dirty jokes about cakes and pies, its hucksters would sell dirty postcards of fruits and vegetables, and people would have dreams in which male genitals figure as primary-process symbolic substitutes for the cucumbers and carrots that are the dreamer's real objects of desire.

What about this Freudian account of the origin and function of consciousness? We will present two criticisms—one related to function, the other to origin. First the functional point. The question here is: what is consciousness for? Freud's answer is that consciousness enables us to figure out how to obtain the instinct object when this task requires problem solving. The id is evidently endowed with sufficient mental powers to acquire instinct objects when the acquisition is in some sense routine. But consciousness is necessary to adapt one's behavior to unexpected circumstances.

This view of the function of consciousness antedates psychoanalysis. Between the eras of introspectionism and behaviorism, American psychology went through an intervening movement known as *functionalism* (yes, the history of psychology sketched in Chapter 2 is a drastic simplification of the historical reality). This turn-of-the-century functionalism should not be confused with another, much more recent theory of cognitive science that goes by the same name (recent functionalism will be discussed in Chapter 6). Like the introspectionists before them, the early functionalists regarded consciousness as the main subject matter of psychology. Introspectionists wanted to study consciousness for its own sake. They sought to describe the qualities of conscious states in isolation from their nonmental causes or effects. The functionalists, however, strove to ascertain what difference being in a particular conscious state makes in our subsequent behavior. What conscious states are *like* was deemed to be a less important question than what conscious states are *for.* In their concern with behavior, the functionalists foreshadowed the coming behaviorist revolution but they didn't go so far as to throw consciousness out of psychology altogether. Most functionalists followed William James (1890/1950), their leader, in regarding consciousness in general to be the process that enables us to adapt our behavior to novel circumstances. Freud says essentially the same thing.

Our criticism is that neither Freud nor James tries to explain why the capacity for adapting to novel circumstances—what Freud calls secondary process thinking—requires consciousness. According to Freud, there can be *primary* process thought without consciousness. Then why can't there also be unconscious secondary process thought? What is it about problem solving that requires consciousness? At this juncture, it's relevant to say a few words about the enterprise of artificial intelligence (AI) research (the topic will be discussed at length in Chapter 7). AI is the attempt to write programs that enable computers to simulate human intellectual performances. For example, it's easy to write a program for alphabetizing a list of names or playing a legal game of chess. A far more difficult AI task is to write a program for summarizing longer texts. In fact, a program that can do so as well as humans has not yet been devised. Nevertheless, many AI researchers believe that computers can, in principle, be programmed to perform any intellectual task that human beings are capable of. Suppose, just for the sake of the argument, that these AI researchers are right. Then computers would be capable of any and all instances of the secondary process thought that Freud attributes to consciousness. But if a computer can do it, then it doesn't require consciousness! One could claim that a computer programmed to think like a human being in every way would ipso facto become conscious. But it's unclear what explanatory advantage is purchased by this additional postulate. The structure of the program itself already explains the problem-solving capacities of the computer even if the computer *doesn't* become conscious. So the question remains: what is consciousness for? Of course, the optimistic AI researchers may be wrong—it may turn out that there are human intellectual capacities that can't be programmed. But that's by no means been proven as yet. Moreover, even if we admit that human thought is unprogrammable, Freud and James would still owe us an explanation of how consciousness is supposed to help us to perform the unprogrammable tasks.

We turn now to Freud's account of the origin of consciousness. Some, including psychoanalyst Heinz Hartmann (1958), have claimed that the psychoanalytical theory of ego development is logically flawed. The argument is very brief—too brief to do justice to its importance. We'll make up for this deficiency by presenting Hartmann's point twice in different ways.

The first pass: Freud's developmental theory, in essence, is that the id can't adapt to the constraints of reality, so it develops a rational device—the ego—that *can* take these constraints into account. Hartmann's point is that this response of growing an ego is *already* an adaptive, rational response to the constraints of reality. There's nothing in the pleasure principle that would explain such a reaction to experiencing a conflict with reality. Hartmann's conclusion is that we've got to be capable of adaptive responses *before* the first conflict occurs. If we weren't—if we started life working solely in accordance with the pleasure principle—then when conflict with reality occurred, we wouldn't develop an ego. We would die.

The same argument in another form: why do we acquire knowledge about the world? (That's what the ego is basically for.) Freud's view is that we *don't* acquire knowledge at first—we just do what gratifies our instinctive needs. But we learn that knowledge *helps* to gratify our instinctive needs—and that's why we embark on the enterprise of acquiring knowledge. The problem with this account is that if we aren't acquiring knowledge at the beginning, then we could never come to know that knowledge is useful in the quest for instinctive gratification. The fact that we learn that knowledge is useful shows that we are busy acquiring knowledge before we know that knowledge is useful. The conclusion, once again, is that we must be born with the capacity and desire to acquire knowledge already in place.

Hartmann claims to have shown that the ego doesn't develop as a result of conflict. It must be there right from the start. Also, the wishes that initiate behavior aren't all for the gratification of biological instincts like sex and hunger (reread the last sentence of the previous paragraph). That means that Freud's analysis of culture as produced by the sublimation of ungratified instinctive desire is rendered superfluous. Despite his major theoretical divergence from Freud, Hartmann is still considered to be a psychoanalytic theorist, because he still accepts the most basic tenets of psychoanalysis: the existence of unconscious mental processes and the tripartite division of the mind into id, ego, and superego. However, making the ego innate is so enormous a change that this revised theory goes by the name of *ego psychology,* in recognition of the greater importance placed on the activity of the ego. Hartmann's revision has been widely accepted in the psychoanalytical community. Most people who consider themselves to be orthodox psychoanalysts are ego psychologists.

4.3. Moral Behavior

So far as we've taken our account of psychoanalysis, there's no place yet for considerations of morality. The ego won't take food away from an ill-tempered gorilla because it judges that the resultant pleasure would be outweighed by the resultant pain; but it *would* take food away from a little child who can't retaliate. What about cases such as the hungry mother who gives her food to her children? According to the reality principle, the only restriction on instinctive gratification is the avoidance of painful consequences. If you can safely get away with a self-serving behavior, then you'll do it. If this is so, then wouldn't all impoverished mothers eat their fill and let their children die?

These reflections bring us to the subject of the *superego,* which is the third and final mental structure postulated by psychoanalytic theory. According to psychoanalytic orthodoxy, the ego is fully developed in the first or second year of life, the superego is developed by age five or six, and that's it—there are no important mental developments after the superego appears. According to Freud, your psychological make-up is pretty much set for life by the age of six.

The superego's function is to erect barriers to instinctive gratification beyond those imposed by reality. This needs some explaining. What happens when parents punish a child for a certain behavior—say, for lying? Assume that the child already has an ego but doesn't yet have a superego. Now parental punishment is an aversive consequence of lying that the ego is capable of taking into account. The child thus learns to avoid punishment, just as he learns to avoid sticking his fingers in the fire to retrieve a toy. At this stage, if the ego judges that it can tell an advantageous lie *without getting caught,* the reality principle dictates that it will do so. However, as children grow older, almost all of them begin to display a different behavioral pattern: they sometimes avoid a previously punished behavior even when they're sure that they *won't* be caught. This is the type of behavior that needs to be explained. As was the case with the imageless-thought controversy, the frequency of the phenomenon is not important. It can be granted for the sake of the argument that almost all students would almost always cheat on exams if they were assured of not being caught. So long as at least one student doesn't cheat on at least one occasion, we have a theoretical problem.

Freud's explanation of moral behavior is that the punishing behavior

of the parents is *internalized* in the following sense. A new mental structure, the superego, is put in place and functions as a *representative* of the
parents. The superego metes out the punishment that the parents *would*
administer if they were around. This punishment is in the form of an
unpleasant emotional state that goes by the name of *guilt*. After you've
grown a superego, you're in effect walking around with the punishing
agent inside your head. So it may look as though you refrain from doing
the thing you were punished for even though you won't be found out;
but in reality you're *always* found out, because the punishing agent is
always right there.

It's theoretically important that even after the superego is in place,
the ego is still supposed to be functioning hedonistically. It's still
trying to minimize pain—but now it has a new form of pain to take
into account. Before the superego, the ego only had to worry about
whether instinctive gratification would lead to harm from reality such
as getting hit by a truck. After the superego, it also has to worry about
whether gratification will impel the superego to inflict the harm of
guilt. The ego's ordained task is to satisfy all three masters: (1) to give
the *id* what it wants while avoiding (2) harm from *reality* and (3) guilt
from the *superego*. Of course, talk of "reality" as an agent is metaphor-
ical. Id, ego, and superego, however, are literally personages, each with
an agenda of its own. Bannister aptly summarizes their character and
relationship:

> . . . psychoanalytic theories suggest that man is essentially . . .
> a dark cellar in which a maiden aunt and a sex-crazed mon-
> key are locked in mortal combat, the affair being refereed by
> a rather nervous bank-clerk. (Bannister 1966, 363)

According to Freud, nobody can survive into adulthood without
an ego; but it is possible to grow to adulthood without developing a
superego. This is what makes a person a *psychopath*. Psychopaths are
people who will lie, cheat, steal, and kill without any sign of remorse,
so long as it's to their advantage to do so. The psychoanalytic theory
of psychopathy is that such a person has never developed a superego.
The result is that the ego, working purely hedonistically—as all egos
do—is unrestrained by the threat of guilt.

Like the ego, the superego is at least partly conscious. The way
Freud sees it, we are all split personalities (except for those of us who

are psychopaths). Sometimes the pronouns "I" and "me" refer to the ego, sometimes to the superego. The ego "me" is the one who calculates consequences, makes decisions, and acts on them; the superego "me" is the one who passes judgment on the correctness of the action. This dissociation explains the puzzling but commonplace phenomenon wherein a person consciously does something (e.g., masturbates) while at the same time consciously castigating himself for doing it. The puzzle is why we would do something that we ourselves disapprove of. Freud's solution is to say that the "me" who decides to perform the action is not the same entity as the "me" who does the disapproving.

How does the superego develop? We've seen that the ego develops out of a conflict between the id and reality. We've also seen that the Freudian theory of ego development is subject to very damaging criticism. The same can be said about the developmental theory of the superego. It, too, is supposed to develop as the result of a conflict; and the story that Freud tells about its development is also subject to damaging criticism. In fact, the theory of superego development is the least tenable part of psychoanalysis. But the story has been extremely influential on contemporary arts and literature. So despite its untenability, it's really unthinkable that an introduction to psychology should leave it out. We're talking about the infamous *Oedipus conflict*. That's the name of the story that Freud tells about little boys. The corresponding story for little girls—the *Electra conflict*—is slightly different. As many recent authors have noted, Freud was a notoriously sexist thinker. The difference between the Oedipus and Electra conflict is one of many places where this sexism manifests itself. Let's start with little boys.

Freud begins with the observation that the male child sees his father as a rival for his mother's affection. But the child also sees father as an all-powerful figure capable of delivering the direst of punishments. Consequently, he fears that if he wins the contest for mother's affection, father will wreak terrible vengeance on him. (Freud identifies the feared punishment as a fear of being castrated. This colorful and implausible detail isn't essential to the theory—any terrible punishment will fit in with the rest of Freud's account just as well.) The child thus finds himself in a no-win situation: if he loses the contest with dad, he's deprived of mom's affection, and if he wins the contest with dad, he loses a highly prized member. What's the best course for him to take? That's the Oedipus conflict. (Oedipus was a mythological Greek king who murdered his father and married his mother.)

Recall that the earlier conflict between the instincts and reality is resolved by growing an ego. Similarly, the Oedipus conflict is resolved by growing another mental structure—the superego. What happens is that the child *identifies* his sense of self with his father. This means that he experiences father's successes and failures as his own successes and failures. In this way, the rivalry with father is short-circuited: if father wins the affection of mother, then by virtue of identification, so does the child. In this way, he gains mother's affection *and* placates father at the same time. Because of identification, the child begins to act toward *himself* in the same way as his father would: if he does something that father would punish, then *he,* being identified with the father, does the punishing—and that's what it is to have a superego.

The Electra conflict for little girls is almost the same, but with the roles reversed: the little girl see mother as a rival for the affection of father, and resolves the conflict by identifying with mother. The difference is that mother is a much less fearsome rival than father. Therefore the conflict is less severe and the identification that resolves it is less complete. This explains the well-known fact that women are morally inferior to men—they have a weaker superego because the Electra conflict that produces it is weaker!

In this account, the superego and moral behavior are a mere *byproduct* of the resolution of the Oedipus and Electra conflicts. We don't abstain from lying, stealing, and killing because of a moral insight or feeling that these things are bad—we do it ultimately to gain the affection of mom or dad.

We will discuss three criticisms of the Freudian account of the superego, in order of increasing severity. The least telling criticism is the complaint that the key concept of identification is very obscure. What exactly happens when you extend your sense of self to another person? One searches in vain through the literature of psychoanalysis for a suggestion as to the mechanism that effects such a change. This deficiency is regrettable, but obscure as the mechanism may be, there's very little doubt that identification happens. The two most obvious examples are identification with countries (patriotism) and with sports teams (fandom). When the home team wins, the fan is elated; and when the home team loses, he gets depressed. That's exactly the property of Freudian identification: experiencing the successes and failures of the other as one's own. The clincher is that when the home team wins, fans never exclaim, "They won!"—it's always "*We* won!"—even if their participation in the game was restricted to viewing it on television.

The second, and more telling, criticism is that it's difficult to reconcile Freud's theory of the superego with some of his more general theoretical assumptions. On Freud's account, the ego sometimes finds itself weighing the pain of continuing hunger against the pain of guilt for eating forbidden food. Guilt is not a form of pain that the id recognizes. According to the Freudian version of hedonism enshrined in the pleasure and reality principles, the only pain that motivates behavior is supposed to be the pain of ungratified biological instincts like hunger and sex. However, in light of the theory of the superego, this formulation of hedonism needs amendment. Evidently, the ego's decisions can be motivated by forms of pain (guilt) that are not biological need-states. In fact, the desire to avoid guilt can trump instinctive desires: we sometimes choose to prolong our state of hunger rather than eat forbidden fruit. But then the ego is not just a manager that figures out how to get the id what it wants. Its own desire to avoid guilt, which means nothing to the id, may determine a course of action.

The foregoing critique has some of the same consequences as Hartmann's critique of the Freudian ego theory. According to Hartmann, we have to accept the thesis that human beings are born with an innate propensity to acquire knowledge. The most radical consequence of accepting this thesis is that there's no longer any reason to suppose that all cultural activity is based on the sublimation of instinctive needs. Similarly, we've just seen that the Freudian theory of the superego requires us to postulate guilt-avoidance as a noninstinctive need. The way Freud tells it, children can be made to feel guilty about *anything*. Hence guilt-avoidance is available as an alternative to sublimation for explaining any cultural activity. We may engage in scientific or artistic pursuits in order to avoid the guilt of living unproductive lives.

Like the sublimation hypothesis, this alternative account of culture still depicts cultural activity as an indirect means of gratifying another desire: we don't engage in scientific or artistic pursuits for their own sake, but merely to avoid guilt. However, once we've postulated the existence of *one* nonbiological motive, it becomes extremely plausible to postulate the existence of others. If we're going to make one exception to the rule that only instinctive needs motivate behavior, why not make two, or three, or four? We will see in Chapter 5 that this route was actually taken by later psychoanalysts. Hartmann's thesis that we have an innate knowledge-seeking propensity is a major step down this path. This thesis provides a direct, nonreductive explanation for knowledge-seeking activities like science. If Hartmann is right, then we don't need any other advantage to engage in knowledge seeking. We're built to value knowledge for its own sake.

A note on the logical structure of the foregoing critique: the argument isn't that Freud's theory of the superego is flawed in and of itself—it's that there's an incompatibility between what Freud has to say about the superego and his hypothesis that the only source of motivation is ungratified instinctive need. Rationality compels us to abandon one or the other. Hartmann's argument already forces us to reject Freud's general theory of motivation. So the fact that the superego theory is incompatible with the general theory of motivation doesn't really count against the superego theory. When we characterize this critique as "telling," we mean that it highlights a problem for psychoanalytic theory taken as a whole.

The third, and most telling, criticism of the superego theory is that it's based on the child-rearing practices of a particular time and place—early twentieth century Europe—where monogamy was strictly enforced, father was the sole disciplinarian, and discipline was severe. If the Oedipal story is a universally valid account of how moral behavior develops, then moral behavior *wouldn't develop* in cultures and eras in which this set of circumstances doesn't exist. For example, the anthropologist Bronislaw Malinowski described a Pacific Island culture where the roles of father and uncle were reversed (Malinowski 1927). In this culture, the discipline of children was entirely in the hands of their mother's brother, while father functioned as little more than a playmate. The Oedipus conflict is supposed to arise when the child sees himself as competing with a stern disciplinarian for the prize of mother's affection. But on the island described by Malinowski, the person he's competing with and the stern disciplinarian are two different people! The child has reason to fear uncle, but no reason to identify with him—identification with uncle doesn't buy him anything. Conversely, the child has no reason to fear a no-holds-barred contest with affable dad. In sum, the Oedipus conflict doesn't arise. So if Freud's account were the only way that morality develops, we would expect the members of Malinowski's culture to have no conception of morality. This is, of course, not the case. Different cultures have different notions about what *is* moral and immoral; but they all have *some* conception of morality. That is to say, they all specify certain sorts of activities that are to be performed (or not) regardless of one's personal inclinations. The fact that some cultures don't provide any space for the Oedipus conflict to arise means that the Oedipus conflict is not a necessary prerequisite for morality.

4.4. Anxiety and Defense

In classical Freudian psychoanalysis, the function of the ego is to satisfy the id's demands for instinctive gratification while at the same time taking into account the constraints of reality and of the superego. Obviously, this mission can't be accomplished unless the ego knows what the id wants. For the ego to know what the id wants is for us to be conscious of our instinctive needs. This is very often the case. When the id wants food, the ego consciously experiences the sensation of hunger; and when the id wants sex, the ego is aware of being sexually aroused. The central idea of psychoanalysis, however, is that some desires remain unconscious. In fact, some desires *resist* becoming conscious even if they're pointed out by another person. Chapter 3 ended with the assertion that the main goal of Freud's theoretical endeavors was to provide an explanation for this sort of resistance. We're finally ready to see what Freud was able to come up with.

Suppose that the id wants sexual gratification, but the superego condemns all available forms of sexual activity as bad and threatens to inflict a stiff dose of guilt for indulging in any of them. It's the ego's job to figure out a mode of action that satisfies both the id and the superego. But what if it can't find one? What if the conflict is *irresolvable?* Freud says that if the ego remains in this state of irresolution, it begins to fall apart. This is a new and independent postulate of psychoanalytic theory—it doesn't follow from anything that was said before. What does it mean for the ego to fall apart? Well, the ego is the mental organ that engages in secondary process thinking—thinking that's rational, and that distinguishes objective events from subjective experiences. An impairment of this function therefore produces *ir*rational thinking and a diminished capacity to distinguish objective reality from subjective experience. In a phrase, the impairment of ego functions produces *loss of contact with reality*. According to psychoanalysis, loss of contact with reality is the defining characteristic of *psychosis*. It's not the only conception of psychosis that's in play among psychologists. Another is the social conception according to which a person is psychotic if her experience and behavior are radically different from the norm in her society. But Freud's is "loss of contact with reality."

So, according to Freud, the danger of an ungratifiable wish is that it can make you go crazy! When this danger threatens, the ego abandons the futile program of delaying gratification and searching for a safe instinct-object. It becomes concerned only with its own preservation. What it does to preserve itself is to distort or completely push out of consciousness the ungratifiable wish. The idea is that it's the ego's awareness of its own incapacity to fulfill the id's demand that causes the breakdown. Evidently, the ego can't continue to function under the burden of knowing that it's unable to fulfill its mission so it protects itself from breakdown by not letting itself know about its own impotence. There are various ways of doing this. Each one is called a *defense mechanism*. Freud offered slightly different lists of the defense mechanisms at different times. Some of them, however, are present in all the lists. Here are a few of the most famous.

In *displacement,* you continue to be aware of *what* you want to do, but you distort your awareness of *who* you want to do it to. You'd like to remonstrate angrily to your boss, but you're afraid you'll lose your job. Moreover, you can't admit this to yourself, for then your superego would condemn you as a coward. In displacement, you continue to be aware of your anger, but you change the object. Yes, you're angry—but it's no wonder you're angry when the dog keeps chewing up the furniture!

In *projection,* you remain conscious of the *thought* of the unacceptable wish, but you attribute the *feeling* to others. The classic example is the projection of homosexual impulses. You're aware that your mind is continuously flooded with thoughts of homosexuality—but it's no wonder you keep thinking about homosexuality when every same-sex person you meet makes sexual advances toward you!

In *reaction formation,* you drown out the unacceptable wish by flooding your mind with thoughts of the opposite kind. Whistling in the dark is a type of reaction formation. Another example: when little boys first get sexually interested in little girls, they have a problem admitting their interest, even to themselves. Their way of dealing with the situation is to become extraordinarily nasty to little girls—playing pranks on them, pulling their pigtails, and so on. As little girls know, this is all a device to cover up the boys' attraction.

In *repression,* the ego loses all awareness of the ungratifiable wish. The issue simply disappears from consciousness. All the other defense mechanisms can be thought of as partial and imperfect repressions wherein some element of the irresolvable conflict leaks through into consciousness. Repression is therefore theoretically the most important defense mechanism. We'll have a lot more to say about it later in this chapter.

Freud thinks that we all have defense mechanisms. A *neurotic* is someone who's burdened with an extraordinarily large number of them. So the difference between a "normal" person and a neurotic is one of degree. It's often thought that the difference between neurotics and psychotics is also one of degree. If this were so, then normals, neurotics, and psychotics could all be located on a continuous dimension of mental disturbance. But according to Freud, psychosis is *qualitatively different* from neurosis, not just different in degree. A neurotic is someone who's burdened by a lot of defenses, while a psychotic is someone whose defenses have *failed.* The neurotic defends too much to be functioning optimally; the psychotic hasn't defended enough.

How do the defense mechanisms work? We'll discuss only the perfect defense of repression. To explain Freud's theory of repression, we need to introduce one more concept: *anxiety.* Anxiety is an aversive sensation related to a potential danger in the future. For example, you turn a corner and see a tiger in front of you, whereupon you experience an intense negative feeling. Why does this reaction take place? After all, the sight of a tiger doesn't do any physical damage to you. To be sure, the sight of a tiger is a signal of a *potential* damage—it tells you that you've got to take action in order to avoid getting killed— but why does the *signal* hurt? Wouldn't we have been better off if the signal of impending danger had been a harmless flashing red light instead of a painful dose of anxiety? Well, one benefit of a painful danger signal is that it immediately motivates you to get out of the situation. If the signal were a red light, you might be impelled to think about what your reaction should be, and then it might be too late— the tiger will have pounced on you before you've made up your mind to run away. The pain of anxiety, on the other hand, calls for immediate relief: your present circumstances make you feel bad, so you immediately escape from them—and by escaping the lesser pain of anxiety, you manage to avoid altogether the greater misfortune of being killed by the tiger. It's this escape-avoidance dynamic that's essential to the Freudian notion of anxiety—anxiety gives you something bad to escape, and as a result you totally avoid something that's even worse.

Freud distinguishes three types of anxiety: *realistic, moral,* and *neurotic.* All three types work the same way. They differ only in the location of the danger being signaled. The three locations correspond to the three entities that the ego has to take into account in making its decisions: reality, the superego, and the id.

1. Realistic anxiety is a signal of danger coming from "reality"; i.e., the external world of colliding trucks and murderous tigers.

2. Moral anxiety arises when you contemplate doing something that the superego forbids; it impels you to decide *not* to do it in order to terminate the anxiety. By escaping the pain of moral anxiety, you avoid the greater pain of guilt that you would experience if you succumbed to temptation.

3. Neurotic anxiety is a signal of danger coming from the id. The danger in this case is the irresolvable conflict coming to consciousness and producing a breakdown of ego function. In brief, neurotic anxiety is a signal of impending psychosis.

Neurotic anxiety works the same way as the other two. Let's retrace the steps involved in realistic anxiety: (1) the sight of a tiger produces realistic anxiety; (2) the anxiety impels you to run away in order to escape it; (3) by escaping anxiety, you manage to avoid being killed. Neurotic anxiety begins with thinking of an *associate* of the irresolvable conflict—that is to say, an idea that in the normal course of events would lead you to thoughts of the irresolvable conflict. For example, suppose that the ungratifiable wish is the desire to kill a rival, and suppose that this rival has an unusually large number of cats. In the normal course of events, if you thought of cats, it would be natural for that idea to cause you to think about your cat-owning rival and your desire to terminate him. But what happens is that the thought of cats itself produces anxiety—and just as anxiety at the sight of a tiger makes you run away physically, here the thought of the associate makes you run away mentally. To escape the anxiety, you *change the direction of your thoughts,* and thereby avoid thinking the forbidden thought. If you keep doing this with every associate of the forbidden thought, then the forbidden thought never manages to enter consciousness; that's how repression works. Resistance is just another way of talking about repression: to turn away from any line of thought that leads to consciousness of the forbidden impulse *is* to resist the imputation that one harbors the impulse.

Neurotic anxiety is also the key to the psychoanalytical theory of phobias. In the example of the previous paragraph, you end up with an irrational fear of cats—you feel anxious at the sight or the very mention of cats, even though you may concede that a cat is very unlikely to inflict serious harm. But the only reason that neurotic anxiety seems to be more irrational than realistic anxiety is that the danger signaled by the latter is out in the external world for everybody to see, whereas the danger signaled by the former is an event that takes place in the inner recesses of your mind. While it may be true that a cat is unlikely to inflict *physical* harm on you, it may very well inflict *mental* harm by introducing the idea of cats into your mind, which can make you think of your cat-owning rival, which can make you think of your ungratifiable desire to kill him, which can precipitate a psychosis.

We've covered enough theory now to make sense of the therapeutic practice of free association. What the therapist looks for is an idea that elicits anxiety and breaks the flow of associations. When the idea of cats comes up, the patient takes an uncharacteristically long period of time to come up with an associated idea. Perhaps she insists that nothing comes to mind. Moreover, when something does come to mind, the new idea seems to represent a discontinuous change in the direction of her thinking. Such hesitations and discontinuities, along with the appearance of anxiety, are treated as evidence that the idea of cats is an associate of the ungratifiable wish. By obtaining a series of clues of this type, the psychoanalyst may be able to zero in on the forbidden wish.

What if the therapist finds the hidden wish? The therapist is then in a position to guide the patient to a realization of what she's defending against. But should he do it? Remember that the idea was repressed in the first place because of the danger of psychosis. If the patient's situation is still the same now as it was when the repression was imposed, the therapist does *not* help the patient to a realization of what she's been defending against. In fact, he might help to *strengthen* her defenses against such a realization. It's often the case that the irresolvable conflict is repressed in childhood but a conflict that a child can't resolve may very well be resolved easily by an adult. For example, a child may be unable to admit consciously that her parents aren't perfect. After all, her very existence depends on her parents doing the right thing. As an independent adult, however, it may be easy for her to accept that her parents sometimes make mistakes. The problem is that the topic, being repressed, is never brought forward for reexamination. Thus, even if the original reason for the repression is no longer valid, the patient never discovers that the circumstances have changed. It's as though you encountered a tiger in a particular place and stopped going there. After some time, the place might have been cleared of tigers and may now be completely safe but because you never go there any more, you never find out. In any case, it's only when the tigers are gone—when the therapist thinks that the repressed idea can now be dealt with—that he helps the patient to lift the repression.

Theoretically, the benefits of de-repression therapy are twofold. First, uncovering a repressed wish produces a decrease in anxiety: you no longer fear cats when you've consciously realized that you hate your cat-owning rival. At least that's what the theory says should happen. Secondly, the fewer your defense mechanisms, the less distortion there is in your perception of the world and of yourself (assuming that the ego remains intact). This is a consequence of the definition of "defense mechanism." Of course, the definition doesn't ensure that anybody actually uses defense mechanisms, any more than the definition of "mermaid" tells us whether there are any mermaids. But if we do indulge in defense mechanisms, then surely we would see things more clearly when we give them up.

Let's assume that people do repress certain ideas. Even so, it's not clear that Freud's theory of repression provides an adequate explanation of the phenomenon. There's a difference between neurotic anxiety and the other two forms of anxiety that Freud doesn't take into account. In the case of realistic and moral anxiety, you (the ego) *know* what danger the anxiety signals. When you encounter a tiger, you become anxious about the prospect of getting killed; when you contemplate engaging in naughty sexual activities, you get anxious about the fact that you'll be made to feel guilty. Neurotic anxiety, however, is an anticipatory signal of becoming conscious of the forbidden wish. Here you're *not* conscious of what you're anxious about. If you were, then the dangerous circumstance that's being signaled would already have happened.

But if you don't know what you're anxious about, then you wouldn't know how to *eliminate* the anxiety. For example, suppose that the sight of a tiger produces realistic anxiety, but you don't know the source of your anxiety. Then the impulse to get away from the anxiety wouldn't necessarily lead you to run away from the tiger. Suppose there's a tiger to the left of you and a tree to the right. For all you know, the anxiety might be due to the *tree,* in which case the way to eliminate it would be to run away from the tree and toward the tiger! But this is exactly the state you're in when you experience neurotic anxiety. You don't *know* that the anxiety is about the imminent arrival in consciousness of the forbidden wish. Therefore you can't know that the way to eliminate the anxiety is to *change your thoughts.* For all you know, what you should do to eliminate anxiety is to *change your location.*

On the other hand, if you *do* know what your neurotic anxiety is about, then the repression has failed. In realistic and moral anxiety, there's a *gap* between consciousness of the danger and the danger itself: you can be aware that the tiger is the source of danger before the danger materializes. But in neurotic anxiety, there is no gap between consciousness of the danger and the danger itself. To become conscious of the danger *is* for the calamity to befall you.

The foregoing criticism doesn't mean that Freud is necessarily wrong about the claim that we repress unacceptable impulses. It just means that he wasn't able to come up with an adequate explanation for how repression works.

We will close this chapter with a few words on a topic that's already come up in several previous discussions: Freud's rejection of the methodology of the controlled experiment. Freud, as well as the overwhelming majority of later psychoanalytic theorists, relied exclusively on *naturalistic observation*—the observation of phenomena as they occur naturally in everyday life and in the clinical setting, rather than in prearranged experimental situations. The method of naturalistic observation is open to standard criticisms. These are mainly that it's subject to various biases. First there's the *personal bias* due to the fact that we tend to notice, remember, and record what fits with our preconceived notions, rather than what shows our beliefs to be false. There's also a *population bias:* the range of phenomena that a given researcher comes "naturally" into contact with may be unrepresentative of the total class of phenomena. This is an especially acute problem for Freud's methodology, because the subjects he observed intensively were almost all patients seeking psychological help. It's quite plausible to suggest that generalizations based on a clinical subpopulation may not apply to the general population. In Chapter 5, we'll see that humanistic psychologists make precisely this argument. They take the view that psychoanalysis covers half of psychology—the sick half—and that to obtain a complete psychological theory, the clinical observations of psychoanalysts have to be supplemented with the study of healthy, optimally functioning individuals.

These are valid criticisms of Freud's naturalistic method. It's because of criticisms like these that the experimental method was adopted. But Freud claims that the experimental method is also subject to biases—primarily to a *situational bias*. Almost all psychology experiments have in common the fact that the subject knows that she's in a psychology experiment. The problem is that behavior undertaken with this knowledge may not be representative of the behavior that takes place in other, less artificial situations. For example, if you're in a psychology experiment you can be pretty sure that your life won't be threatened. But in the real world that's not so. Sometimes people die. Freud had no confidence that when our behavior really matters—when it's a matter of life or death, marriage or divorce, career success or career failure—our actions can be extrapolated from what we do in contrived experimental settings. This is also a valid criticism. The moral is that psychological theories should ideally be tested against both naturalistic and experimental data.

5. Psychology Loses Its Mind: The Behavioral Revolution

5.1. Behaviorism and Behavioral Psychology

We've been using the terms "behaviorism" and "behavioral psychology" interchangeably; but now we need to make a distinction between them. *Behavioral psychology,* like psychoanalysis, refers to a family of conceptually similar theories. The recurring concepts in psychoanalytic theories are id, ego, superego, anxiety, defense, and others. The recurring concepts in theories of behavioral psychology include stimulus, response, reinforcement, conditioning, and extinction. Theories of behavioral psychology are also called *S-R theories,* in honor of their most central concepts (stimulus and response). *Behaviorism,* on the other hand, is the name of a single proposition. It's the thesis that psychology should deal only with the behavior of organisms, because reference to mental states and processes is illegitimate or ill-advised.

Behavioral psychology and behaviorism go well together. Theories of behavioral psychology make no reference to mental events; hence they qualify as behavioristic. Nevertheless, behavioral psychology and behaviorism are logically independent ideas. For one thing, it isn't necessarily the case that every behavioristic theory is a theory of behavioral psychology. A theory that employs some set of nonmentalistic concepts other than stimulus and response would obviously not be an S-R theory, but it could still be behavioristic. Also it's logically permissible to accept an S-R theory without endorsing behaviorism. All you'd have to say is that the S-R theory is true as far as it goes, but that it isn't complete—it leaves mental phenomena out of its account. In actual practice, however, behaviorism and behavioral psychology have gone hand in hand, like dualism and voluntarism, or introspectionism and structuralism.

This droning litany of "behavioral psychologies" and "behaviorisms" makes for dull reading but it's important to keep the two ideas apart, especially when dealing with criticisms of the approach. Some of the criticisms are directed at the tenets of behavioral psychology, and some at the (single) tenet of behaviorism. If the critique of behavioral psychology succeeds, then we have to give up the S-R way of talking about behavior, but we don't necessarily have to give up behaviorism. We could instead come to the conclusion that we have to devise a new behavioristic theory.

Of course, the main appeal of behavioristic psychology—the reason it became so popular at mid-century—was because it satisfied the tenet of behaviorism. Stimulus and response—S and R—are purely materialistic concepts. This is obvious in the case of R: a response is a physical movement of the organism in space and time. It's not so obvious in the case of S. There's a nonbehavioristic use of the term "stimulus," according to which the present stimulus is what the organism presently *perceives*—and perception is a mental state if anything is. That's *not* what behaviorists mean by S. For them, the stimulus is the *physical setting* in which the behavior takes place—the choice point of the maze, or the button that the pigeon is being trained to peck.

Behavioral psychology represents a much greater departure from the common-sense psychology of the nonpsychologist than does psychoanalysis. Freud departed from common-sense psychology by extending the common-sense mentalistic concepts of belief, desire, perception, and so on, to unconscious processes. Both common-sense psychology and psychoanalysis assert that what causes you to behave the way you do is what you desire and what you believe. It's just that in psychoanalysis, the beliefs and desires don't have to be conscious. Behavioral psychology, however, proposes to explain behavior without any reference to the mentalistic concepts of common sense.

When contemplating behavioral psychology, it's always necessary to keep the following methodological principle in mind: if mental or cognitive processes are alluded to in a behavioral theory, the behavioral psychologist regards it as a *mistake* that has to be rectified. Behavioral psychologists want to explain behavior without any reference to what the organism believes or desires. We'll see that it sometimes requires a lot of ingenuity to circumvent mentalistic explanations. Moreover, the attempt to do so sometimes results in convoluted explanations for phenomena that seem simple and straightforward from a mentalistic perspective. Why do behavioral psychologists resist the simple and straightforward in this case? Because they're convinced by the arguments for behavior*ism* that psychology *can't* avail itself of mentalistic concepts.

Here's the agenda for the next two chapters. In this chapter, we'll try to assess how successful behavioral psychologies have been in explaining behavior. If they have been successful, then they don't stand in need of any further justification. In particular, there's no need to consider the merits of the arguments that purport to show that psychology *must* be behavioristic—for even if our theories don't *have* to be behavioristic, the fact that a particular behavioristic theory is successful is reason enough to adopt it. But if behavioral psychology *doesn't* succeed—and it doesn't—then we need to see if the restriction on theorizing imposed by behaviorism is the culprit. This is the topic of the next chapter.

5.2. Classical Conditioning

The major figures in the history of behavioral psychology, in rough chronological order are René Descartes, Ivan Pavlov, John B. Watson, E. L. Thorndike, Clark Hull, and B. F. Skinner. You might be surprised to find the dualist Descartes on the list but remember that Descartes had different accounts of the causes of human behavior and of animal behavior. His theory of animal behavior—the *reflex* theory—was the first behavioral theory. It's said that this theory was inspired by his observation of the moving statues in the French royal gardens. The statues were built so that when strollers in the gardens stepped on certain tiles, hydraulic pressure would be conveyed to the statues in such a way that they would dart in and out of hiding. In the seventeenth century, this was a high-tech tour de force. Many visitors commented that the movement gave the statues an eerie appearance of being alive.

Descartes thought that the mobility of the statues was a good model of how animals might behave given that they had no mentality and no free will. Stepping on the tiles was akin to light energy entering the eyes. The conveyance of hydraulic pressure to the statue was like the conveyance of some form of physical energy from the eyes to the muscles—maybe even hydraulic pressure conveyed through tubes filled with liquids, just like the statues in the royal gardens. Descartes called such a connection between a physical stimulus (stepping on a tile, light entering the eyes) and a behavioral response a reflex.

According to Descartes, the reflex theory could account for animal behavior, but not for human behavior. The reason for its failure in the case of human beings is that the stimulus-response connection of a reflex is fixed: every time the same tile is stepped on, it elicits exactly the same behavioral reaction. Human beings, however, by virtue of having free will, could choose to respond to a stimulus one way on the first occasion of its occurrence and an entirely different way on the second.

Whether or not it's attributed to free will, there's no doubt that human beings do sometimes react differently to different presentations of the same stimulus. That's enough to show that the reflex theory can't explain human behavior. But the reflex theory doesn't explain animal behavior either, and for the same reasons: cats and dogs don't always react to the same stimulus in the same way. At first, the verbal command "sit!" has no effect on the behavior of a dog; but, if the right regimen of training is followed, the same stimulus is eventually followed by the response of sitting. The fact that dogs can be trained already shows that the reflex theory, with its rigid S-R connections, can't explain everything about animal behavior.

Twentieth-century behavioral psychologists universally agreed with the foregoing conclusion. They often expressed the point by saying that the reflex theory can't explain the phenomenon of *learning*. In its everyday sense, learning is the process of acquiring new information (learning that the capital of Canada is Ottawa) or new skills (learning to ride a bicycle). The acquisition of information is obviously a mental process so behavioral psychologists, being behaviorists, couldn't have been using the term "learning" in its standard, everyday sense. For the behavioral psychologists, learning referred to the process of behavioral change—going from reacting to a stimulus-type S with a response R1, to reacting to S with a different response R2. The second part of the everyday definition—the acquisition of new skills, such as riding a bicycle—qualifies as learning in this technical sense. But behavioral learning more generally includes *any* form of behavioral change—any process whereby a new response is substituted for an old response to the same stimulus situation. So *losing* the ability to ride a bicycle is also learning in this sense. In the behavioral sense of the term, the statues in the royal gardens can't learn. Human beings and dogs *can* learn; therefore, the reflex theory doesn't fully explain human or canine behavior.

After the formulation of the reflex theory, nobody had anything new to say about the causes of behavior until the turn of the twentieth century. The reason, of course, was that psychology in the nineteenth century was overwhelmingly introspective and had nearly completely eliminated behavior from its scope. Then, at the turn of the century, a Russian physiologist named Ivan Pavlov announced the discovery of a law of behavioral change: the principle of *classical conditioning* (Pavlov 1927/1960). Before describing this principle, it needs to be pointed out that there *are* reflexes—fixed S-R connections—in dogs and humans. For example, neurologically normal human beings exhibit the patellar reflex, which is a fixed kicking response to the stimulus of a sharp tap on the tendon below the knee. Another reflex, common to humans and dogs, is the response of salivating when the stimulus is food in the mouth. We can't choose not to salivate when there's food in our mouth—that's how we're wired up. What's wrong with the reflex theory is that it says that *all* behavior is reflexive.

Now for the principle of classical conditioning. Start with a reflex S-R connection, like the connection between food and salivation. Pavlov called the stimulus of a reflex an *unconditioned stimulus* (UCS) and the reflex response an *unconditioned response* (UCR). So salivation is a UCR to the UCS of food. Suppose now that the UCS is repeatedly presented to the subject together with a *neutral* stimulus, i.e., a stimulus that *doesn't* elicit any UCR. For example, place food in a dog's mouth while at the same time ringing a bell. The law of classical conditioning says that after several such pairings of an unconditioned and a neutral stimulus, the (previously) neutral stimulus is able to elicit the same response as the unconditioned stimulus *even if it's presented without the UCS*. So, after pairing food and the ringing of a bell, just ringing the bell will make the dog salivate. When this process of conditioning is complete, the previously neutral stimulus is called a *conditioned stimulus* (CS), and the response elicited by the CS is a *conditioned response* (CR).

Most people know about Pavlov's experiments with salivating dogs. After a few pairings of food (the UCS) and the ringing of a bell (the CS), the bell alone produced the salivation response (the CR). Pavlov also reported experimental evidence for several subsidiary principles relating to classical conditioning. One of these is the principle of *extinction:* as the CS continues to be presented without the UCS, the CR gradually fades in intensity. In Pavlov's laboratory, the dogs salivated less and less with repeated ringings of the bell, and they eventually stopped salivating altogether.

Another subsidiary principle is the law of *stimulus generalization,* according to which a neutral stimulus that's *similar* to the CS is able to elicit the CR even though it has never been paired with the UCS. Moreover, the intensity of the CR varies directly with the degree of similarity to the CS. In the Pavlovian situation, dogs who have been conditioned to salivate to a tone of a given pitch would also salivate to a tone of a different pitch; and the more dissimilar in pitch to the original CS, the less the salivation.

Then there's the principle of *higher-order conditioning.* Suppose that you pair food and bell-ringing until the bell-ringing alone produces salivation. Then suppose that you pair the bell-ringing with another neutral stimulus, such as a flash of light. What happens is that the second neutral stimulus also comes to elicit the CR of salivation, even though it had never been paired with the UCR for salivation (i.e., food). In sum, a CS can play the same role in conditioning as a UCS.

Meanwhile, back in the United States, John B. Watson was formulating and arguing for the principle of behavior*ism* (Watson 1913). Unlike the principle of classical conditioning, the principle of behaviorism is not a scientific law from which empirical predictions can be derived and tested. It's a philosophical principle about how the science of psychology should proceed. Watson's early writings on the subject were broadly programmatic. He argued for the general proposition that psychology should be behavioristic, but he didn't have any specific scientific principles to propose. Classical conditioning was exactly what he was looking for. Note to begin with that the principle of classical conditioning is a principle of behavioral change: before conditioning, the neutral stimulus has no effect on behavior; after conditioning, the same stimulus (now called a conditioned stimulus) elicits the conditioned response. Hence classical conditioning qualifies as a law of *learning,* in the behavioral psychologist's sense of the term. So do the subsidiary principles of extinction, stimulus generalization, and higher-order conditioning.

Moreover, classical conditioning is a *behavioristic* law of learning. None of the four concepts needed for its formulation—UCS, UCR, CS, and CR—adverts to mental states. This is sometimes misunderstood. Upon learning about classical conditioning, nonpsychologists tend to describe what happens in Pavlov's experiments in mentalistic terms. For example, they say that the dogs come to *expect* that the bell means that food is coming, and that this expectation is implicated in the production of the conditioned response. This is not Pavlov's account. There's no reference to expectations in the law of classical conditioning. The law merely states that if a UCS and a CS are presented together, the CS comes to elicit the same response as the UCS when it's presented alone. Maybe the mentalistically inclined nonpsychologist is right in supposing that the behavioral change is due to changing expectations. But the reason that Watson was excited about classical conditioning was that it enables you to predict behavior *without* making any reference to mental states.

At this point, Watson made a huge conceptual leap. He not only asserted that the principle of classical conditioning was both behavioristic and true—he also hypothesized that it was the *only* principle needed to explain all of behavior. Watson suggested that classical conditioning and its subsidiary principles are the *basic* laws of behavior in the same sense as Newton's laws of motion are the basic laws of classical physics: everything else in the field follows from them. If this hypothesis had worked out, it would have been a spectacular scientific success—one can't imagine a simpler psychological theory.

On the face of it, it seems highly implausible to suppose that the complexities of human behavior—of language, for instance—could be accounted for by the subjects' conditioning history. To make it more plausible, Watson set out to demonstrate how simple conditioning could produce a complex behavioral phenomenon. He chose phobias. As the reader knows, Freud had expounded a very complex theory of phobias, according to which they were due to the neurotic anxiety produced by an associate of a wish that the ego couldn't gratify. Watson argued that you don't need this elaborate theoretical apparatus—simple conditioning accounts for it. His demonstration of the classical conditioning of a phobia is a classic bit of psychological history (Watson and Rayner 1920). The subject in whom a phobia was implanted was a baby known in the literature as Little Albert. The UCS was a sudden, loud sound, to which the UCR is the "fear" response—not, of course, the felt emotion of fear, but the behavioral manifestations that nonbehaviorists attribute to the emotion (hence the scare quotes). The CS was a rat, which initially didn't produce any "fear" in Little Albert. After a few pairings of sudden noise and rat, however, merely seeing the rat was enough to make Little Albert cry. Voilà—"rodentophobia."

Watson understood that a single demonstration of this type couldn't establish the truth of his general hypothesis. The aim of the demonstration was merely to show that classical conditioning had more explanatory power than one might at first suppose. Of course, connecting classical conditioning to phobias isn't that much of a conceptual stretch. One would have liked to see a similar derivation from conditioning principles of the behavioral phenomenon of talking grammatically, or of the behavior of delusional schizophrenics. Moreover, even the conditioning explanation of phobias is open to criticism. For example, the power of the CS to elicit the CR is supposed to extinguish with continued presentation of the CS; but people who suffer from an irrational fear (or "fear") of rats continue to exhibit this fear rat after rat, ad infinitum.

The strongest criticism of Watson's hypothesis is the general argument that purports to show that classical conditioning can't possibly explain everything about behavior. Earlier in this section, we showed that the reflex theory can't explain the phenomenon of learning, or behavioral change. Classical conditioning does allow for some types of behavioral change: at first, Pavlov's dogs didn't salivate when a bell was rung, and then they did. But the kind of learning that's allowed by classical conditioning is much too narrow to provide an account of all behavior. What classical conditioning does is shift responses from one stimulus to another. But the total *behavioral repertoire*—the sum of all behaviors that the organism emits to any and all stimuli—remains unchanged. However, it's incontrovertible that as a person grows from infancy to adulthood, he adds *new responses* to his behavioral repertoire. An adult does things—riding a bicycle, speaking a language, and playing the piano—that an infant doesn't do at all, regardless of the stimuli that impinge upon him. The principle of classical conditioning seems unable to account for this phenomenon of *response novelty*.

In reality, the issue is more complex than our presentation suggests. Confronted with the response novelty argument, Watsonians countered that what appears to be a novel response might turn out to be just a novel stringing together of old responses that were already in the behavioral repertoire. For example, there's a time in all our lives when we've never uttered the word "bag" before; but that doesn't necessarily mean that saying "bag" for the first time is a novel response. We can think of the response of saying "bag" as a sequence of three responses: making the sound "b," then making the sound "a," and then making the sound "g." So long as all three of these responses are already in the child's behavioral repertoire, saying "bag" for the first time is not really doing anything new. On this account, what happens is that some complex series of conditioning experiences strings the old responses together to form what *looks* like a new response.

Let's look at this explanation more closely. It frequently happens that while you are talking or performing some other complex motor skill, the environment in which you're behaving remains entirely static. For example, the environment in which you utter the "b" of "bag" may be identical to the environment in which, a moment later, you utter the "a" of "bag." If Watson is correct in supposing that it's all classical conditioning, then uttering the "b" of "bag" and uttering the "a" of "bag" are both conditioned responses. But what are their respective conditioned stimuli? It's been assumed that the environment is the same on both occasions. Then any aspect of the environment that might be the CS to the CR of uttering "b" is also going to be present at the next moment, when you utter "a." But then why don't you utter "b" a second time, instead of "a"? If your surroundings remain constant while you say "bag," it seems that one and the same CS must elicit one CR on one occasion and another CR on the next occasion. But to say this is to deny the principle of classical conditioning.

Watsonians had a reply. They noted that there's one way in which your-environment-when-you-utter-the-"b"-of-"bag" can't ever be identical to your-environment-when-you-utter-the-"a"-of-"bag": when you begin to utter the "a" of "bag," your environment includes the stimulus that you just finished uttering the "b" of "bag." That is to say, your response of uttering "b" is also a stimulus; therefore it's available for playing the role of CS for the CR of uttering "a." This analysis suggests a general recipe for accounting for complex and apparently novel behaviors in terms of classical conditioning. The novel response R is broken up into a series of old responses that are already in the behavioral repertoire: R1-R2-R3-R4. Their chaining is then attributed to their being CRs, which are conditioned to the *stimulus* of performing the prior response:

$$R1 \rightarrow S1 \rightarrow R2 \rightarrow S2 \rightarrow R3 \rightarrow S3 \rightarrow R4 \rightarrow S4$$

This clever solution was shown to fail in a famous article by the physiological psychologist Karl Lashley (1951). Let's look at the initial portion of the complex chain, R1 → S1 → R2. Lashley pointed out that for this sequence of events to occur, neural impulses originating from the performance of R1 have to travel to the brain and then back again to the muscles involved in the production of R2. But neural impulses travel quite slowly—too slowly, in fact, to account for the rapid sequence of responses involved in such skilled performances as speech, or playing arpeggios on the piano. In cases like these, the component responses run themselves off so rapidly that there simply isn't enough time for the successive neural round trips between brain and periphery that are required by the Watsonian analysis.

It took a few decades for the issue to sort itself out but eventually the community of behavioral psychologists came to agree that Watson's vision of a complete psychology based entirely on the principle of classical conditioning was untenable. This isn't to say that there's any problem with the principle of classical conditioning itself. The problem is with the far stronger Watsonian thesis.

5.3. The Law of Effect

E. L. Thorndike's research provided the basis for a second behavioristic principle (Thorndike 1911). Thorndike placed cats in various "puzzle boxes," escape from which was rewarded by food. In order to get out of the box, the cat had to emit a particular response, such as pushing open a trap door. At first, the cat's behavior was random. However, by sheer chance the cat eventually emitted the response leading out of the box, whereupon it obtained food. Thorndike observed that on the second trial, the cat got out of the box a little bit faster than on the first trial, and on third trial, it got out a little bit faster still. In the end, when placed in the box, the cat would quickly and smoothly run through the required movements for exiting and obtaining food without any wasted motion. The same learning pattern was exhibited by every tested cat and every tested escape response.

Thorndike proposed a theory to account for these data:

> Of several responses made to the same situation, those which are accompanied or closely followed by satisfaction to the animal will, other things being equal, be more firmly connected with the situation, so that, when it recurs, they will be more likely to recur. (1911, 244)

Punishment, on the other hand, decreases the probability of recurrence. In the discussion that follows, we'll deal only with the "satisfaction" half of the principle. Thorndike called his principle the *law of effect*. Most later behavioral psychologists called it the principle of *instrumental conditioning*. B. F. Skinner called it *operant conditioning* (he also referred to classical conditioning as *respondent conditioning*).

How, exactly, does the law of effect explain Thorndike's data? Suppose there's a point in the puzzle box where the cat can turn either to the left or to the right. A turn to the left will lead to satisfaction; a turn to the right won't. Suppose also that the two responses are equally likely on the first trial. If the cat turns to the right, nothing happens, and the two responses remain equally likely on the second trial. Eventually, by chance alone, the cat will turn to the left. This response will be followed by satisfaction, and so the probability of its recurrence will go up. Thus on the next trial, the cat will have a somewhat greater tendency to turn to the left than to the right. Of course, the cat may still turn to the right, but every time it turns to the right, probabilities remain unchanged; whereas every time it turns to the left, the probability of turning to the left *again* is increased. In this way, the probability of turning to the left gradually gets higher and higher, until it's emitted every time.

As we noted in the previous section, virtually all behavioral psychologists eventually conceded that classical conditioning alone couldn't explain everything about behavior. But the orthodox view in the decades of the 1930s, 40s, and 50s was that the conjunction of classical conditioning and the law of effect (equivalently, classical and instrumental conditioning, or respondent and operant conditioning) provides a complete behavioristic theory of animal and human behavior.

Is the law of effect behavioristic? There's no doubt that it specifies conditions under which organisms will exhibit behavioral changes. But these conditions, as Thorndike formulates them, seem to be mentalistic: responses increase in probability if they're followed by "satisfaction"—and what is satisfaction if not the acquisition of something that the organism *wants?* If behavioristic psychology were to avail itself of the law of effect as an explanatory resource, the law had to be reformulated in such a way that it avoided reference to mental states.

Various ways of behaviorizing the law of effect were tried. Here's one that didn't work, though it was relied on by a lot of behavioral psychologists. Instead of "satisfaction," they talked about "reinforcement"; the law of effect became the principle that the probability for a response goes up when that response is followed by reinforcement. And what is reinforcement? Here's a purely behavioristic definition: an event is a reinforcement if its occurrence increases the probability of a preceding response. So why is food reinforcing? If you say that it's because the organism *wants* it or *likes* it, you violate behaviorism. According to the new definition of reinforcement, however, there's no need to advert to wants and likes. To establish that food is reinforcing, you just need to set things up so that a particular response produces food. For example, you might place a rat in a box equipped with a bar that's connected to a dispenser of food pellets. Every time the rat presses the bar, the dispenser delivers a pellet in a little dish. Now simply look to see if the frequency with which the rat presses the bar increases. If it does, then you've established that the food pellets are reinforcing (for this rat)—and you've done so without having to mention any of the organism's mental states.

What's wrong with this approach is that if you define reinforcement as above, then the law of effect becomes a logically *necessary* truth, like "black cats are black" or "bachelors are unmarried." Necessary propositions are true solely by virtue of the meanings of the concepts that make them up. You don't have to do any empirical research to establish that bachelors are unmarried—you need only know the meaning of "bachelor" and "unmarried." Given that the meanings are what they are, there's no conceivable circumstance in the world that would justify the rejection of "bachelors are unmarried." It's a proposition that's true in all possible worlds. In contrast, *contin-*

gent propositions are made true or false by the fact that the world possesses or fails to possess some feature. An example is "the average bachelor is six feet tall." Contingent propositions are true in some possible worlds and false in some possible worlds. Thus we have to examine the real world in order to ascertain whether it possesses the features specified by the contingent proposition: we have to measure a random sample of bachelors in order to see whether their average height turns out to be six feet.

Scientific laws purport to tell us the way the world is. They are therefore intended to be contingent propositions. But look at what happens to the law of effect if you use the behavioristic definition. The law of effect can be expressed as follows:

> If a response is followed by reinforcement, its probability goes up.

Here's the behavioristic definition of reinforcement:

> Reinforcement is an event that causes the probability of a preceding response to go up.

But if that's what reinforcement is, we can simply say so in the statement of the law of effect. This yields:

> If a response is followed by an event that causes the probability of a preceding response to go up, its probability goes up.

On this reading, the law of effect is undoubtedly true; but it's *necessarily* true, like "bachelors are unmarried." It doesn't specify that the world possesses or fails to possess any particular feature. No matter how rats behave or fail to behave, the law of effect is still going to be true. For example, its truth would not be called into question if food *didn't* increase the probability of the preceding response—we would simply conclude that food is not a reinforcement. Thus this version of the law of effect isn't a scientific principle at all.

What behaviorists needed at this juncture was a definition of reinforcement that made the law of effect contingent. This was supplied by Clark Hull's enormously influential *drive theory* (Hull 1943).

5.4. Drive Theory

The basic concept that gives drive theory its name is of course the concept of *drive,* which Hull tended to represent by the single letter D. D is defined as the organism's overall level of activity—the sheer amount of movement displayed, irrespective of the nature or direction of the activity. So an organism doesn't have a plurality of drives; its drive state is specified by a single quantity. If you want to ascertain whether one organism is in a higher or lower drive state than another, you can place each of them in a situation in which its range of motion is restricted to a single measurable dimension. Hullians were particularly fond of the "activity wheel," in which the organism could only run forward, thereby causing the wheel to spin in the opposite direction. The number of revolutions per minute was taken as an index of drive.

Hull postulated that the determinant of the organism's drive state is the severity of its *biological deficit state.* This is exactly what causes activity to take place according to the pleasure principle of psychoanalytic theory. (We will have much more to say about this parallelism later in this chapter.) In order to show that the biological deficit of food deprivation increases drive among rats, you can divide your rats into two groups. The rats in group 1 are allowed to eat their fill just before the experiment; the rats in group 2 are deprived of food for a few hours. Then all the rats take a turn in the activity wheel. If you do this experiment, you'll find that the food-deprived rats of group 2 are more active than the sated rats of group 1. This means that they're in a higher drive state. Hypothesis confirmed.

The most important principle of drive theory is the law of effect: the probability of a response R to stimulus S is determined (in part) by how often R has previously been reinforced in the presence of S. In drive theory, however, reinforcement isn't Thorndike's behavioristically dubious "satisfaction," or the circular definition that turns the law of effect into a trivial logical necessity. According to drive theory, *reinforcement is drive reduction*—an event that diminishes the organism's drive state. Given the postulated connection between activity and biological deficit, this is tantamount to saying that reinforcement is what diminishes a biological need.

The law of effect thus claims that the probability of R increases if R is followed by an event that diminishes a biological need. This principle may or may not be true but at least it is contingent—you need to observe the world in order to find out if it's true. First you need to establish that a particular event is drive-reducing. It may or may not be true that what decreases drive level also *increases* the probability of a preceding response—that's what makes drive theory contingent. In order to confirm (or disconfirm) drive theory, you have to set things up so that the emission of some response (e.g., pressing a bar) results in the drive-reducing state of affairs (e.g., the acquisition of food). The drive-reduction theory is confirmed if the probability of the response goes up. If the probability of the response *doesn't* go up, the theory can't be saved by concluding that food is simply not a reinforcer—for it's been independently established that food *is* a reinforcer by virtue of its drive-reducing propensity.

Let's run through the theory again, this time adding more theoretical detail. Suppose that R and R' are the only two responses that the organism is capable of performing in the stimulus situation S. According to drive theory, the probability that R will be emitted in the presence of S is determined by the relative values of the excitatory potentials, $_sE_R$ and $_sE_{R'}$, of those particular stimulus-response pairs. Given stimulus S, the response with the higher excitatory potential is more likely to be emitted; moreover, the greater the difference between the excitatory potentials, the greater the probability of the higher-potential response. The excitatory potential of an S-R pair is in turn determined primarily by two factors. One of them is the number of times R has previously been reinforced in the presence of S. Hull calls this quantity the habit strength of the S-R pair, and he abbreviates it $_sH_R$. To say that $_sH_R$ is a determinant of $_sE_R$ is to say that the likelihood of emitting R in the presence of S is in part determined by the number of times R has been reinforced in the presence of S. This is the principle that was discussed in the previous paragraph. It is, in fact, precisely the law of effect.

But drive theory also postulates a second determinant of $_sE_R$: the organism's *drive state,* abbreviated as *D.* Thus if you want to increase the likelihood that an organism will emit response R to the stimulus S, you can do either of two things: (1) increase the number of times R is reinforced in the presence of S, or (2) increase the organism's drive state. To increase the organism's drive state is to increase its activity level, and you do that by increasing its level of biological deficit (e.g., by depriving it of food). The idea is that if the organism becomes more active—

i.e., if it produces more behavior—then the likelihood of *every* response goes up. Hull sums up his theory with a famous equation:

$$_SE_R = {_S}H_R \times D.$$

This equation plays the same central role in Hull's theory as the pleasure principle does in Freud's. D needn't be flanked with little Ss or Rs, since every stimulus-response pair gets multiplied by one and the same quantity: the organism's unitary drive state.

On this account, drive reduction has two simultaneous and opposite effects. On the one hand, drive reduction reinforces the response R that produced it, thus increasing the value of $_SH_R$. This results in an increase in $_SE_R$, hence also in the likelihood of R. On the other hand, drive-reduction obviously involves a decrease in the value of D, which has the effect of *decreasing* $_SE_R$, hence also in the likelihood of R (as well as of all other responses). Suppose, for example, that a rat presses a bar and is rewarded with an unlimited quantity of food. The habit strength of the bar-pressing response goes up by virtue of its having been reinforced by drive reduction. But the amount of drive-reduction is so enormous that the decrement in D more than offsets the increment in $_SH_R$. The result is a net decrease in $_SE_R$, hence in the likelihood of pressing the bar again. The rat is reinforced for bar-pressing, but it eats so much that it becomes inactive and doesn't press the bar again. So if you want to increase the likelihood that the organism will emit R, you should reinforce R frequently, but make sure that drive is reduced minimally on each occasion. A single pellet of rat chow is more effective than the whole bag. The frequency of reinforcement produces a substantial elevation of $_SH_R$, while the small magnitude of each instance of drive reduction produces a relatively small decrement in the value of D. When $_SH_R$ and D are multiplied together to get $_SE_R$, the result will be a net increase in excitatory potential.

An important consequence of Hull's equation is that if D = 0, then $_SE_R = 0$ for all responses R and all stimuli S. This in turn entails that when D = 0, the probability of emitting any response at all is zero, no matter how often the response has been reinforced. This makes internal sense: D's being equal to zero means that the organism is totally inactive. Recall, however, that D is determined by the level of the organism's biological deficit. Thus drive theory tells us that when all of an organism's biological needs are met, the organism lapses into complete inactivity. We've heard this before. Freud says exactly the same thing!

There are deep similarities between drive theory and psychoanalytic theory. What Hull calls "drive" is very similar to what Freud calls the "instincts." In fact, the word that got translated as "instinct" in the standard English versions of Freud's German is "Trieb," which is the cognate of "drive." Both theories say that all behavior begins with a biological need, and that if there is no biological deficit, the organism remains inert. Both have apparent counterexamples to contend with— examples of behavior that doesn't diminish any biological needs. Freud explains this kind of behavior as sublimation—the production of primary process *associates* of the instinct-object that the id can't distinguish from the real thing. Hull has a similar theory: any stimulus that is temporally associated with a drive-reducing stimulus acquires the capacity to act as a reinforcer (it becomes a "secondary reinforcer"). So, money works as a reward even though it doesn't directly diminish drive (you can't eat money) because it's associated with drive-reduction, as when you use it to buy food. Thus both Freud and Hull say that the cases in which behavior is *not* directed at overcoming biological deficits are cases in which the behavior is directed at *associates* of biological-deficit reduction. The difference between them is that what's associated are *ideas* in Freud, and objective *stimuli* in Hull.

Drive theory, like psychoanalysis, is an instance of the noncommon-sensical kind of hedonism that lops off the positive part of the pleasure-pain or attraction-aversion continuum. Both regard behavior as directed solely toward overcoming an aversive state. Once all biological deficits are eliminated, behavior stops—there's nothing more for the organism to do. In the next section, we'll see that it's this feature that gets both of the theories into the same serious difficulties. Our discussion of these parallel critiques will closely follow the definitive treatment by R. W. White (1959).

5.5. Critique of Drive Theory and Psychoanalysis

In the 1940s and early 1950s, American experimental psychologists reported literally hundreds of experimental confirmations of predictions deduced from drive theory. But in the mid-1950s, a few experimental results were reported that seemed to disconfirm the theory. By the mid-1960s, this trickle of disconfirmations had turned into a tidal wave. The experiments that were thought to be the most troublesome were those that seemed to show that response frequency could be increased without the reduction of a biological need. One of the earliest of these was J. Olds' and P. Milner's (1954) classic study of electrical stimulation of the brain. These researchers found that an electric current passed through certain portions of rats' brains had a powerful behavioral effect: rats would readily learn a bar-pressing response that turned on the current. In fact, they would keep on pressing for more electrical stimulation until they dropped from exhaustion, ignoring food, rats of the opposite sex, and all the other more conventional sources of motivation.

Olds and Milner's discovery was widely discussed in lay circles. It inspired quite a few science fiction stories of future dystopias in which people live out their entire lives hooked up to electrodes implanted in their brains. The phenomenon is inherently fascinating. But what Olds and Milner themselves emphasized was its theoretical implication for drive theory. What are we to say about Olds' and Milner's discovery from a drive-theoretical point of view? According to drive theory, response frequency increases when the response is followed by the reduction of a biological need, or by a secondary reinforcer (a stimulus that's been associated with drive reduction). But it's implausible to suppose that electrical stimulation of the brain diminishes a biological need. After all, countless generations of rats had managed quite well without it. Nor has this novel form of stimulation ever been associated with the diminution of a biological need (or with anything else, for that matter). Here's how Olds sums it up:

> Now we have to ask what the reward finding contributes to motivational psychology. In the first place it categorically answers the main question which we asked at the outset. It *is* possible to reward an animal without . . . satisfying some physiological need. . . . For, by no stretch of the imagination, could we suppose that our animals would perish without this electrical input to the septal area of the brain. . . . Our reward stimulus is *not* a drive reduction, and it is also not a stimulus which has so far as we know any previous association with a drive reduction. (Olds 1955, 141)

The same theoretical conclusion follows even more immediately from a family of much less flashy investigations of what came to be called *exploratory behavior.* The basic phenomenon is very simple. You start with a rat that's in a low drive state—a rat that's just eaten its fill, copulated to its heart's content, and so on. Such a rat will be lazily lolling about its cage. Now you place this rat in a *novel environment*— for example, a complex maze with lots of twists and turns that the rat hasn't been in before. This change of scenery will invariably perk the rat up. It will start to wander around, exploring the maze. This phenomenon isn't nearly as surprising as the effect of brain stimulation. But it's just as much of an embarrassment for drive theory. Exploratory behavior didn't diminish any biological need; therefore, from the viewpoint of drive theory, its frequency should not have increased. Like electrical stimulation of the brain, novelty seems to elicit activity in a manner that has nothing to do with drive reduction.

Drive theorists tried various ways to explain exploratory behavior that were compatible with their theory. Often this involved adding new items to the list of needs that increase an organism's drive state. For example, some drive theorists introduced the notion of a *novelty* drive. The idea is that novel stimulation is inherently aversive, like receiving an electrical shock. If a rat is shocked, it will learn to behave in a manner that turns off the shock. Similarly, if you inflict a novel stimulus on the rat, it will learn to behave in a manner that eliminates the novelty. One way of doing this is to explore the new environment until it becomes familiar. In brief, exploratory behavior occurs because it's reinforced by a decrease in novelty.

The problem with this explanation is that it doesn't account for some other basic facts about exploratory behavior. Consider the following elegantly simple experiment. Montgomery (1953) placed rats in a Y-maze where—instead of food—one side held a large, novel, and complex maze. In this situation, rats quickly started to turn into and explore the complex maze on every trial. There's an important difference between this phenomenon and the basic phenomenon of exploratory behavior described above. The basic phenomenon is that organisms explore novel environments when they find themselves in one. This is compatible with the view that novelty is a drive state that's diminished by exploration. In Montgomery's experiment, the rats *choose* to enter into the novel environment. This is certainly incompatible with view that novelty is aversive. It would be like choosing to turn the electric shock apparatus *on,* and then doing everything you can to turn it *off.*

So drive theorists gave up the notion of a novelty drive and switched to a *boredom* drive. Saying that novelty is aversive didn't work, so they tried to say that lack of novelty is aversive—it produces a negative state of "boredom" that's alleviated by performing responses that *produce* novelty rather than eliminate it. On this account, exploratory behavior is the manner in which the reinforcement of novelty is appropriated: exploring the novel environment is our way of consuming its novelty. This theory can explain why Montgomery's rats turned into the complex maze: this response was reinforced by the reduction of their boredom drive. But the theory gets into trouble in other ways. It postulates that *prior* to turning into the complex maze, the rats were in a high drive state as a result of boredom. But high drive is defined as high activity level, yet these rats didn't exhibit a high activity level prior to finding the novel environment. Back to the drawing board.

Through the 1950s and 1960s, drive theorists continued to tinker with their theory to make it compatible with recalcitrant data. Such changes to a theory to make it fit the facts are called *ad hoc adjustments.* They're a common feature in the history of science, and to a certain extent they're entirely acceptable. It may be that your theory is on the right track, but just needs a little after-the-fact adjustment to make it perfect. But if the need for ad hoc adjustments persists—if every time somebody does a new experiment, you have to change the theory to make it fit the new data—people start to lose confidence in the theoretical approach. This is what happened to drive theory in the 1950s and 1960s. In 1950, drive theory was by far the most influential theory among American academic psychologists. By 1970, it was practically extinct.

Most of the disconfirmations requiring ad hoc adjustments had to do with the same theme. Like the data on brain stimulation and exploratory behavior, things that didn't fit were instances of behavior that couldn't be related to biological deficit states. Interestingly, psychoanalysis was undergoing parallel developments. To be sure, psychoanalytical psychologists didn't do experiments but a lot of psychoanalysts began to report the same type of naturalistic observation: they saw in their patients instances of positive striving that couldn't easily be related to the elimination of biological deficit states. Such accounts were especially prominent in the reports of psychologists who specialized in the psychoanalytical study of children. These psychologists observed that children expend enormous amounts of energy in mastering new skills, particularly in learning to walk and to talk. They do this even in institutional environments where they get little or no encouragement or reward for doing so. In fact, it seemed to the psychoanalysts that children would strive to walk and talk even if they were *punished* for their attempts. But the inability to walk or talk isn't a biological deficit state. Once again, it's true that the ability to walk and talk greatly *helps* us to overcome our biological deficits. But the observation was that the efforts to acquire new skills *preceded any evidence of their utility.*

Very few psychoanalysts tried to deny the naturalistic observation that children strive to master skills prior to having any knowledge of their utility but they responded to this disconfirmation just as drive theorists did to the disconfirming data on exploratory behavior. The latter invented new drives; the former invented new instincts. They postulated a "mastery instinct," according to which a lack of cognitive and motor skills was an aversive state to be eliminated. This move initiated several rounds of disconfirmations and ad hoc adjustments, as happened in drive theory. Hartmann's argument that the motivation to acquire knowledge has to be innate (see section 4.2) was part of this development. The end result was the same in psychoanalysis as in drive theory: the rejection of the orthodox theory.

A lot of this criticism of psychoanalysis came from humanistic psychology, which had its birth around the same time—the late 1950s or early 1960s. The humanistic critique culminated in the theoretical work of Abraham Maslow (1968), the most important figure in the movement. According to Maslow, we have to distinguish between two classes of needs. In addition to the *deficit* needs discussed by Hull and Freud, we're also motivated by *growth* needs. These include such non-deficit-related activities as the acquisition of new skills, expanding our knowledge, and doing things for pure pleasure. Deficit needs come first: so long as one suffers from a serious biological deficit, growth needs won't manifest themselves. Very little poetry has been written by people who are on the verge of dying from hunger, thirst, or cold. But what happens when all or most of our deficit needs are met? According to both Freud and Hull, nothing happens—when all of our deficit needs are met, we lapse into inactivity. According to Maslow, an entirely different set of needs comes into play. Maslow reinstituted the missing positive part of the motivational spectrum that's already in common-sense psychology.

In effect, Maslow accused the first two "forces" of psychology of providing only half of the picture and he thought he knew why they had committed this particular error of omission. It was because each of them had studied a subject population in which deficit needs are likely to be particularly strong, and growth needs correspondingly weak. For psychoanalysis it was patients seeking psychological help, and for drive theory it was infrahuman organisms. In both these populations, it's reasonable to expect that growth needs would be weaker than in well-functioning human beings (though it seems that even rats have some growth needs).

The main lesson of all this is that life isn't just a matter of eliminating deficits. There is such a thing as positive striving. This is something that we common-sense psychologists knew all along.

5.6. The Refutation of the Strong Law of Effect

In section 5.2, we saw that a prevalent definition of reinforcement turns the law of effect into a logically necessary truth. Hull's definition of reinforcement avoids this pitfall: if reinforcement is drive reduction, we can't tell whether the law of effect is true without looking at behavior. Unfortunately for drive theory, its version of the law of effect turns out to be false. The data on brain stimulation and exploratory behavior show us that we can increase the frequency of a response by connecting it to a nondrive-reducing stimulus. There's a small conceptual knot here that needs unraveling. We need to distinguish between two forms of the law of effect. The *weak* form says that reinforcement (for Hull, drive reduction) increases the frequency of a preceding response; the *strong* form says that it's *only* reinforcement (for Hull, drive reduction) that increases the frequency of a preceding response. The weak law of effect allows that there may be mechanisms other than reinforcement that affect response frequency; the strong law of effect doesn't. When it's claimed that the data on exploratory behavior show the law of effect to be false, it's clearly the *strong* law that's at issue. Exploratory behavior shows that drive reduction can't be the only mechanism of behavior change. Henceforth, when we refer to the law of effect, we'll be talking about the strong version.

The problem of defining reinforcement in a way that makes the (strong) law of effect come out contingently true was never resolved by behavioral psychologists. Moreover, there are reasons to suspect that the law of effect is going to be false no matter how the concept of reinforcement is defined. The law of effect has this form: when *some sort of event is produced by a response,* the frequency of the response increases. Different definitions of reinforcement amount to different specifications of what that sort of event is like. The fundamental problem is that there's evidence of learning (i.e., behavior change) under conditions in which the response that's learned doesn't produce *any* event. We will discuss three studies that make this point. Curiously, two of these were conducted at the dawn of the behavioristic era. The evidence they provided was ignored because it didn't fit in with prevalent theoretical views.

The first study concerns the *latent learning phenomenon.* By the 1930s, the law of effect had become enshrined as the best-established theoretical principle in psychology. Yet E. C. Tolman and his colleagues had provided as clear a disconfirmation of the law as can be imagined. Tolman demonstrated that response frequency could be altered in the absence of any rewards or punishments. In one of Tolman's numerous demonstrations of this "latent learning effect" (Tolman and Honzik 1930), two groups of rats were run in a complex, multiple-unit maze. One group found food in the end box on every daily trial. The other found nothing at all for the first ten days. For this second group, the only thing that differentiated the "end box" from any other point in the maze was the experimenters' future intentions. At the end of the first ten days, the rewarded group was making much fewer errors in navigating to the end box than the unrewarded group. This is, of course, what the law of effect would have predicted. On the eleventh day, the previously unrewarded group began to find food in the end box. According to the law of effect, this group should then have begun to recapitulate the history of the always-rewarded first group—their errors should have gradually begun to drop at about the same rate as the rewarded group's did during the first ten days of the experiment. What happened, however, was that the previously unrewarded group's errors plunged *immediately* to the level that had been painstakingly achieved in ten days of trial and error by the always-rewarded group.

From a cognitive point of view (of which Tolman was an early champion), these results are not at all surprising. Evidently, in their unrewarded explorations of the maze during the first ten days, rats in the unrewarded group learned something (in the cognitive sense of the word) about the layout of the maze. When, on the eleventh day, they unexpectedly found food at what the experimenters had designated as the end box, they immediately knew how to get back to the same spot. But this is not what should have happened if response frequency were a function of the number of times the response has been rewarded. This powerful disconfirmation had no perceptible effect on the history of psychology. By the early 1930s, the latent learning phenomenon had been frequently replicated in a variety of experimental arrangements. Yet the law of effect continued to be the centerpiece of the most influential theories of learning through the 1940s and well into the 1950s.

Actually, D. A. Macfarlane (1930) had made Tolman's point even more elegantly in an experiment in which he trained rats to turn the right way in a maze to obtain a food reward. Then he flooded the maze with water. He found that the rats immediately began to swim to the arm of the maze that led to food. Once again, we commonsense psychologists are not at all surprised at this behavior. If asked for an explanation, we would say that in the earlier part of the experiment, the rats learned where the food was. Then when the maze was flooded, they simply did what they had to do in order to get where they wanted to go. But from viewpoint of a behavioristic law of effect, this shouldn't have happened. In behaviorism, there's no learning of facts, such as the fact that food is to be found at the end of the left arm of the maze. For behaviorists, "learning" just means changing the probabilities of certain *movements*. In the first part of the experiment, certain movements involved in running were reinforced. But swimming involves a completely different set of movements—a set which hadn't been reinforced in the first part of the experiment. Therefore, the strong law of effect leads to the incorrect prediction that the rats would have to start all over again to "learn" to swim to the food.

Tolman's and Macfarlane's studies show that the law of effect alone (or together with the principle of classical conditioning, for that matter) can't explain every kind of learning. The strong law of effect is false. What happens next? One possible response—the one foreshadowed by Tolman—is to go the cognitive route and allow psychological theories to refer to organisms' mental states. However, if you're convinced that psychology needs to be behavioristic, you might try a different route. You might try to formulate new behavioristic laws that either replace or supplement the law of effect and the principle of classical conditioning. The most influential example of such a proposal is Bandura's and Walters' (1963) law of *observational learning*. As its date indicates, Bandura's and Walters' book appeared rather late in the behavioristic era, when the storm clouds of the impending cognitive revolution were already on the horizon. The law of observational learning asserts that human beings, and to a lesser extent other organisms as well, have a tendency to *imitate* the behavior they see exhibited by others—the law of "monkey see, monkey do." The imitative tendency is independent of any rewards or punishments that may be associated with the observed behavior. A monkey will tend to do what it sees even if it's never reinforced for performing the observed behavior. It will tend to do what it sees even if it's never reinforced for imitating *any* behavior. Punishment may overwhelm the tendency to imitate a particular observed behavior; but the punishment would have to be greater than that needed to inhibit the behavior if it *hadn't* been observed. In sum, the law of observational learning is basic.

Bandura and Walters demonstrated the presence of the imitative tendency in a variety of experimental settings. In the most widely cited of these experiments, children watched adults playing with dolls. One group of children saw the adults play with the dolls aggressively, kicking and punching them; the other half saw the adults interact unaggressively with the dolls. Then all the children were left alone with the dolls and given the (erroneous) impression that they were not being observed. In this situation, the children who had observed aggressive play exhibited much more aggression than the children of the other group. As in the latent learning experiments, this is a behavioral difference between two groups whose members had not been exposed to different reinforcement contingencies. The law of effect doesn't explain the difference in aggressive play, but the law of observational learning does.

The law of observational learning has the obvious practical implication that we should be careful about what sorts of behaviors our children are exposed to. For example, Bandura and Walters noted that their theoretical and experimental work supported the view that violence portrayed in films and on TV *would* tend to produce violent behavior in imitation. Observational learning also explains away an old problem for behavioristic S-R theory. It had long been known that children who are physically punished for aggressive behavior actually show *more* aggressiveness than other comparable children. This finding is incompatible with the second part of the law of effect—the part that we've said very little about. The law of effect says (roughly) that reward increases the frequency of a preceding response, and that punishment *decreases* the frequency of a preceding response. The same problems are encountered in attempting to define punishment as in the definition of reward. But however you define punishment, being beaten is certainly going to be included.

So why don't children who are beaten for aggression show less aggressive behavior? Bandura and Walters note that physical punishment does two things simultaneously. First, by virtue of the fact that it is a punishment, it should, as per the law of effect, cause the aggressive behavior to diminish. But beating the child also provides him with a model of the very behavior he's being punished for. According to the law of observational learning, the parents' aggressiveness should foster imitative aggressiveness by the child. The punishment effect weakens the child's tendency to aggress, and the imitative effect strengthens it. In any given situation, either effect might overwhelm the other. The newly expanded behavioristic theory that contains both the law of effect and the law of observational learning doesn't *predict* that aggressive behavior would increase; but neither does it incorrectly predict, like the law of effect alone does, that aggressive behavior would *decrease*. At least the facts about aggressive behavior don't disconfirm Bandura and Walters' theory.

The law of observational learning was a significant addition to S-R theory. It enabled that theory to account for a number of phenomena that the classical S-R theory (law of effect plus classical conditioning) couldn't deal with. But it didn't resolve *all* the problems of S-R theory. For example, it didn't help to explain the latent-learning phenomenon, or why Macfarlane's rats swam to the goal box on their first aquatic trial.

5.7. The Refutation of Behavioral Psychology

We will close this chapter with an argument that shows that behavioral psychology can't be saved by the addition of any number of new behavioristic laws. It's difficult to say where this argument comes from—it was in the air in the 1970s. It especially informed the work of Noam Chomsky and Jerry Fodor. The argument *doesn't* show that behavioristic theories generate false predictions; rather it purports to show that strictly behavioristic theories don't make any predictions at all. Behavioral psychologists certainly suppose that they're deriving predictions from their theories but according to the coming argument, their predictions are unavoidably dependent on their intuitions about their subjects' mental processes. If this argument is sound, behavioral psychology can't be saved by any purely behavioristic theoretical maneuvers. It's the end of the line for S-R theory.

Suppose you seat your subject before a monitor on which a succession of geometrical shapes is displayed. You want S to press a button every time the displayed shape is a triangle, and at no other time. So you present a triangle on the screen, wait until S presses the button, and then provide her with a reward. Then you blank the screen and start the next trial. To ensure that S will respond *only* to triangles, you intersperse the triangle trials with trials in which the monitor displays a circular shape. If S presses the button during a circle trial, she receives an electric shock. It won't take human subjects very long to catch on to the contingencies of reinforcement in this situation, whereupon they will press the button as soon as a triangle appears on the screen, and they will refrain from pressing the button as long as a circle is on the screen.

Suppose now that you present S for the first time with a square. Will she press the button? We might reason as follows. S has previously been rewarded for pressing a button in the presence of triangles and punished for pressing in the presence of nontriangles. Squares are a species of nontriangle; so it seems that the law of effect leads to the prediction that she *won't* press the button when there's a square on the screen. But there are other ways to describe S's reinforcement history. For example, it's also true that she's been rewarded for pressing at *polygons* and punished for pressing at *non*polygons. Squares are a species of polygon; therefore the law of effect leads to the prediction that S *will* press the button when there's a square on the screen.

So what did S really get rewarded for: pressing a button for triangles, or pressing for polygons? Clearly, the answer can't be found by examining the objective, physical stimuli that were available in the button-pressing situation. The shapes that were occasions for reward were triangles, and they were also polygons. Given the amount of training that S received, it's impossible to predict how she'll react to a square. If we want to know that S will respond to all—and only—triangular shapes, we have to disambiguate the reinforcement contingencies. We could, for example, include training trials in which squares are displayed on the screen and button-pressing, if it occurs, is shocked. This would clearly establish that the class of stimuli that are occasions for reward is not the class of polygons. It could, however, still be the class of triangles.

But there are multiple ways to describe S's newly augmented reinforcement history as well. One way is to say that pressing for triangles is rewarded and pressing for nontriangles is punished. Another way is to say that pressing for *any polygons other than squares* is rewarded, while pressing for *any square or nonpolygonal figure* is punished. If the first description is right, S would not press the button if presented for the first time with a *pentagon;* if the second description is right, she would. So we still can't predict that S will press a button for all and only triangles. That is to say, we can't predict it *from the law of effect.* Of course, we all know that a human subject will try the triangles-versus-nontriangles hypothesis before resorting to baroque structures like nonsquare-polygons-versus-squares-or-nonpolygons but it isn't the law of effect that tells us this. We know it on the basis of our informal, intuitive, "street" knowledge of human nature.

If we want the law of effect to generate the prediction that S will press at all and only triangles, we need more data. In particular, we need to include some trials in which pentagons are displayed and button-pressing, if it occurs, is shocked. But the same dilemma can be repeated almost verbatim. One way to describe the twice-augmented reinforcement history is still to say that pressing buttons for triangles is rewarded and pressing for nontriangles is punished. Another way is to say that pressing for *any polygons other than either squares or pentagons* is rewarded, while pressing for *any square or pentagon or nonpolygonal figure* is punished. If the first description is right, S would not press the button if presented for the first time with a hexagon; but if the second description is right, she would. So we still can't predict that S will press for all and only triangles.

It should be clear that the dilemma can be repeated ad infinitum. Given any finite number of stimuli, there are going to be various ways of embedding them all in a superordinate category. It follows that after any finite regimen of reward and punishment, there are going to be alternative ways of describing what category of stimuli has been the occasion for reward or for punishment. Generally speaking, these alternative descriptions will lead to different behavioral predictions from the law of effect. Moreover, there's nothing about the physical stimuli that enables us to pick out the *right* description, the one we should use for making predictions. Therefore we can't use the behavioristic law of effect to make any predictions at all.

Can't the law of effect at least enable us to predict that S will press for triangles? For the sake of the argument, we've assumed that this is so but the same dilemma can be run backward, as it were. Suppose S has experienced three rewarded trials with triangles. Suppose also that all three trials were with equilateral triangles. Then the reinforcement history can be described either as (1) pressing buttons for triangles is rewarded, or as (2) pressing for equilateral triangles is rewarded. With the first description, the law of effect predicts that a scalene triangle will elicit the button-pressing response; with the second, the law of effect predicts that a scalene triangle *won't* elicit the button-pressing response. The same argument works with *any* triangles in the training set. Suppose that the three triangles that were occasions for reward were an equilateral triangle T1, an isosceles triangle T2, and a scalene triangle T3. This reinforcement history could still be described either as (1) pressing for triangles is rewarded, or as (2) pressing for triangles that have exactly the dimensions of T1 or T2 or T3 is rewarded. With the first option, the law of effect predicts that an equilateral triangle twice the size of T1 will elicit the button-pressing response; with the second description, the law of effect predicts that such a triangle *won't* elicit the button-pressing response. It's clear that rewarding responses to any additional number of triangular shapes isn't going to make any difference. So long as the stimuli are finite in number, they're always going to be amenable to alternative descriptions that yield divergent predictions. Therefore, the behavioristic law of effect can't be used to make predictions.

Entirely similar remarks apply to any other S-R law that might be proposed. Consider the law of observational learning. There are indefinitely many ways to describe what behavior is being observed. In Bandura's and Walters' experiment, the children could be said to have observed the adults acting aggressively with dolls, or punching dolls with their fists, or punching this particular doll, or moving energetically, or simply moving. Each of these descriptions leads to different behavioral predictions from the law of observational learning, and there's no way to tell which is the correct description by examining the objective, physical dimensions of any stimuli or responses. This problem is going to infect any theory that restricts its theoretical concepts to stimuli and responses behavioristically conceived. Therefore behavioristic S-R theory makes no behavioral predictions.

If we want our theories to predict behavior, we need more information to help us pick the appropriate description of the relevant stimuli and responses. The physical properties of the stimuli and responses aren't enough. There's only one place to look for further information: *inside the subject*. What determines whether S has been rewarded for pressing for triangles or for pressing for any polygons other than squares can only be an internal state of the subject. In some way or other, the rewarded stimuli are *internally represented* either as triangles or as nonsquare polygons. We're forced to say this by default: there's no other candidate for determining which category the rewarded stimuli belong to. But an internal representation of a category sounds very much like a mental state; thus ends the history of behavioral psychology.

6. The Transition from Behaviorism to Cognitive Science

In the previous chapter, we saw that S-R theory got itself mired in all sorts of conceptual and empirical difficulties. Some of these problems, like the latent-learning phenomenon, were discovered and widely discussed from the earliest days of the behavioral era. Why did behavioral psychology endure as long as it did despite its patent shortcomings? Because of American psychologists' adherence to the philosophy of behaviorism. This philosophical thesis functioned as a restriction on the theories that were deemed to be scientifically legitimate. With the behavioristic restriction in place, it proved to be impossible to formulate any theories that could adequately deal with the well-known difficulties. But behavioral psychologists thought that the case for behaviorism was ironclad. If this was so, then there was no choice but to live with the difficulties, hoping that they might be eventually be resolved by some presently unimaginable development. After living in this vain hope for several decades, psychologists and philosophers of science began to look for—and to find—cracks in the ironclad case for behaviorism.

The critique of behaviorism in this chapter will show that there's no basis for forbidding psychological theories to refer to mental states. Behaviorism isn't compulsory. The flip side of this conclusion is that the mentalism of cognitive science is at least philosophically permissible. This chapter is therefore simultaneously the finale of our discussion of S-R theory and the start of our discussion of cognitive science.

6.1. Methodological Behaviorism

Recall the distinction that we made in section 2.2 between two broad types of behaviorism: *methodological* and *metaphysical*. The two behaviorisms share the same conclusion: psychology can't refer to mental states. But each offers a different reason for coming to that conclusion. Methodological behaviorists admit that there are—or may be—mental states, but say that they're not suitable for scientific investigation. Methodological behaviorists are, or at least can be, dualists.

The argument for methodological behaviorism is short, simple, and very powerful. It consists of two simple premises and a direct conclusion.

> Premise 1. Scientific data must refer to publicly observable events.

By definition, a phenomenon is *publicly observable* (*public,* for short) if any properly situated observer would be able to detect it. An observer is "properly situated" if (1) she's in the right place at the right time to observe the event, and (2) she possesses the normal complement of cognitive and perceptual skills. (For a more thorough discussion of this important concept, see Kukla 1983.) The rationale for the first premise is that what distinguishes scientific from nonscientific claims is that the former needn't be accepted or rejected on faith. If somebody makes a claim in science, anyone who is interested in it ought to be able to confirm or disconfirm it for herself. This requirement rules out divine revelation to a prophet as a source of scientific data. If premise 1 is accepted, one can't use divine revelations—even one's own—to support or criticize a scientific theory.

Private events are events that aren't public. Divine revelations are a type of private event. The second premise delineates another type:

> Premise 2. Physical events are public; mental events are private.

Suppose someone claims that a physical event takes place under certain conditions—e.g., that rats who receive food after pressing a bar will emit this response more frequently than rats who receive an electric shock for bar-pressing. If it's important for you to know whether this claim is correct, you can check it out for yourself: you can reward some rats with food and shock other rats when they press the bar, and observe whether the rewarded rats press the bar more often than the shocked rats. In fact, you and the claimant can both stand side by side and observe the *same* rats. The rats' bar pressings are publicly observable events. The same is true of any behavioral response. But if someone claims to have a certain mental image or feeling, you can't confirm the claim for yourself. There's no sense in which you and she can stand "side by side" in order to observe the occurrence or nonoccurrence of her mental state. The only mental states that you can observe are your own, just as the claimant is the only being who can observe her own mental states. That is to say, mental states are private. But then, by premise 1, reports of one's mental states can't legitimately play the role of scientific data.

> Conclusion. Reports of physical events (like behavior) can be scientific data, but reports of mental events can't.

And that's methodological behaviorism.

Before launching into a critique of the argument, we should pause to appreciate its force. It's undoubtedly the most influential piece of reasoning in the history of psychology. It persuaded several generations of psychologists to become behaviorists. In fact, American psychologists were so certain of the soundness of the argument that they presented it without critical comment in the first chapters of their introductory psychology texts. They did this as late as 1968:

> . . . the terms used in any science must, at least in the final analysis, refer to events . . . that are publicly observable, verifiable, and testable. Events that do not meet this criterion are not part of science. . . . Among the events that are logically inaccessible to public examination is the whole world of private experience. I can never know whether your experiences of red, amusement, and embarrassment are the same as mine; nor, if I see you scratch or weep, can I verify your itch or woe directly. (Kimble and Garmezy 1968, 10-11)

For a methodological behaviorist, all science is physical science. Psychology is the physical science that studies the publicly observable behavior of organisms; that is, their physical movements. To be sure, human organisms sometimes tell us that they are in certain mental states. But the publicly observable data that can be derived from such events aren't that certain experiences have occurred, but that someone has emitted certain verbal responses:

> Most subjects will give a report of seeing an afterimage and a "flight of colors" after looking at a bright light for a while. What must now be stressed is that we do not (and cannot) really know that the subject *sees* the sequence of colors. All that we can say for sure is that subjects consistently *report* seeing a sequence of colors. This is the important point. It is not the subject's private experience that counts, for that is forever beyond our direct observation. It is, rather, the report of such experiences that is open to public inspection, verification, and test. (Kimble and Garmezy 1968, 11)

Despite its evident persuasiveness, the methodological behaviorist's argument commits a relatively simple logical error: adoption of its first premise is incompatible with the adoption of its second premise. More precisely, if you accept premise 1, you eradicate the grounds upon which the methodological behaviorist wishes to adopt premise 2. For suppose you do accept premise 1—you resolve to study only the publicly observable events. So which are they? For you to know that an event is *publicly* observable, you have to know that *someone else* can observe it. Is a rat pressing a bar a publicly observable event? To establish that it is, you have to be able to stand side by side with someone else in front of the rat and ascertain that she observes the same behavior as you do. But observing that a physical event takes place is itself a private mental event. The other viewer's *seeing* that the rat presses the bar is as hidden from you as her feelings, thoughts, and images. You can observe the bar-pressing rat yourself, and you can observe that she *reports* observing the bar-pressing rat but you can't observe *that she observes it*. Yet this is just what's required before you can say that the rat's bar-pressing is *publicly* observable. The argument in brief is that if we agree that our knowledge is restricted to publicly observable states of affairs (premise 1), we are left with no basis upon which to conclude, as per premise 2, that physical events *are* publicly observable.

A corollary of this conclusion is that subjects' verbal reports of experiences are in the same "untestable" boat as the experiences themselves. Consider once again the quoted passage on afterimages. Let's agree that you can't verify that someone else sees an afterimage, and also that you *can* verify that she says, "I see an afterimage." This is not yet enough to get the second fact into science. According to premise 1, you must also establish that *others* can verify the same fact. But, to paraphrase the foregoing disquisition on afterimages, you do not (and cannot) really know that others *observe* someone's saying, "I see an afterimage"; all you can say for sure is that they *report* observing it. Thus you have no grounds for claiming that the physical event that consists of someone saying, "I see an afterimage" is "open to public inspection."

Methodological behaviorists are guilty of wielding an inconsistently selective skepticism. When they're told that someone experienced a thought or an afterimage, they reject this claim because they can't independently verify it. But they're evidently prepared to accept another's claim to have observed a physical event, for otherwise they couldn't conclude that physical events are publicly observable. Yet the one claim is no more verifiable than the other. Logic compels us to treat them both the same. There are two ways of treating them both the same. We may say that our willingness to accept others' reports of their observations of physical events commits us also to accepting reports of their thoughts and images. Or, we may reject both types of claims on the basis of their unverifiability. The first of these courses amounts to an explicit repudiation of methodological behaviorism. The second course leads to a consistent *solipsism;* that is, a thoroughgoing skepticism concerning whether others can be known to have any sort of mental life. Solipsists don't, however, distinguish between public and private events—so far as they can tell, there is no *public* to which events may be observable. Therefore, solipsists can't be methodological behaviorists. In sum, methodological behaviorism is incompatible with an even-handed treatment of all mentalistic reports, regardless of whether that treatment is skeptical or credulous.

6.2. Metaphysical Behaviorism

Metaphysical behaviorism is supposed to be what you get when you approach the problems of psychology from a *materialist* perspective. According to materialism, the only events that exist in the world are physical events. Therefore there are no immaterial mental events for psychologists to study. Psychology must be behavioristic by default. Philosophers of the behaviorist era tended overwhelmingly to be metaphysical (as opposed to methodological) behaviorists. Psychologists, however, more often inclined toward the methodological doctrine.

The case for metaphysical behaviorism obviously depends on the premise that dualism is false. In Chapter 1, we argued that this premise is not entirely secure: dualism has its unresolved problems, but it's still a rational option. In fact, it made something of a comeback in the 1990s. But for almost all of the twentieth century, dualism was in utter disrepute in the philosophical community. Philosophical discussions of the problems of psychology generally *presupposed* materialism. Nevertheless, metaphysical behaviorism was abandoned well before the mini-resurgence of dualist sentiment in the 90s. What happened in the 70s and 80s is that it gradually came to be realized that materialism doesn't rule out the possibility of a mentalistic psychology. Mentalistic psychology is *compatible* with materialism. As a consequence, fans of the mind don't have to worry about the dualism versus materialism issue: they get to talk about mental events if dualism is right, and they *still* get to talk about mental events if materialism is right. The second part of the foregoing claim is by no means obvious—it's a foreshadowing of the conclusion that will be arrived at by the end of this chapter.

There are two subvarieties of metaphysical behaviorism. The more drastic *radical* behaviorism is the thesis that attributions of mental states are always false. On this view, to say that someone is experiencing a mental image or feeling thirsty is akin to claiming that Santa Claus lives at the North Pole, or that goblins are responsible for a broken vase: it's to impute existence to fictional entities. If this is so, then what were the nineteenth-century introspectionists doing? Radical behaviorists are committed to saying that the introspectionists were trying systematically to investigate a subject-matter that didn't exist. Is it plausible that a normal adult could be so thoroughly confused? Well, in the Middle Ages it was widely believed that there could be a systematic body of knowledge pertaining to demons and demonic possession. The radical behaviorist's claim is that introspective psychology is like demonology. This is an extreme minority viewpoint, even among metaphysical behaviorists. To most people, philosophers and nonphilosophers alike, it seems crazy to say that when somebody tells you that he's thirsty or has a headache, he's invariably mistaken. However, radical behaviorism turns out to be very difficult to refute.

The preferred variety of metaphysical behaviorism was the doctrine that goes by the name of *logical* behaviorism. Logical behaviorism is a *semantic* theory—i.e., a theory about the meaning of mentalistic terms. It hypothesizes that talking about mental states is really a roundabout way of talking about behavior. For example, a logical behaviorist might hypothesize that the apparently mentalistic sentence,

(1) Bob is thirsty.

has the same meaning as the purely physicalistic sentence,

(2) Bob is drinking a lot.

Unlike the radical behaviorists, logical behaviorists concede that imputations of mental states, as in "Bob is thirsty," are sometimes true. But they agree with radical behaviorists that mentalistic psychology is based on a deep confusion: the introspectionists mistakenly thought that sentences like "Bob is thirsty" were rendered true by the occurrence of events in an immaterial realm.

Here's another way to draw the distinction between the two metaphysical behaviorisms. Radical behaviorists say that the mentalistic term "thirst" has the same status as the term "Santa Claus"; logical behaviorists say that "thirst" is akin to "the average person." There are true things to be said about the average person. Here (let us agree) is one of them:

(3) The average person has 2.3 children.

Despite the fact that (3) is a true sentence, *the average person does not exist*—nowhere in the universe will we find an entity that has a fractional number of offspring. Sentence 3 *looks* grammatically as though it were imparting information about an entity that's named by the term "average person." In reality, however, the sentence is a succinct equivalent to a much longer sentence, namely:

(4) If you add up the number of children that every person has and divide by the number of persons, the result is 2.3.

Note that sentence 4 makes no reference to "the average person." If sentence 4 is indeed an adequate translation of sentence 3, it follows that sentence 3, when properly understood, doesn't entail that the average person exists. The term "average person" is introduced merely for the sake of being able to state the content of sentence 4 more succinctly. Similarly, "Bob is thirsty" may very well be true, even though there's no such thing as thirst. Presumably, "Bob is thirsty" is an alternative way to say something about Bob's behavior, such as that he's drinking a lot. The important point is that the facts about Bob can be exhaustively stated without making any reference to Bob's thirst. The reference to thirst, when we make it, merely provides a stylistic alternative to behavioral description. Psychology is still all about behavior.

The thesis that mentalistic sentences have behavioral equivalents runs into an immediate (but reparable) difficulty: the language of mental states allows that one can be in a mental state without behaving at all. You can sit perfectly still and be thirsty. The logical behaviorist's reply is that mental states aren't equated with overt behaviors, but with behavioral *dispositions.* Dispositions are conditional properties that tell us that the object possessing them will react in a particular way *if* something happens. Dispositional properties crop up routinely in all of the sciences. Chemists, for example, talk about the solubility of certain substances. To say that a substance is soluble is to say that it would dissolve if it were placed in water. But the substance can be soluble even when it's sitting high and dry in a jar on the shelf. That's how to reconcile the thesis that mentalistic talk is translatable into behavioral talk with the observation that you can be in a mental state without behaving: the behavioral talk is talk of behavioral dispositions. For example, to say that Bob is thirsty isn't to say that Bob is drinking, or even that he's drinking a lot. Travelers lost in the Sahara Desert are presumably thirsty; but they may not be drinking at all for the simple reason that they have no access to anything drinkable. A better translation of "Bob is thirsty" than "Bob drinks a lot" is the conditional,

> (5) If Bob had access to something to drink, then he would drink it.

Note that the proposed translation of "Bob is thirsty" still makes no reference to mental states. Mentalistic talk is "translated out," or *reduced* to talk about behavioral dispositions.

The logical behaviorist project of reducing the mental to the behavioral is well-illustrated in the following passage by Skinner (elsewhere, Skinner sounds more like a radical behaviorist):

> When the man in the street says that someone is afraid or angry
> or in love, he is generally talking about predispositions to act in
> certain ways. The "angry" man shows an increased probability
> of striking, insulting, or otherwise inflicting injury and a low-
> ered probability of aiding, favoring, comforting, or making love.
> The man "in love" shows an increased tendency to aid, favor, be
> with, and caress and a lowered tendency to injure in any way.
> "In fear" a man tends to reduce or avoid contact with specific
> stimuli—as by running away, hiding, or covering his eyes and
> ears; at the same time he is less likely to advance toward such
> stimuli or into unfamiliar territory. (Skinner 1953, 162)

Logical behaviorism was the majority viewpoint among English-
speaking philosophers in the 1950s and 1960s but eventually it succumbed to a number of powerful counterarguments. In fact, logical
behaviorism proved to be more clearly refutable than either dualism
or radical behaviorism. The first counterargument is that no one has
ever been able to give an adequate translation of any mentalistic term
in purely behavioral language. For example, consider the dispositional
translation given in sentence 5 of "Bob is thirsty." Bob would *not* drink
a liquid that he had access to if he thought that the liquid was poison-
ous. So translation 5 has to give way to the more complicated,

(6) If Bob had access to something to drink and if he
believed that it was nonpoisonous, then he would drink it.

In this case the behavioral translation fails! You're defining the mentalistic term "thirsty" in terms of another *mentalistic* term, namely
"believes." You could try to translate out the reference to belief by
claiming that,

(7) Bob believes that X.

is itself equivalent to the behavioral disposition,

(8) If Bob were asked whether X is true, he would say "yes."

But Bob would answer "yes" to this question only if he *wanted* his
interlocutor to know what he believed (a murderer asked whether he's

responsible for his victim's death wouldn't necessarily answer affirmatively). Once again the behavioral translation of a mentalistic term has to use another mentalistic term—in this case, "wanting." So it's not a behavioral translation at all. As far as anyone has been able to tell, this *always* happens with would-be behavioral translations: you always get another mentalistic term on the other side of the equation. This is a strong argument against logical behaviorism. It isn't totally conclusive, however, since the failure of any number of attempts to translate out mentalistic language doesn't show that the task is impossible but it's been a long time since anyone even tried to translate out mentalistic talk.

A second counterargument purports to show, in one fell swoop, that any behavioral reduction that anyone might propose in the future is bound to fail. Consider any behavioral definition of love. However elaborate the specification of love-behavior might be, it's possible for someone to act it out for a large cash reward, or because it's part of a fraternity initiation, or simply because the actor is portraying someone in love in a play. Since the behavioral definition of love is satisfied in these scenarios, the logical behaviorist is committed to saying that the actor is in love. But, in practice, that isn't how the mentalistic term "love" is used. We don't count love-behavior that occurs in a play as an instance of true love. Now the *radical* behaviorist wouldn't be surprised or discomfitted by these observations. His view is that "love" refers to an immaterial mental state, and that, moreover, imputations of *being* in love are always false (because there are no immaterial mental states). Thus the question whether there is a behavioral scenario that's correlated with true love doesn't even arise. But the *logical* behaviorist claims that what we say about love can be captured by a behavioral definition. The argument against this view is that our concept of love allows us to distinguish between true love and pretending to be in love but this distinction can't be captured by any behavioral criterion.

A third argument against logical behaviorism is that it clearly doesn't apply to *first-person* claims about one's own mental states. If the logical-behaviorist account were correct, then your utterance "I have a headache" would mean that you're disposed to behave in a certain manner. But then if someone were to ask you whether you have a headache, you would have to observe your own behavior in order to reply: if you find yourself groaning, holding your head, and taking aspirin, then you conclude that you have a headache! It's at least initially plausible to suppose that *someone else's* groaning, head-holding, and aspirin-taking behaviors are grounds for *your* concluding that *she* has a headache; but it clearly isn't the basis on which you make the corresponding judgment about yourself. An exercise for the reader: explain the following joke. Two logical behaviorists meet in the street. One of them says to the other: "You're fine. How am I?"

6.3. Central State Identity Theory

By the early 1980s, disillusionment with the various forms of behaviorism had become widespread. The underlying philosophical commitment to materialism, however, remained unshaken. Fortunately for materialists, there's another approach to the mind-body problem that both satisfies the tenet of materialism and avoids the difficulties of behaviorism—the *central state identity theory*. Like logical behaviorism, central state identity theory equates mental states with purely physical states of affairs but the physical equivalents of the mental are different. According to logical behaviorism, to have a belief or a desire is to be disposed to behave in a certain manner; according to central state identity theory, it's for one's central nervous system (particularly one's brain) to be in a particular neurophysiological state.

Predictably, there are several varieties of central state identity theory. The first, *semantic identity theory,* says that a mentalistic statement such as "S believes that P" *means* that S is in a particular brain state. This is totally implausible. For suppose that your claim "I believe that Lima is the capital of Peru" means that your brain is in the neurophysiological state X. Then to be justified in claiming that you believe that Lima is the capital of Peru, you would have to establish that your brain is in state X. But surely you don't have that kind of detailed neurophysiological knowledge about the state of your brain! Therefore you're not justified in claiming that you believe that Lima is the capital of Peru. If you were asked whether you believe that Lima is the capital of Peru, you'd have to work out a way to observe your own brain in order to ascertain whether it's in state X. This is, of course, absurd. You don't need to examine your brain in order to know what you believe.

For that matter, even being able to observe your brain wouldn't help. Everyone agrees that we don't yet know what brain states correspond to various mental states. But then, if your claim "I believe that Lima is the capital of Peru" means that you are in some unknown brain state, it would follow that you don't even know what "I believe that Lima is the capital of Peru" *means*. This is even more outrageous than the consequence that you wouldn't know whether the sentence is true. In fact, if we didn't have a prior understanding of what believing that Lima is the capital of Peru means, we would have no way of ever discovering a corresponding brain state—for what is the sought-after brain state supposed to correspond to?

For these reasons, central state identity theorists have preferred to endorse the *contingent identity theory*. Like all central-state theorists, contingent identity theorists maintain that mental states are identical to brain states. But they don't say that terms referring to mental states are *synonymous* with the terms that refer to the corresponding brain states. The identity is asserted to be *contingent*, as opposed to logically necessary (see section 5.2). An example of a logically necessary identity is the identity between the class of all bachelors and the class of all unmarried male human adults. Anyone who understands the language is in a position to know that this identity holds. No empirical evidence is needed. This is the kind of identity that's involved in the semantic identity theory. An example of a contingent identity is the identity of the president of the United States in the year 2005 and the president of the United States whose father was also a president of the United States. Here a knowledge of the language isn't enough to establish the truth of the identity—empirical evidence is required.

Another example: it was discovered through scientific research that water is identical to H_2O. But "water" doesn't *mean* the same thing as "H_2O"—if it did, then it would follow that before it was known that water is H_2O, people didn't know what the word "water" meant. The identity discovered through scientific research is contingent. Contingent identity theory in psychology is the theory that the relationship between mind and brain is like the relationship between water and H_2O. There is, however, one important difference between the two relationships. The empirical evidence that water is H_2O is already in; but the identity between mental states and brain states is a guess about the results of *future* scientific research. Nobody knows, or even claims to know, what brain state is equal to the mental state of believing that Lima is the capital of Peru. Contingent identity theorists are people who bet that future neuropsychological research will discover a corresponding neural state for this and every other mental state.

Suppose that future research does discover perfect correlations between mental states and neural states: every time a mental state X occurs, there's a specific neural state Y that takes place, and vice versa. Such perfect correlations would constitute the best data that a contingent identity theorist could hope for. But a *dualist* could explain these data with the hypothesis that the neural state Y is not identical to the mental state X, but that it's the unique *cause* of X. Both the identity theorist's and the dualist's hypotheses provide adequate explanations of the mind-brain correspondences. So the identity theorist can't win the argument on the grounds of empirical data alone. She also has to appeal to the greater simplicity of her hypothesis relative to the dualist's.

6.4. Type and Token Identity

The contingent identity theory comes in two flavors: *type* identity theory and *token* identity theory. In this context, a type is a general category of entities, and a token is a specific, individual entity. The dog Fido is a token of the type "dog." The token identity theory is the theory that every token mental state is (contingently) identical to a token brain state. If this is so, then Bob's thinking, at 3:25 p.m. on May 23, 1998, that Lima is the capital of Peru is identical to some specific neurons in Bob's brain firing in a particular manner at that time. According to type identity theory, every type of mental state is identical to some type of brain state. If this is so, then the belief that Lima is the capital of Peru, whenever and wherever the belief occurs, is identical to some type of neural assembly firing in a certain manner.

Suppose that the type identity theory is true: every type of mental state is identical to a type of brain state. Then, obviously, the token identity theory is also true: every specific mental state is identical to a specific brain state. But the converse proposition doesn't hold. The truth of the token identity theory doesn't ensure the truth of the type identity theory. That's the point of making the distinction between the two theories. An analogy will help to make this elusive point clear. Let's define a *b-thing* as any physical object that, at some time or other in the history of the universe, is designated by an English word that starts with the letter b. Thus bison are b-things, as well as bicycles, bread sticks, and balloons. Obviously, every token b-thing is a token physical object—indeed, the fact that it is a physical object is part of the very definition of "b-thing." Nevertheless, it would be impossible to formulate a type in the language of physics that's coextensive with the type "b-thing": the b-things simply have no physical properties in common. It's remotely possible that we might find an enormously complex physical-state description that's coextensive with the class of all the things that have ever had a b-name *to date*. But even if we did find such a description, the type-to-type identity could be falsified simply by selecting any physical object that didn't fit the physical description and dubbing it a "beezle."

In the same way, it's logically possible that all the tokens of the belief that Lima is the capital of Peru have no physiological properties in common, even though each token, taken individually, is a neurophysiological event. What goes on in your brain when you believe that Lima is the capital of Peru may simply not be the same kind of thing as what goes on in your neighbor's brain when he believes that Lima is the capital of Peru, and so on. But—and this is the payoff—token identity is enough to satisfy the tenet of materialism. To say that the token identity theory is true is to say that every token mental state is identical to a token physical state. But that's just a long-winded way of saying that every mental state is a physical state—and that's materialism. So you can repudiate the thesis that there's a neurological description of every *type* of mental state and still be a card-carrying materialist.

The foregoing remarks show that mind-body token identity without type identity is a conceptual possibility. Is that the way things really are? The cognitive science community is more or less evenly split on this issue. Neuropsychologists tend to endorse the type identity theory, while cognitive psychologists tend to repudiate it. The main reason one might want to reject the type identity hypothesis is that it entails a dubious sort of human chauvinism (Putnam 1975). It seems plausible to suppose that there could be intelligent extraterrestrials who have drastically different physiologies, but who are nevertheless capable of having beliefs. In fact, it seems plausible that beliefs can find a home in indefinitely many exotic physiologies. If this is so, then the type identity theory is false: as in the case of b-things, it would be impossible to specify any physical properties that are shared by all beliefs.

The same point has been made in relation to artificial intelligence—AI—instead of intelligent extraterrestrials. On some accounts, AI is the thesis that a properly programmed computer can have mental states like beliefs (see Chapter 7). But one and the same program can be run on computers of widely different construction. In principle, even a system composed of tin cans connected with bits of string can run any program that an IBM mainframe can run (albeit somewhat more slowly). If the AI thesis that computers can have beliefs turns out to be true, it follows that types of beliefs can't be equated with types of physical states.

In addition to qualifying as a materialist, the token identity theorist who rejects type identity can also consistently maintain that the laws of psychological science are independent of the laws of neurophysiology. Until the 1980s, it was widely believed that a commitment to a materialist ontology also committed one to the view that psychology can ultimately be reduced to physiology, in the strong sense that the laws of psychology would eventually be derived from neurophysiological principles. This was not a happy conclusion for most psychologists, since it meant that their science was merely a stopgap enterprise, doomed to obsolescence by the advance of neurophysiology. One sees this resistance to reductionism in even so outspoken a proponent of materialism as Skinner (1976). But if materialism entails reductionism, then the denial of the latter requires us to repudiate the former as well. Most psychologists were unwilling to abandon materialism, and therefore became reluctant reductionists. However, a famous argument, attributed mainly to Donald Davidson (1970), establishes the logical independence of the two doctrines. Here's how the argument goes.

First let's note that if the type identity theory is true, then psychology *does* reduce to neurophysiology. Consider any psychological law—say:

(9) Believing that Lima is the capital of Peru causes one to giggle.

If type identity theory is true, then there will be a neurophysiological equivalent to the type of mental state designated by "believing that Lima is the capital of Peru." Call that neurophysiological equivalent N. Then we have:

(10) Believing that Lima is the capital of Peru = being in neurophysiological state N.

Then, substituting equals for equals, the psychological law (10) can be rewritten as:

(11) Being in neurophysiological state N causes one to giggle.

Note that 11 makes no reference to any mental states. If the type identity theory is true, we can subject any psychological law to the same treatment—all mentalistic terms can be replaced by their neurophysiological equivalent. Thus an exhaustive account of human nature needn't make any reference to mental states. If type identity theory turns out to be true, psychology will have been revealed to be indeed a stopgap enterprise: we formulate psychological principles only as long as we don't know the neural correlates of mental states. Once we know them, we won't need psychology any more—it will all be neurophysiology. No wonder neuropsychologists favor type identity theory!

Now what if only the token identity theory is true? You still satisfy the requirement of materialism, since every mental state is identical to a neural state. Thus you can translate out every *specific* mentalistic claim. Suppose that at 3:25 p.m. on May 23, 1998, Bob believed that Lima is the capital of Peru. The token identity theory assures us that this token belief had a neural equivalent. But without type identity, there's no assurance that we can find a neural equivalent N that's coextensive with the class of all beliefs, at all times and by all persons, that Lima is the capital of Peru. Thus laws like 9 may very well be irreducibly mentalistic. The token identity theory gives you a way to be a materialist and to have an autonomous, irreducible mentalistic psychology at the same time.

6.5. Functionalism

If beliefs have no physical properties in common, then what is it that makes a state a belief? The answer that has gained the most favor among postbehavioristic psychologists goes by the name of *functionalism*. Functionalists maintain that what all the different tokens of the type "belief" have in common is the way they function. The import of this claim is best explained by a nonpsychological example. What's the definition of the word "heart"? The physical composition of hearts isn't a part of the definition—for while most of the hearts that we know of are composed of protoplasm, there are also artificial plastic hearts. The fact that our hearts are located on the left side of the chest isn't a defining characteristic either—extraterrestrials might have their hearts on the right, or even in their feet. Regardless of its composition, location, or any other physical characteristic, an organ qualifies as a heart so long as it causes the blood to circulate. A heart is any device that plays that *causal role* in the broader system of a living organism. A concept that, like "heart," is defined in terms of what it causes rather than its physical properties, is called a *functional concept.* "Blood" is also a functional concept—it's the medium that carries nutriments to different parts of the body, whether this medium is a red liquid or a greenish gas.

According to functionalism in psychology, beliefs, desires, and other mental states are also defined by their causal role in a system. Here's an example of a functional definition of the mental state of *wanting:*

> (12) Wanting ice cream = whatever state it is that causes a system to obtain ice cream.

Actually, the state of wanting is much more complex than this (for one thing, you may want something that you're unable to obtain) but formula 12 will serve as an example of a functional definition. According to 12, *any* state that causes ice-cream-obtaining behavior counts as an instance of wanting ice cream. It may be a neural event of a particular kind for you, a neural event of a very different kind for your neighbor, a siliconal event for Martians, and so on. It could even be something *non*physical, like the activity of an immaterial Cartesian mind. Functionalism is agnostic on the dualism-materialism issue—it's just that it *allows* you to be a materialist while denying that psychology can be reduced to neurophysiology.

It's important to distinguish the functionalist treatment of mental states from the logical behaviorist's treatment. A logical behaviorist might say something like the following:

> (13) Wanting ice cream = obtaining ice cream.

Again, this is an oversimplification (you may want ice cream and be unable to obtain it); but 13 serves as an example of the logical behaviorist's characteristic reduction of the mental to the behavioral. The logical behaviorist's formula 13 *equates* the mental state with a behavioral state. Like the type identity theory that equates mental states with neural states, logical behaviorism entails reductionism: if wanting ice cream is identical to obtaining ice cream, then any general statement that adverts to wanting ice cream can be rewritten as a general state-ment about ice-cream-obtaining behavior. For example, the law,

(14) Everybody wants ice cream after dinner.

is translated into,

(15) Everybody obtains ice cream after dinner.

In the functional definition 12, however, the mental state isn't identi-fied with behavior, but with the *cause* of the behavior. Since causes are distinct from their effects, the project of translating out mentalistic terms is a nonstarter.

A good way to understand the enterprise of functionalist psycholo-gy is to work out the functionalist theory of a very simple device: a Coke machine (the example is an adaptation of Fodor's [1981]). Suppose you encounter a Coke machine, but have no idea how it works. You try subjecting it to various stimuli, such as verbally request-ing a Coke, sticking your hand up the dispenser, and kicking it; but none of these stimuli elicits any response. When you put a dime in the coin slot, however, the machine dispenses a Coke (it's a very old machine). You try this a few times, and find this S-R connection to be reliable. So you adopt it as the First Law of Coke Machine Behavior: when it receives a dime, the machine gives you a Coke. Then you try inserting a nickel: nothing happens. You try a few more stimuli—you insult the machine and spit on it: no response. Then, perhaps because you've run out of ideas, you try putting in a nickel again. This time, however, you're rewarded with a Coke. A third nickel gets no response, but a fourth nickel produces another Coke. Evidently, inserting a nickel sometimes causes Coke-dispensing behavior, and sometimes it doesn't. Whatever the Second Law of Coke Machine Behavior might be, it won't be in the form of an invariable S-R connection. But the machine's reaction to nickels isn't probabilistic either: experimentation reveals that a Coke is dispensed on every *second* nickel that's inserted. That means that the machine must have some way of representing the fact that it's already received one nickel since it last dispensed a Coke. Whatever we ulti-mately make of this notion of "representing," it's at least clear that it's an internal state of the machine. This is what we have learned so far: to predict the behavior of even so simple a system as a Coke machine, you have to postulate that the system may be in any of several internal states.

One way of summarizing these (and a few other) behavioral facts about the Coke machine is to devise the following table:

(16)	S1	S2
input a nickel	go to S2	give a Coke and go to S1
input a dime	give a Coke and stay in S1	give a Coke and a nickel and go to S1

The items on the left, "input a dime" and "input a nickel" are the two types of environmental stimuli that are relevant to the operation of the machine. But you can't just specify a unique response that will be elicited by each stimulus. The machine's reaction also depends on which of two internal states it's in, S1 or S2. Moreover, the reaction called forth may involve a change of internal state as well a behavioral response.

What are these internal states, S1 and S2? They're functionally defined by the foregoing table. S1 is *whatever* state it is that plays the specified causal role in the system of the Coke machine—i.e., whatever state it is that causes a Coke to be dispensed upon receipt of a dime, and so on. Table (16) is a complete theory of Coke-machine behavior: you don't need to know anything more than it tells you in order to predict the behavior of the Coke machine. It doesn't matter if the machine works electronically, or mechanically, or if there's an elf inside that dispense Cokes according to these rules. The physical details of how S1 and S2 are realized are irrelevant to the work of Coke-machine psychologists. What matters is their functional relationships. According to functionalists, the laws of human behavior are like the laws of the Coke machine, and its internal states are the mental states of belief, desire, and so on. What this comes to in practice will become clear in Chapter 7.

Functionalism has been subjected to several criticisms, the most damaging of which is that it fails to account for the qualitative content, or *qualia,* of mental states. Some mental states have no qualia. For example, there's no clear qualitative content to having a belief. Right at this moment, it might be true that you believe that Lima is the capital of Peru; but there needn't be any experience or "feel" (in the broadest sense of the term) associated with your having this belief. Acts of will also seem to be devoid of qualitative content. These cases stand in contrast to emotional or perceptual states, which are thick with qualia. The distinction has sometimes been described as follows: there is something it is like to be having an emotion or a perception, but there's nothing it is like to be believing or willing.

If functionalism is right, mental states are all defined by the causal role they play in a system. But it's been argued that two mental states can play exactly the same causal role, and yet be qualitatively different. Of course, if they are qualitatively different, they must be counted as different mental states—and then there's more to (some) mental states than a causal role.

There are two ways to argue for the foregoing conclusion. The *inverted spectrum* argument asks us to imagine two observers, X and Y, who are exactly alike, except that the perceptual experience that X calls "red" is what Y calls "green," and vice versa. It may be assumed that their behavioral responses to various environmental stimuli are the same in every respect. For example, they both call the color of the top traffic light by the name of "red." But if X were to see what Y sees when he (Y) looks at the top traffic light, he (X) would call that color "green." Thus X's and Y's perceptions of the top traffic light are two different mental states, even though they're functionally identical. If this scenario is even logically possible, then there can be no functional definition of qualia-laden states.

The same point is made even more simply by the *absent qualia* argument, also known as the *zombie* argument. A zombie is a creature who behaves just like an ordinary human being, except that he has no qualia whatsoever. When his eyes are directed to the top traffic light, he says that the light is red but he doesn't have the accompanying experience of redness, or of anything else. Zombies can behave in ways that satisfy any proposed functional definition of a mental state. Therefore, if functionalism is true, they can *be* in any mental state. But they can't be in any qualitative state. Therefore functionalism is not true.

There are also problems relating to the functionalist theory of thin, qualia-less mental states but these are not usually deemed to be as damaging to functionalism as the problem of qualitative content. A reasonable position for a contemporary cognitive scientist to take is that functionalism provides us with a good account of nonqualitative mental states like beliefs, but not of qualia-laden states like perceptions. This is to admit, however, that qualia are entirely mysterious from the perspective of functionalist psychology. This admission in turn weakens the functionalist claim to have shown that one can account for mental states without giving up materialism—for if functionalism has nothing to say about the nature of qualia, one can't rule out the possibility that an adequate account of them will require some form of dualism after all.

7. Mind Regained: The Cognitive Revolution

7.1. Folk Psychology

Cognitive science came into being in the 1960s and 1970s following the downfall of behaviorism and behavioral psychology. As its name suggests, it's a scientific approach to studying the mind that permits the mentalistic language of inner ("cognitive") states, like beliefs and desires. The research tradition that goes by the name of "cognitive science" differs from the previously discussed traditions—introspective psychology, psychoanalysis, behavioral psychology, and so on—by virtue of its *interdisciplinarity*. It's not only psychologists who are cognitive scientists—the field also includes contributions from philosophers, computer scientists, linguists, and anthropologists. As the following discussion will show, it's not always easy to separate these different strands into the contributions of traditionally compartmentalized university departments. That's part of the *point* of interdisciplinarity. Cognitive science is an attempt to combine all the insights from different fields into a single approach. The ideal cognitive scientist argues like a philosopher, experiments like a psychologist, and programs like a computer scientist. The repertoire of methods is substantially more diverse than the traditional psychologist's. The goal, however, is the same: an understanding of the nature of the mind. Let's get started.

In the previous chapter, we dealt with the philosophical objections to a psychology of mind. We assume now that these objections have been adequately addressed, and that there's no reason to prohibit the scientific investigation of mental states. This general conclusion is an *invitation* to do cognitive science; but it isn't yet cognitive science itself.

It provides us with no clue as to what the fundamental concepts and principles of cognitive science might be. Now there is a specific cognitive theory that the reader is sure to be familiar with. This theory goes by the name of *folk psychology*. The laws of folk psychology are the (mostly implicit) principles that nonpsychologists and psychologists alike use to explain their own and other people's behavior in everyday life. Contemporary cognitive scientists are of the opinion that folk psychology is more uniform and more systematic than folk psychologists themselves believe. Most cognitive scientists also believe that folk psychology is at least approximately correct—that it undoubtedly needs revision and supplementation, but that it's on the right track. The general (but not universally held) opinion is that folk psychology is at least closer to the truth than is behavioral psychology.

So what is folk psychology? What does it tell us about the causes of behavior? Let's examine an entirely pedestrian behavioral episode: you see someone running down the street and you ask why that person is running. What kind of an answer might you get from a folk psychologist? You would most definitely *not* get a behavioral-psychology story about the person's reinforcement or classical conditioning history, which led her to emit a running response to the stimulus of this part of the street. You might, however, get something like this: the runner *wants* to get to the grocery store before it closes, and she *thinks* that she won't get there in time unless she runs the whole way. Or perhaps this: she *believes* that a bomb is about to go off in the vicinity. These explanations may or may not be true in the particular case at hand but they're good examples of the type of account that's deemed to be adequate by us folk psychologists.

In both examples of folk-psychological explanation, the account is framed in terms of what the agent *believes* (that the store is about to close, that a bomb is about to explode) and what she *desires* (to get into the store). No desire is mentioned in the second account, but it's there implicitly. We don't feel its omission because the operative desire is thought to be obvious: it's that the runner doesn't want to get blown up! Belief and desire are the most fundamental concepts of folk psychology, like stimulus and response are in behavioral psychology. In fact, folk psychology is sometimes referred to as *belief-desire psychology*.

Needless to say, a theory that makes use of the concepts of belief and desire qualifies as a cognitive or mentalistic theory. Indeed, folk psychology employs quite a few mentalistic concepts. According to folk psychology, people not only believe and desire things—they also *wish* that things were a certain way, *fear* that they might not be a certain way, *wonder* whether they are a certain way, *hope* that they are a certain way, and so on. Some claim that all the mentalistic concepts relevant to the folk-psychological theory of behavior can be defined in terms of belief and desire. For example, to "wish" that something were so is to *desire* that it be so, but to *believe* that it isn't or won't be so. If this definitional claim holds up, it would mean that folk psychology enjoys a degree of conceptual simplicity that rivals that of S-R theory.

To say that belief and desire are the central concepts of folk psychology is not yet to state any folk-psychological *principles*. What's the relation between belief, desire, and behavior supposed to be? These principles are rarely formulated explicitly by folk psychologists. In this respect, they're like the laws of grammar. We all "use" the laws of grammar in that the sentences we utter conform to the laws but we usually can't state explicitly what the laws are that we're following. In fact, they have to be discovered by linguists. Similarly, our explanations of behavior follow laws that we can't make explicit. These laws have to be discovered by cognitive psychologists.

An important folk-psychological law—arguably the most important—is the *practical syllogism*. This principle, which was discussed in ancient times by Aristotle, relates beliefs and desires to behavior. Here's a drastically simplified formulation:

(1) If a person P wants a state of affairs X to obtain, and if P believes that he can bring it about that X obtains, then P does bring it about that X obtains.

According to this principle, it's the conjunction of a belief and a desire that generates action. If P wants X, but doesn't believe that he can get X, then he won't get X. For example, you might like to visit distant stars, but you might not believe that you can do anything that could gratify this desire. Therefore the desire doesn't get converted to behavior. Similarly, P's belief that he can obtain X isn't by itself sufficient to cause him to obtain it. You might believe that you are capable of throwing your wallet out of a swiftly moving car, but you might not do it because you don't want to.

Principle 1 is merely a first approximation to a plausible folk-psychological law. It's easy to find exceptions to it, an exception being a scenario wherein folk psychologists would not endorse one of the consequences of principle 1. Here is one of them: you may want to get X and believe that you can get X, but your belief may be erroneous—in reality, you *don't* have the power to obtain X. In that case, you *won't* bring it about that X obtains, even though you have the requisite desire and belief. All that can be predicted is that, given the requisite desire and belief, you'll *try* to get X.

The principle needs other refinements as well. For example, you may want X and believe that you can get X; yet you may not even try to get X because there's another state of affairs Y that you want *more* than X and you believe that you can't have both X and Y. This example highlights the need to take into account the fact that beliefs and desires come in degrees. When you quantify these concepts, and polish up the statement of the practical syllogism some more, you get a highly sophisticated cognitive theory of human action called *decision theory*.

It's important to keep two levels of theorizing distinct here. You could claim that the practical syllogism or some other principle is a rule of folk psychology, or that it's a valid law of human behavior (or both). To establish empirically that it's a folk-psychological principle, one would have to ask people to make various sorts of judgments about others' behavior and see if what they say conforms to the principle. A lot of this work has been done by social psychologists under the name of *attribution theory*. Now it might be true that the practical syllogism is a rule of folk psychology, and yet it might also be false as a law of human behavior. That is to say, folk psychology might be *wrong*. But it might also be *right*: it might provide correct behavioral explanations and predictions. "Decision theory" is the name of the theory of behavior that you get when you (1) polish up the practical syllogism, and (2) take it to be true—not just in the sense that people *use* it to explain and make predictions about behavior, but also in the sense that it *does* correctly explain and predict behavior.

So how good a theory is folk psychology? Can it be used to make predictions, and are its predictions correct, or at least more often correct than can be attributed to chance? There's no doubt about the answer: we folk psychologists predict other people's behavior accurately and with confidence all the time. For instance, we wouldn't go driving on highways unless we were confident that the overwhelming majority of other drivers aren't going to intentionally start driving the wrong way. Why do we believe that? Because we believe that the over-whelming majority of other drivers don't want to die, and that they believe that if they drive the wrong way on a highway, there's a good chance that they will die. Or, suppose you want to meet a friend. You call her up and make arrangements to meet at a particular time and place. On the basis of what she tells you, you make the prediction that she'll be there at the designated time and place. What's involved in this prediction, inter alia, is that people generally tell the truth and do what they say they will do, at least when it's not to their disadvantage to do so. On the basis of this bit of folk-psychological lore, you go to the designated place at the designated time, and—lo and behold!—your friend is usually there. At least you succeed in meeting up with your friends more often via the folk-psychological route than if you went to look for them at a random location or a random time. In fact, you'd have a better chance of finding them this way than by studying what movements they've previously been reinforced for performing.

There's a persuasive demonstration of the predictive success of folk psychology that we've conducted in many classes. We tell the students that they're subjects in an experiment. Here are their instructions: they're to take the number five, add three to it, then add one to that sum, and then write the final total in the margin of their notepaper. We then show them a previously prepared slide in which we announce our behavioral prediction that Ss in this experiment will write the number nine in their margins. Finally, we ask the students to indicate what they wrote. Our prediction is overwhelmingly con-firmed every time! Even in classes of over one hundred students, no one has ever reported writing anything in the margin other than the number nine. The statistical significance of these results is astronomi-cal; it's certainly beyond any level obtained by any other means of gen-erating behavioral predictions. How did we arrive at our prediction? Not by our knowledge of arithmetic. Our arithmetical knowledge tells us that $5 + 3 + 1 = 9$; but it doesn't tell us that when people are *asked to add* $5 + 3 + 1$, they will *say* that the sum is 9. That prediction comes once again from our folk-psychological knowledge of what other people *believe* (that $5 + 3 + 1 = 9$), and of the conditions under which they'll tell the truth about what they believe.

Of course, folk psychology isn't a perfect theory. We'll discuss some of its shortcomings later in this chapter. At present, we'll only say a few words about one objection that readers of this book may already be entertaining—the psychoanalytic objection. In Chapter 2, we noted that the basic psychoanalytical insight is that human behavior is sometimes irrational. What does it mean for behavior to be irrational? To quote our earlier selves:

> . . . your behavior is reckoned to be rational if you're doing what *you* believe will get you what *you* want.

Clearly, this is to say that rational behavior is behavior that accords with the practical syllogism. Freud's basic insight—the conclusion that he draws from his ruminations on phobic behavior, compulsions, addictions, and posthypnotic suggestions—is that the practical syllogism is sometimes false! It seems to us that this insight is incontrovertible. Thus it has to be admitted that folk psychology gets some things wrong. But so does every scientific theory that has ever been proposed. The enormous predictive success of folk psychology is reason enough to use it to guide our practical affairs, even though it will occasionally lead us astray. In any case, we possess no better guide.

7.2. Rational Belief

The practical syllogism is an example of a principle that relates mental states to action. Folk psychology also contains principles that relate mental states to other mental states. Here's a trivial example:

> (2) If a person P believes that X is true, and if P also believes that Y is true, then she believes that the conjunctive proposition "X and Y" is true.

Thus if someone answers the questions "Is Tom in New York?" and "Is Mary in Los Angeles?" affirmatively, and if you know that they're not deliberately lying, principle 2 gives you license to predict that they'll give an affirmative answer to the single conjunctive question "Is it the case that Tom is in New York and Mary is in Los Angeles?"

Principle 2 is reminiscent of an elementary rule of deductive logic, namely:

(3) If X is true and Y is true, then the conjunctive proposition "X and Y" is true.

But although principle 3 *mirrors* principle 2, it certainly isn't *identical* to 2. Principle 2 permits us to infer that persons who have certain beliefs will also have another belief, whereas principle 3 tells us that if certain propositions are true, then another proposition is true. In fact, principle 2 isn't a rule of logic at all. It's a contingent claim, the truth of which requires empirical evidence. Of course, if we're rational, then our beliefs will mirror the laws of logic in precisely this way. Principle 2 tells us that people are rational at least to the extent of obeying the logical rule formulated in principle 3. This principle may or may not be true. Please note: the conception of rationality and irrationality that's at issue here isn't the same as the psychoanalytic irrationality that was discussed in section 2.1 and reviewed at the end of the previous section. The latter is a property of *actions*—it stipulates the conditions under which it's crazy to *do* something or not to do it. In the present context, rationality is a property of *beliefs*—it stipulates the conditions under which it's crazy to believe or not to believe in a certain proposition.

If we could assume that people's beliefs are *perfectly* rational, we would have an elaborate cognitive theory of belief already worked out: whatever the logical consequences of someone's beliefs may be, we could predict that the person would believe those too. Principle 2 would be a special case of this more general principle. Another case would be:

(4) If P believes that X is true, and if P also believes that "X implies Y" is true, then she believes that Y is true.

This *psychological* principle mirrors the *logical* principle:

(5) If X is true and "X implies Y" is true, then Y is true.

A system of beliefs that mirrors all the rules of logic is said to have the property of *closure*. Here is a more precise statement of what it is for beliefs to "mirror" logic: if any set of propositions X1, X2, X3 . . . are believed, and if proposition Y follows logically from X1, X2, X3, . . .

then Y is also believed. Perfectly rational belief systems, if they exist, have the property of closure. They also have the property of *consistency:* if a proposition X is believed, then not-X, the negation of X, is *not* believed. If you discover that someone believes that Paris is the capital of France, then, if you assume that that person is perfectly rational, you can predict that he *won't* also believe that Paris is *not* the capital of France.

Unfortunately for the advancement of cognitive science, people *aren't* perfectly rational. Take closure: if we had it, there would be no such thing as mathematical discovery. The theorems of a mathematical system like Euclidean geometry are all logical consequences of the axioms. Thus if our beliefs had the property of closure, anyone who knew the axioms of the system would also know all the theorems, and there would be no employment for mathematicians. In reality, we *don't* know all the logical consequences of our beliefs, because some of these consequences aren't nearly as obvious as those of principles 3 and 5—they require lengthy and difficult proofs. As for consistency: it's so common for human believers to subscribe to *in*consistent propositions that a number of theories have been proposed that try to specify what happens when the believer is confronted with his own inconsistencies (e.g., Festinger 1957).

There are three ways to account for irrational beliefs. The first way is to attribute them simply to *malfunctions* of our cognitive machinery. No mechanism is perfect—there's always the chance of slipping a gear. Even though you may know that $8 \times 7 = 56$, you might get confused in the midst of a bout of mental arithmetic and equate it with 63.

Second, some irrationalities may be due to *inherent limitations of the mind.* Even if there are no malfunctions, it's impossible for there to be a perfectly rational cognitive device. For example, closure is impossible in a real-world device for the simple reason that our belief system has infinitely many logical consequences. It's a consequence of our numerical beliefs that $2 + 2 = 4$, that $758 + 21 = 779$, that $1000 + 3 = 1003$, and so on to infinity. No matter how many of these calculations we carry out, there are always more that haven't yet been done. The result is that our belief system is always going to lack closure. This failure of rationality has nothing to do with malfunctions. Our belief system is going to lack closure even if our minds work with all the lucidity and efficiency of which they're capable. In this case, the irrationality is *built into* the system. Let's call it *structural irrationality.*

The work of Daniel Kahneman and Amos Tversky provides a good example of the cognitive-scientific approach to structural irrationality (Tversky and Kahneman 1974). These authors argue that since we can't be perfectly rational, we have to deploy procedures for acquiring new beliefs that are less than perfect. Rules of this type, called *heuristics,* give us many of the right answers that we need much of the time, but they don't give us all the right answers all of the time. The *representativeness heuristic* is a good example. For most of our conceptual categories, we have an idea of the *typical* representative of that class: a gray-striped tabby is more representative of the class of all cats than a Siamese, a sparrow is more representative of birds than a penguin, and so on. Kahneman's and Tversky's data suggest that we use the representativeness of a subcategory to make judgments about its relative frequency in the broader class. Thus we tend to suppose that there are more sparrows than penguins. This inferential strategy often leads us to correct conclusions. But not all the time. Kahneman and Tversky have been very clever in uncovering circumstances in which our heuristics fail us and give the wrong answer.

The third kind of irrationality is a type that looms large in psychoanalysis. As noted above, a lot of what Freud has to say about irrationality applies to actions rather than beliefs. But Freud has important things to say about irrational beliefs as well. The *defense mechanisms* are ways that we distort the consequences of our beliefs because we don't want to know what they are. This phenomenon has nothing to do with malfunctions or with structural limitations of the cognitive apparatus. In the case of the defense mechanisms, we *have* the cognitive apparatus to acquire a certain piece of information about ourselves, but we don't acquire it because we don't want to know. Let's call this *motivational irrationality.* It's a major point of similarity between psychoanalysis and cognitive science that both approaches have a lot to say about irrationality. In contrast, the topic doesn't even arise in behavioral psychology. But cognitive scientists have dealt almost exclusively with structural irrationality, whereas Freud talked mostly about motivational irrationality. There's scope here for a mutual enrichment of these two perspectives on the mind.

7.3. The Representational Theory of Mind

The majority of contemporary cognitive scientists subscribe to the *representational theory of mind* (affectionately known in the field as RTM). Like many of the ideas in cognitive science, RTM is closely patterned after folk psychology. This is why a lot of it sounds obvious—it's your grandmother's and your uncle's theory of mind. Among professional psychologists, however, these theoretical ideas were presented in a climate of opinion where S-R theory dominated; and in relation to this intellectual backdrop, RTM was considered very radical. Also, we will see that RTM has some surprising consequences that folk psychology never drew.

The basic assumption of RTM is that the mind contains *representations*. These are essentially the entities that English-speaking folk psychologists call "ideas." Representations derive their name from the fact that they represent various objects or processes in the world. For example, your idea of Ronald Reagan is a representation of a person who was president of the United States after Jimmy Carter. You might also have a *general* idea of what it is to be a man. This idea represents not any specific man but the class of *all* men—past, present, and future. Moreover, you can put your ideas together to form more complex ideas. You can put together your ideas of Reagan, of a man, and of class membership, to come up with the idea that Reagan is a man.

Finally, you can operate on these complex representations in a variety of ways. Having constructed a representation of the fact that Reagan is a man, you can put a copy of that idea in a bin that contains all the ideas that you believe to be true. The official name of this bin is *long-term memory*. You can also put another copy of the same representation in a bin that contains the representations of all the states of affairs that you *want* to be true. There's no standard name for this location; let's call it the *desire store*. A current inhabitant of your desire store might be the idea of your lolling on a Hawaiian beach.

According to RTM, the mind is composed of many bins containing representations. The contents of these bins interact in various ways. Whenever you see a cognitive theory of memory or attention or action that's represented by boxes connected by arrows, you're dealing with this kind of bin. The boxes contain representations, and the arrows indicate a flow of information—copies of the representations being sent from one bin to another. The bins are often called *proposi-*

tional attitudes, since each one is differently related to the propositions it contains. If a proposition is in long-term memory, then your attitude toward it is one of belief; if the same proposition is in the desire store, then your attitude toward it is one of desiring that it be true; and so on.

The *laws* of RTM are rules that specify what happens when particular representations are located in particular bins. They might specify that a copy of the representation be sent to another bin, or that a representation be taken out of a bin. Consider the mini-law formulated in principle 2 above: believing X and believing Y causes you to believe the conjunction "X and Y." RTM would formulate this claim as follows: when a representation of X and a representation of Y are both in the belief store, a more complex representation of "X and Y" is constructed and added to the belief store. The practical syllogism would look like this: when (1) a representation of X is in the desire store, and (2) a representation of the idea that you can bring it about that X is in the belief store, then another representation of X is constructed and placed in what may be called the *executive store.* The contents of the executive store are what folk psychologists refer to as our current intentions: to place the idea of having a cup of coffee in the executive store is to decide to get a cup of coffee.

In many ways, this is all like a computer following a program: symbols are shunted from place to place, and combined and separated. Some people have suggested that the inspiration for RTM comes from computers. On this view, computers have acted as a model for human nature, just as the statues in the French royal gardens were a model for animal behavior in Descartes' time. But the roots of RTM go back long before the computer revolution. RTM is a picture of human nature that's implicit in folk psychology. Maybe the similarity between computers and RTM is due to the fact that we constructed computers to function after our own image of ourselves: having set out to build thinking machines, we were guided by our own theories of what it is to think.

7.4. The Language of Thought

What's the relation between thought and speech? When we introspect on the process of thinking, we often catch ourselves engaging in an internal monologue conducted in our native tongue. In cases like these, to construct a representation of the fact that Reagan is a man seems to be a matter of constructing an English sentence like "Reagan is a man." If this is so, then the units of thought—the simple representations out of which more complex ideas are constructed—are arguably coextensive with the *words* of our vocabulary.

But most cognitive scientists believe that RTM applies to nonhuman, as well as to human, organisms. On this view, lions and tigers also have representations. They may not have as many ideas as we do, and they may be capable of only very simple constructions but if a lion can think at all, then it follows that there's a way to represent objects and facts *without language*. If a lion can believe that the gazelle in front of him is good to eat, there has to be a "language of thought" that contains nonverbal symbols representing gazelles and things that are good to eat. Those who are skeptical about lions and tigers having beliefs are invited to contemplate another kind of nonlinguistic organism: human infants before they've learned to speak. The fact that preverbal infants are capable of *learning* the meanings of words and the grammar of their native tongue strongly suggests that they're antecedently capable of thinking. But if you concede that a baby can think, then you also have to concede the existence of nonverbal representations.

Let's look more closely at what's involved in learning one's first language. What happens when you learn the meaning of a new word, such as "sibling"? Well, you might simply be told that a sibling is a brother or a sister. Of course, to profit from this instruction, you must already know the meaning of the words "brother," "sister," and "or." More generally, understanding the verbal definition of a new word requires a prior understanding of the meanings of other words (namely, those employed in the definition). It's clear that this process of providing definitions isn't going to account for how semantic learning begins. The meanings of the first few words, at least, have to be conveyed by nonverbal means such as pointing. Let's suppose that the process succeeds: the infant learns her first word, "mama," through nonverbal means. Let's also suppose that by "mama" she means the person who feeds and takes care of her. Since "Mama" is her first word, how can the infant think that thought? From the perspective of RTM, there's only one plausible answer: the thought that the word "mama" refers to the person who feeds her is constructed out of *nonverbal symbols* for "person," "feeds," and so on.

The system of nonverbal symbols in which at least some of our thinking is conducted is often referred to as the *language of thought*. The language of thought has even been given a proper name: *Mentalese*. According to proponents of Mentalese, the process that we call first-language learning is more appropriately conceived as learning a second, foreign language. When we're in a foreign country and are trying to learn the vocabulary of its language, we do so by trying out various hypotheses framed in our own language. From the way the natives use the word "homme," we guess that it means the same thing as our English word "man," and so on. We learn the vocabulary of our "first" language the same way, i.e., by framing semantic hypotheses and seeing whether they fit the informants' usage. Nobody knows of any other way in which a language can be learned. So when trying to figure out what "daddy" means, the infant may initially hypothesize that "daddy" refers to any person other than mama. What if, as is often the case, "daddy" is the second English word that's learned after "mama"? In that case, how can the infant formulate any hypothesis about "daddy" at all? The theoretical suggestion is that the infant begins her language learning by formulating hypotheses in Mentalese.

Where does Mentalese come from? How is it learned? Jerry Fodor, the foremost proponent of the language-of-thought hypothesis, says that the concepts of Mentalese have to be *innate:* we're born with certain concepts already built into our cognitive machinery (Fodor 1975). We have to be prewired for Mentalese, because otherwise we couldn't get the process of language learning off the ground. If learning a concept involves making hypotheses about its meaning and seeing if these hypotheses work out, then we have to start with at least some innate concepts, or else we couldn't make the first hypothesis.

7.5. Universal Grammar

Cognitive scientists have hypothesized that we're born prewired with innate *beliefs* as well as concepts. The most influential claim of this type is Noam Chomsky's contention that we're born with some built-in knowledge of grammar (Chomsky 1986). According to Chomsky, a child who is learning the grammar of his native language comports himself like a scientist who is trying to discover the true theory of the universe based on the available data. In the case of the language learner, the data are the sentences he hears spoken around him. From these linguistic data, the child hypothesizes what the rules of grammar are that generate these sentences, and constructs his own sentences accordingly. Chomsky argues that the data that are available are invariably inadequate to the task. No being, however intelligent, could parlay the linguistic data into knowledge of grammar by a process of rational inference:

> [T]he basic problem is that our knowledge [of grammar] is richly articulated and shared with others from the same speech community, whereas the data available are much too impoverished to determine it by any general procedure of induction. (Chomsky 1986, 55)

Let's make the discussion more concrete by considering a particular deficiency in the linguistic data. Chomsky notes that children learn many aspects of language without going through a prior process of trial and error—they seem to get it right on the very first trial:

> There is good reason to believe that children learn language from positive evidence only, (corrections not being required or relevant), and they appear to know the facts without relevant experience in a wide array of complex cases. . . . (Chomsky 1986, 55)

One of Chomsky's examples concerns the formation of interrogatives in English (Chomsky 1980). He asks us to imagine a "neutral scientist" observing a child learning English. The scientist observes that the child has learned to form such questions as those of (A), corresponding to the associated declaratives:

> (A) The man is tall—is the man tall? The book is on the table—is the book on the table?

On the basis of these facts, the scientist might very well arrive at the tentative hypothesis that the child is following a simple word-transposition rule:

Hypothesis 1: The child processes the declarative sentence from its first word (i.e., from "left to right"), continuing until he reaches the first occurrence of the word "is" (or others like it: "may," "will," etc.); he then preposes this occurrence of "is," producing the corresponding question. . . . (Chomsky 1980, 319)

Further observation, however, would reveal that this hypothesis is false. Consider the following pair of examples.

(B) The man who is tall is in the room—is the man who is tall in the room?
(C) The man who is tall is in the room—is the man who tall is in the room?

Faced for the first time with the task of forming an interrogative out of "the man who is tall is in the room," what will the child say? Hypothesis 1 predicts C. But this is not what the child will say—not even upon first exposure to declaratives containing subordinate clauses:

Children make many mistakes in language learning, but never mistakes such as exemplified in (C). (Chomsky 1980, 319)

According to Chomsky, the correct hypothesis is far more complex. It's:

Hypothesis 2: The child analyzes the declarative sentence into abstract phrases; he then locates the first occurrence of "is" (etc.) that follows the first noun phrase; he then preposes this occurrence of "is," forming the corresponding question. (Chomsky 1980, 319)

Now, if, as we agree all around, hypothesis 1 was a reasonable hypothesis for a neutral scientist to make on the basis of the data contained in statement A, the same hypothesis should also have been a reasonable one for the *child* to make at that stage in its language learning when its only linguistic information was of the type contained in A. But if a child ever *did* adopt hypothesis 1, he would guess that C is right. Presumably, he would then receive correction, whereupon he would recognize that hypothesis 1 is inadequate and begin to look for alternative rules. But this never happens: children never make mistakes of type C. This means that they never entertain hypothesis 1—not even when the data available to them are all of type A. However, no matter how smart you are, there's no way that you can know on the basis of A-type data alone that hypothesis 2 is better than hypothesis 1. "The only reasonable conclusion," according to Chomsky, is that we possess innate information on the basis of which hypothesis 1 can be ruled out a priori.

So, the logic of the argument runs as follows. Children learn their language on the basis of linguistic data that are demonstrably inadequate for the task. Therefore they must bring innate information to the task.

But doesn't every language have its own grammar? How can grammatical knowledge be innate when a child raised in the United States ends up speaking English, while a child who grows up in Japan comes to speak Japanese? Well, if Chomsky's innateness hypothesis is right, it must be the case that all human languages have at least *some* grammatical rules in common. These are the rules that we innately—and correctly—suppose to be true of the language being learned, whether that language is English or Japanese. The set of all innate grammatical rules comprises *universal grammar,* so called because it's a correct, albeit incomplete, formulation of the grammar of every human language in the world.

It's well known among linguists that there are grammatical universals. This important fact about language is sometimes taken as evidence that all languages are historically related. According to this "common origin" hypothesis, language was invented once at one time and place but it diverged into separate languages as the original linguistic group fragmented into communities that fell out of communication with each other. Their common origin, however, explains the lingering universalities. Chomsky's analysis provides an alternative explanation for universal grammar. According to his innateness hypothesis, all human languages follow the same rules because these rules are wired into us from birth. Even if language were invented independently in several places, our innate linguistic equipment would dictate that each invention followed the rules of universal grammar.

The view that human beings are born with a lot of concepts and knowledge already built in is called *nativism.* Its opposite—the view that all or almost all our cognitive furnishings are learned by experience—is *empiricism* (this is one meaning among many of the term "empiricism"). The nativism-versus-empiricism dispute is one of those long-standing philosophical controversies, like dualism versus materialism or determinism versus voluntarism. Empiricism received its classical formulation in the work of the seventeenth-century British philosopher John Locke (1690/1975). According to Locke, the mind of a newborn child is a *tabula rasa,* a blank slate utterly devoid of content. Cognitive science has produced a major counterargument against the tabula rasa theory. The basic point is simple: if you start life as a blank slate, then you can't learn from experience at all. To benefit from experience, you've got to have a certain amount of cognitive content already in place.

7.6. The Modularity of Mind

Nativism is one of two main themes in cognitive science. The other is the *modularity of mind.* The quickest route to understanding the concept of modularity is via a familiar, nonpsychological example: the component-based stereo system (Ellis and Young 1988, 11). A typical system may consist of a CD player, a turntable, an amplifier, and a couple of speakers. These components are the modules of the system. When it's functioning properly, the behavior of this modular system may be indistinguishable from that of an "all-in-one" system. Nevertheless, the relative independence of its several parts makes a difference. For one thing, it's less costly to repair a malfunction. There's no need to replace the entire system if the CD player breaks—you can just unplug the old CD player and plug in a new one. It's also more economical to upgrade. If a new-and-improved CD player comes on the market, you can once again replace the old one—you don't need and wouldn't benefit from the new amplifier that comes with a completely new system. If you want to add a new-fangled mp3 player, it may be easy to plug it directly into the existing amplifier set-up.

From the point of view of psychology, analogous advantages accrue if the mind is structured in a modular fashion. If brain damage is incurred in one module, it may be possible for other areas of the brain to take over the damaged module's function. Similarly, it may be possible to develop new cognitive skills and "patch" them into the existing modular structure. For example, the skills of reading and writing are relatively new in evolutionary terms, yet they seem to be accomplished by relatively independent modules that are integrated with much older systems that control spatial cognition. The modularity hypothesis of cognitive science is the hypothesis that these and other selective advantages have resulted in our component-based minds.

The language module is a good example. The way children learn to speak is very different from how they learn to read or do arithmetic. Language acquisition is effortless for children, whereas mastery of reading or math is often laborious. Moreover, all neurologically normal children learn to speak, in approximately the same amount of time, regardless of huge differences in IQ; but not everybody learns to read or do math. Also, there's a critical age for learning to speak. Older children and adults are *worse* at picking up languages than very young children; yet they're substantially *better* at learning math. These disparities strongly suggest that the two processes utilize different types of cognitive machinery. The clincher is that there are forms of brain damage that devastate the ability to talk, without having any perceptible effect on mathematical skills, as well as brain injuries that have the opposite effect of impairing mathematical performance while leaving language skills unscathed.

The connection between the modularity thesis and brain damage data is worth a closer look. The most persuasive evidence of modularity that we can hope to obtain is, arguably, the occurrence of *double dissociation*. This phenomenon involves a comparison of two patients with different brain injuries. A double dissociation occurs when patient A exhibits impairment in the performance of task X but performs normally on task Y, while patient B performs normally on task X but is impaired on task Y. This pattern is well explained by the hypothesis that patient A's injury damaged the module responsible for performing tasks like X, while patient B's injury damaged the module for Y-type tasks.

What about single dissociations? What if all we know is that patient A is impaired at X but performs normally at Y? Doesn't that already indicate that performance at X is due to the operation of a module that's not implicated in the activity of performing Y? Well, that is a good explanation of the single dissociation, but it's not the only good explanation. A single dissociation can also be explained by the hypothesis that: (1) both the impaired function X and the intact function Y are normally carried out by the same cognitive machinery; (2) the brain injury has diminished the efficacy of this machinery, so that it can no longer perform the most difficult tasks that it used to be able to perform; and (3) X is one of those difficult tasks while Y is relatively easy. Given only that a single dissociation has occurred, either the modularity hypothesis or its alternative might be true. A double dissociation effectively rules out the alternative hypothesis. According to this hypothesis, the fact that patient A is impaired at X but not at Y is due to the fact that Y is easier than X, and the fact that B is impaired at Y but not at X is due to the fact that X is easier than Y. Thus the alternative hypothesis is unable to explain both limbs of a double dissociation without contradicting itself. This leaves the modularity hypothesis as the only plausible account of what's going on in double dissociations.

A good example of double dissociation data at work comes from psychologists' studies of the processes involved in the recognition of faces. Faces carry a huge amount of information—concerning the identity of the person, that person's emotional state, language use via lip-reading, and so on. Psychologists have hypothesized that the cognitive system for processing faces is subdivided into many independent modules, each of which is responsible for one aspect of the process (Bruce and Young 1986). A number of double dissociations have been uncovered which lend support to this hypothesis. To begin with, the ability to recognize faces seems to be quite distinct from the ability to recognize other objects—the former is not merely a special case of the latter. Patients have been found who, following brain injury, were still able to identify objects such as their own possessions, but were unable to identify the faces of even close family members. Other patients, despite being unable to identify everyday objects, could nevertheless recognize familiar faces (De Renzi 1986). This double dissociation suggests that visual information about faces is processed by a module distinct from that which processes visual information about other objects.

Even within the face-processing system, there seem to be a number of more specific modules. Malone and colleagues (1982) describe two different patients who show this. One could recognize the faces of familiar people, but was unable to match pictures of faces that were unfamiliar. The other displayed the opposite pattern of impairment—he could not recognize familiar faces, but performed normally on a matching task for previously unencountered faces. These data provide evidence for the hypothesis that the face-processing system is further divided into two relatively independent "streams" for processing familiar or unfamiliar faces.

There is similar evidence that the ability to analyze a face's emotional expression is also handled by a separate module. Kurucz and Feldmar (1979) describe a patient who was unable to interpret facial expression, despite being able to identify the face. In a different study (Kurucz, Feldmar, and Werner 1979), the same authors discovered a patient who could not identify a face, but was able to recognize the emotional expression on it. Again, this suggests that different modules handle facial recognition and interpretation of facial expression.

Finally, "facial speech analysis" (especially the ability to lip-read) appears to be carried out independently from other forms of facial processing. Campbell, Landis, and Regard (1986) came across two patients who, taken together, demonstrate this. The first could neither recognize faces *nor* read emotional expressions, but performed normally on a task that required the ability to lip-read. The second had intact recognition and emotional-analysis skills, but could no longer judge what was being said on the basis of lip-reading.

With these kinds of dissociations in mind, the most influential models of the cognitive operations involved in face processing have posited separate modules for each of the dissociable functions. The famous Bruce and Young (1986) model features different modules for the analysis of expression, lip-reading, recognition, and so on. This fragmentation of what were thought to be unitary mental processes is a pervasive feature of contemporary cognitive-scientific research. In this respect, cognitive science and folk psychology part company—or so it seems to us. It's our impression that folk psychologists regard a person's performance at any and all cognitive tasks as due to the operation of a unitary mind that does all its work in accordance with a single set of rules. Thus folk psychologists are inclined to believe that we go through the same types of mental processes when we recognize the face of a friend as when we recognize our hat. Moreover, the process of object/face recognition is thought to be a special case of a more general cognitive strategy for drawing conclusions from sensory evidence—a strategy that's employed in picking out grammatical sentences as well as in picking out our hat. The data on language learning and face recognition (inter alia) do not support this view.

In closing, it's worth noting that Freud anticipated the modularity theory. Id, ego, and superego are clearly intended to be modular components of the mind: they have different contents, and the contents are manipulated by different rules (recall the differences between the primary-process thinking of the id and the secondary-process thinking of the ego). By our reckoning, that makes four central cognitive-scientific themes that were foreshadowed in psychoanalysis: (1) the modularity of mind, (2) the pervasiveness of human irrationality, (3) unconscious mental processes, and (4) functionalism.

7.7. Artificial Intelligence

There are several quite different enterprises that go by the name of "artificial intelligence," or AI. Some of them are intimately connected with the goals and methods of cognitive science. All of them involve attempts to write programs that enable computers to perform cognitive tasks, such as alphabetizing lists (which turns out to be easy to program) or writing summaries of longer texts (which turns out to be very difficult). To write a program for a task is to give a series of absolutely explicit instructions—an *algorithm*—for how to do the task. As an example of a set of instructions that illustrate what it is *not* to be an algorithm, here are the directions given in a children's magazine for how to put on an opera: (1) write the opera, (2) get your friends to play all the parts, and (3) charge admission.

Naturally, any form of instruction must presuppose that the instructee is able to perform certain tasks without being told how. These are the *primitive operations* of the system. It's widely believed that any set of instructions that can be followed by a computer of any design can be analyzed into the following primitive operations: (1) recognizing the difference between two symbols (e.g., 0 and 1); (2) following the instruction either to leave the symbol as it is or to change it to the other symbol; and (3) following the instruction to move on to the next symbol to the right or to the left in a series, or to halt. A device that's capable of performing these primitive operations and nothing more is called a *Turing machine,* after the computer science pioneer Alan Turing.

Here's a simple Turing machine program: if the current symbol is 0, leave it alone and move to the symbol on the left; if the current symbol is 1, change it to 0 and move to the symbol on the right. Suppose that the machine starts by reading the underlined symbol of the following series:

... 111<u>0</u> ...

Since the current symbol is 0, the program instructs the machine to leave it alone and move to the left:

... 11<u>1</u>0 ...

Since the current symbol is now 1, the program instructs the machine to change it to 0 and move to the right:

... 110<u>0</u> ...

The next few steps are as follows:

... 11<u>0</u>0 ...

... 1<u>1</u>00 ...

... 10<u>0</u>0 ...

... 1<u>0</u>00 ...

... <u>1</u>000 ...

... 0<u>0</u>00 ...

This particular Turing machine is programmed to be an eraser of 1s.

As noted above, it's widely accepted that a Turing machine can do anything that any computer can do (although it may take much longer to do it than a contemporary PC). Nobody has ever been able to construct a formal proof of this thesis. However, it's believed to be true by the overwhelming majority of discussants of AI. Granting that the thesis is true, it's easy to understand why Turing machines loom large in the theoretical literature of AI: if you want to show that computers can't be programmed to perform a certain kind of task, you need only show that Turing machines can't do that task.

There are various reasons why one might want to write programs that enable computers to perform cognitive tasks. One reason is simply to get the job done so that people don't have to do it. This is *applied AI*. The goal here is a practical one. It's to help people avoid tedium (as when a program is used to alphabetize long lists of names), or to perform essential tasks that human minds are not very good at (such as working out airplane traffic patterns at busy airports). This enterprise has no bearing on the problems of psychology. There are, however, at least two types of AI that are intimately connected to the work of cognitive science. John Searle (1980) has dubbed them *weak* and *strong* AI. We'll devote a separate section to each.

7.8. Weak AI

When we're doing applied AI, all we care about is that the program that we're writing does the cognitive job at hand. If the job is to alphabetize lists of names, "Berger" should come before "Berkowitz," and so on. When we're doing weak AI, however, we want the steps of the program to recapitulate the cognitive steps that a human agent goes through when she's engaged in the task. Weak-AI programmers regard such a program as a *theory* of how human agents perform the task. The difference between the goals of applied AI and weak AI is highlighted by their treatment of cognitive errors. Suppose that we human beings have a tendency to make a characteristic mistake when we try to solve a particular cognitive problem. If we're doing applied AI, our concern is only with getting the correct solution to the problem; thus we'll try to write a program that *avoids* committing the error that we humans are prone to. But if we're doing weak AI, our concern is to lay out the problem-solving procedure that's actually used by humans. In this case, the program fails to achieve the aim of the programmer unless it makes the computer commit the same errors as we do.

A caveat: it can never be claimed of any program that every program line corresponds to a cognitive step taken by human minds. For example, most computers are constructed in such a way that when the task is to do an arithmetic problem like finding the sum of $7 + 3$, the program calls for converting these decimal numbers into binary numbers, adding the two binary numbers, and then reconverting the binary sum to its decimal equivalent. Nobody wants to claim that people perform these binary-decimal conversions when they add. The point is that weak-AI researchers have to specify what aspects of the program are to be treated as theoretically significant.

So, weak AI is a style of psychological theorizing. What are the advantages, if any, of theorizing by writing programs? A common answer is that it enables us to formulate and derive consequences from theories that are too complex to be wielded by the natural human mind. We can write programs that specify how hundreds, or even thousands, of factors interact to influence performance. Even if we could formulate such a theory using only paper and pencil (which is doubtful), the task of calculating a prediction from the theory would surely be beyond our cognitive capacities. If the theory is written in the form of a program, however, deriving predictions is the easiest thing in the world: just run the program on a computer and see what it does. The output of the computer is the theory's prediction of what the human output will be. The bottom line is that weak AI extends the range of psychological theories that are in play.

This putative advantage has been challenged. As is always the case in writing programs, computer simulations of human cognition go through numerous rounds of trial-and-error revisions to get the bugs out of the system. When the program is finally in the form that the programmers want it to have, it's rarely the case that the programmers have a clear vision of how it is that this particular program yields the desired results. In fact, considering both the extreme length and the cobbled-together genesis of all but the most trivial programs, it's fair to say that no human mind *could* comprehend the deductive relation between the program and its consequences. The AI researcher knows only that the program does the job. This knowledge is enough for the practical purpose of finding out what happens next. But if you don't understand why *this* program yields *this* performance, it isn't clear that you can claim to have a theoretical understanding of why this performance took place. At the very least, getting an accurate simulation of a phenomenon doesn't satisfy the conventional goal of scientific work.

A more secure benefit of weak AI is that casting one's theory in the form of a program provides us with a convenient and foolproof method of checking whether the proposed theory really does explain the performance for which it was designed. You need only run the program and see whether the expected performance takes place. If it does, then you can be sure that your theoretical explanation is complete. (An explanation of a phenomenon is complete if it says enough for us to be able to deduce the phenomenon. Of course, the completeness of a theoretical explanation doesn't ensure its truth.) The rigors of

AI have already borne fruit in revealing hidden gaps in theories whose completeness seemed intuitively self-evident. When the theory was put in program form, the machine did not run. The most notable example is undoubtedly the *frame problem,* which, according to Dennett, is a "new, deep epistemological problem—accessible in principle but unnoticed by generations of philosophers—brought to light by the novel methods of AI, and still far from being solved" (1998, 183).

The frame problem arose in the course of trying to devise a program for updating one's stock of beliefs (misleadingly called a "knowledge base") upon receipt of new information. Suppose, for example, that we receive and accept the information that an Antarctic penguin has been found who speaks fluent English. As a result, there are many propositions that we might previously have endorsed, but that we must now repudiate. These might include the propositions that only human beings can master a natural language, that no beings native to the Antarctic speak English, that only featherless bipeds possess the ability to give a passable after-dinner speech, and so on. On the other hand, a great many of our beliefs will remain totally unaffected by the new discovery. These include the belief that penguins are native to the Antarctic, that Paris is the capital of France, and that $2 + 2$ is not equal to 5. What is the procedure followed in making such a revision?

Prior to AI, it had been tacitly assumed that something like the following account is more or less adequate: the new item of information P is checked for consistency against our old beliefs Q1, Q2, . . . Qn. When a Qi is found that is inconsistent with P, it is changed to its negation not-Qi. When AI researchers actually tried to implement this idea, they ran into an immediate problem: any knowledge base comparable to a human being's is so large that the requisite exhaustive check is simply impractical. According to the account we are considering, the discovery that a penguin speaks English is followed by a process of ascertaining that the new information is *not* inconsistent with our arithmetical beliefs, or with our beliefs about the genealogy of the royal houses of Europe, or with the recipes of all the foods that we know how to prepare, and so on.

Evidently, we can't assume that the consistency check of the knowledge base proceeds randomly, or in alphabetical order, or in any other order wherein the items that need to be negated are distributed randomly. We need to develop an algorithm whereby the great mass of knowledge that is clearly irrelevant to the new item is bypassed altogether. But how do you specify a priori what class of beliefs may potentially be affected by the news that a penguin speaks English? Consider the suggestion that we should look at the items in our knowledge base that make reference to penguins, or to English, or to any other nonlogical term that appears in the new item. On the one hand, this recommendation will cause us to overlook indefinitely many necessary changes—for the fact that a penguin speaks English has indefinitely many consequences in which neither "penguin" nor "English" appears. For example, it's incompatible with the proposition that no bird speaks a Germanic language. On the other hand, even the apparently narrow scope of a search through items relating to penguins still leaves us with too many irrelevancies to wade through—for we would have to ascertain that the new item has no effect on our beliefs that penguins are not mammals, that penguins have no credit cards, that no penguin has ever been elected to the U.S. Senate, and so on.

Moreover, suppose that we *could* tell whether a given item in the knowledge base is sufficiently relevant to the new information that it deserves to be checked for consistency. How, exactly, is this capability going to be deployed? To be sure, we now have access to the information that the existence of English-speaking penguins is irrelevant to our belief that Paris is the capital of France but it isn't at all clear how this access helps. On the face of it, it seems that we still have to consider each and every item in the knowledge base in turn. The only difference is that previously we assessed each item in turn for consistency with the new item. Now we assess each item for *relevance* to the new item. Only the items that are found to be relevant are sent along for an evaluation of their consistency with the new item. But because this stage has to be preceded by an exhaustive differentiation of the relevant items from the irrelevant items, there is no theoretical gain.

So we need even more than an algorithm for relevance. We need to come up with a procedure wherein the irrelevant items don't have to be attended to at all—or at least where the number of irrelevant items that have to be attended to is greatly thinned out. But how can you *avoid* the irrelevancies without first having to identify them *as* irrelevancies? Nobody has any idea. It had been thought that the general idea of a search through a memory store would do the explanatory job—that it was just a matter of ironing out the details. But when AI researchers started to work on the details, they found that they didn't know how to proceed. The failure of weak AI in this regard is undoubtedly its most important accomplishment, for it has alerted psychologists to the existence of a major theoretical problem that everyone had previously overlooked.

7.9. Strong AI

The weak-AI style of theorizing is currently flourishing not only in psychology, but in all the sciences. Just as AI researchers try to write programs that simulate cognitive performances, so do meteorologists try to program simulations of weather systems. To the extent that the simulation is accurate, the computer output tells us what the weather in the real world will be like. The advantages of computer simulation over traditional, "manual" prediction are the same in meteorology as in weak AI: (1) it brings complex, multifactor theories into the scope of the manageable, and (2) it reveals implicit, taken-for-granted theoretical assumptions. Weak AI is psychology's adaptation of the new computer technology to scientific ends. As such, it's part of a broad movement that has profoundly affected all the sciences. But there's nothing in the other sciences that corresponds to *strong* AI.

Strong AI isn't merely a style. It's a *hypothesis* that's either true or false. It makes no sense to ask whether *weak* AI is true or false—that would be akin to asking whether psychology is true or false—but *strong* AI is something that one either believes or disbelieves. It's the thesis that a properly programmed computer doesn't just simulate a mind—it *is* a mind. Stated bluntly, it's the thesis that computers can literally think. If strong AI is correct, computer simulations of human cognition are very different from the meteorologists' simulations of weather systems. When the latter program a computer to simulate a hurricane, no one supposes that there really is a hurricane somewhere in the computer. But (if strong AI is correct), a computer simulation of mental processes can itself be a mental process.

The case for strong AI depends essentially on functionalism. According to functionalists, mental states are defined in terms of input-output relations. It follows that a system that perfectly simulates the input-output relations of a human mind will itself be a mind. To get from functionalism to strong AI, you need only [!] show that a perfect simulation of human cognition is possible. This was already clear to Alan Turing as far back as 1950. In a seminal article published at that time,

Turing proposed what has come to be called the *Turing Test* (Turing 1950). Here's how the test works. You, the tester, can freely exchange messages with both a human being and a computer, but you don't know which is which. Your task is to ask questions that will reveal to you which communicant is the computer. Thus if you think that humor can't be programmed, you might send the communicants a joke, ask them to explain what's funny about it, and identify the one who gets it as the human being. Of course, strong AI is committed to the view that humor *can* be programmed. In fact, if strong AI is correct, any and all human cognitive capacities can be programmed. That's what it is for a computer to pass the Turing Test—for it to be impossible for the tester to tell the difference between the computer and the human.

To reiterate: if strong AI is to be true, it has to be possible to program *all* aspects of human cognition. There's a lot about human cognition that AI researchers haven't yet been able to program. The frame problem is a good example. In fact, no computer can currently come even close to passing the Turing Test. But of course, failure to date doesn't establish impossibility. The strategy of strong AI researchers is to divide and conquer: find a program than can simulate one aspect of cognition, then find another program that simulates another aspect of cognition, and so on. The reasoning is that if you keep finding ways to simulate more and more aspects of cognition, this constitutes evidence that a computer will eventually be able to pass the Turing test. To be sure, this inductive inference isn't a sure thing, but it's a reasonable guess.

Some critics of strong AI have presented general arguments to the effect that no computer will ever be able to pass the Turing Test (e.g., Dreyfus 1992). We don't think that any of these arguments is compelling. The most effective critique of strong AI begins by granting, for the sake of the argument, that the Turing Test can be passed, and proceeds to show that the computer that's passed the test still doesn't have mental states. This is John Searle's (1980) famous *Chinese room argument*. Searle asks us to imagine that a person who doesn't speak Chinese is sitting inside a room. This person is given a box of Chinese characters, together with a rulebook. The room also has a mail slot so that the person can send and receive Chinese symbols to and from the outside. The rulebook tells him what symbols to output when he receives certain symbols as input. The person in the room just looks at the shape of the symbols he receives and looks this shape up in the book, and then determines what symbol to produce as output.

To complete the thought experiment, Searle also asks us to imagine that there are native Chinese speakers standing outside the room. These people ask the person in the room questions by entering Chinese characters through the slot. The person in the room takes these symbols, looks them up in the book, and then determines what symbols to produce in response to each question. Thus a Chinese speaker may send the Chinese characters for "how much is seven plus three?" into the room, whereupon the inhabitant of the room looks up those characters in the rule book; the rule book tells him to respond with certain other Chinese characters, which the Chinese speakers outside the room understand to mean that seven plus three is equal to ten. But the person inside the room has no understanding of either the question or the answer—he's just following the book of rules.

Finally Searle asks us to suppose that the rulebook is so sophisticated that for any question the person in the room receives, he is able to produce reasonable answers in Chinese. In fact, the answers are so good that the native Chinese speakers would not be able to distinguish between the responses they get from the person in the room and those that they would get from a native Chinese speaker. The question is: does the person in the room understand Chinese? Most of us would say that he doesn't. The person is just manipulating symbols without understanding what they mean. *But he is doing everything that a computer that passes the Turing test can possibly do!* That is, native Chinese speakers could not distinguish the responses that the person inside the room gives from those that a native speaker would give. Nonetheless, the person in the room does not understand Chinese.

Let us now state the problem more generally. The point of the thought experiment is that computers are *always* in the position of the person in the Chinese room. They are always carrying out formal manipulations of symbols using rulebooks (a.k.a. programs). As the thought experiment makes clear, however, carrying out such manipulations is *insufficient* for understanding. So computers never understand anything. And, if they don't understand anything, they don't have minds. Having a mind involves grasping the *meaning* of symbols. This grasping of the meaning of symbols doesn't happen merely by manipulating them in accordance with formal rules. So the mind can't just be a computer program. Hence strong AI seems to be a false theory about the nature of mental states.

Here's another way to describe the conclusion of the Chinese room argument. The argument for strong AI requires the premises (1) that a computer can pass the Turing Test, and (2) that functionalism is true. Premise 1 asserts that a computer can exhibit all the same input-output relations as a human being; premise 2 asserts that two systems with identical input-output relations are in identical mental states. The Chinese room argument grants premise 1 for the sake of the argument, and purports to show that the second premise—functionalism—is false. Searle's argument is very similar to the qualia arguments against functionalism that we discussed in section 6.5. One of the arguments in that section was that a zombie devoid of qualia could still be functionally identical to a normal human being. Searle's argument is that a system that lacks any understanding of Chinese can still be functionally identical to a native Chinese speaker.

It should come as no surprise that Searle's Chinese room thought experiment has generated a great controversy in the cognitive scientific literature. Examining the huge variety of responses would require a book-length treatment in itself—indeed, there are several (see, for example, Preston and Bishop 2002). The most popular line of response among Searle's critics is the so-called *systems reply.* Proponents of the systems reply note that what does the translating in Searle's argument isn't just the person in the room. The rulebook and the box of characters are just as essential as the person: without any one of these components, there would be no translation. In other words, what does the translating—the equivalent of the computer—is a *system,* of which the person in the room is only a part. Let's grant that the person in the room doesn't understand Chinese. This is not yet to say that the system as a whole doesn't understand Chinese. To suppose that it does is to commit the *fallacy of composition,* which is to attribute properties (in this case, inabilities) to a whole simply because those properties (or inabilities) are present in the parts. In sum, Searle is accused of advancing the following argument:

(6) The man in the room does not understand Chinese

therefore:

(7) The system of which the man is a part does not understand Chinese

This is obviously a non sequitur. If it weren't, you could also conclude that you don't understand English because your kidney doesn't understand English.

Searle says that he's "somewhat embarrassed" to take the systems reply seriously, because, he thinks, it's so wildly implausible. According to Searle, the systems reply amounts to agreeing that the man in the room can't understand Chinese, but saying that somehow the mere addition of the rule book, the boxes of symbols, the pen and paper, the input and output slots, and the bricks and mortar of the room can give rise genuine understanding. He makes the obvious point here that it's difficult to see how the addition of all this extra paraphernalia could give rise to understanding where previously there was none. The only response that's available to advocates of the systems reply is to bite the bullet and aver that this could happen.

Searle also has a crisper and more effective counterargument. Suppose that the man in the room *memorizes* the symbols and the rulebook. Suppose also, that by some impressive (but not impossible) feat of mental agility, he is able to carry out all of the calculations in his head, without recourse to paper and pencil. The man need not, therefore, be constrained to stay in the room, but would be free to walk around with the whole system, as it were, inside his head. In this case, the Chinese-speaking system would consist of nothing more than the man himself. But despite his continued ability to conduct passable "conversations," we would surely want to say that he *still* doesn't understand Chinese. After all, he's still responding to Chinese questions by looking up the answers and parroting what he finds. The only difference is that, the contents of the rulebook having been memorized, he can find the answers in his own memory store. The point is that the systems reply simply doesn't apply to this case. As Searle says: "If [the man in the room] doesn't understand, then there is no way the system could understand because the system is just a part of him" (Searle 1980, 419-20).

The dispute over the Chinese room is by no means settled. It wouldn't be too much of a stretch to regard Searle's argument as dividing cognitive scientists into two broad categories: those who see it as a powerful demonstration of the failure of strong AI and its functionalist underpinnings, and those who regard it as a minor and surmountable confusion. Indeed, the two authors of this volume stand on opposite sides of this divide.

8. Mind Extended: Connectionist, Dynamical, and Situated Cognitive Science

8.1. Connectionism

The theoretical style discussed in Chapter 7 is characteristic of what is now, in the early portion of the twenty-first century, regarded as the classical period of cognitive science. There are still plenty of classicists left—it's arguable that RTM, the representational theory of mind, continues to be the theory of choice for the majority of cognitive scientists. However, large segments of the cognitive science community have moved on to the exploration of substantially different theoretical approaches. One important motive for these defections from RTM is what may be termed the latter's lack of *neurophysiological realism*. For many materialistically inclined psychologists, "mind" and "brain" are more or less the same thing (see Chapter 6 on central state identity theory). However, the computer-like architectures posited by the classical theories bear only a very distant resemblance to the actual structure of the human brain. There is no physiological evidence that physical symbols are literally created, manipulated, and stored in the brain; there seems to be no neural equivalent to the central processor, or to the boxes in which symbolic representations are stored; and although the brain is often characterized in terms of areas of functional specialization, physically speaking, it's mostly made out of one kind of material—neurons (one hundred billion of them by current estimates). The twenty-first-century materialist argues that we ought to be more sensitive to biological reality and consider models that are more like the brain than the symbol-crunching computing machines envisaged by classical cognitive science.

What do cognitive systems look like when they're high in neurophysiological realism? For one thing, they perform many of their operations in *parallel*—that is to say, they do many things at the same time. In contrast, classical systems, like the computer programs that inspire them, work in a *serial* fashion—they perform only one operation at a time. To be sure, a mainframe computer performs a lot of operations per second, but it still does them one at a time. Computers manage to perform complex tasks despite their serial architecture by relying on their blazing speed. Neurons, however, are very slow. In fact, they're so slow that they couldn't account for human cognition if they performed in the serial mode. If cognitive processes are supposed to be neural processes, then cognitive theories that posit serial processing are nonstarters. Parallel processing is the only option. This bit of reasoning is elaborated and refined in what is known as the *hundred-step argument* (Cunningham 2000; Franklin 1998). Here's Cunningham's formulation:

1. It usually takes neurons just a couple of milliseconds (thousandths of a second) to fire.

2. But people can carry out some complex cognitive processes (like recognition) in about 100 milliseconds (about one tenth of a second).

3. If the brain were functioning serially, it would only have time to carry out at most 100 steps to complete a complex cognitive process.

4. But even relatively simple cognitive processes in a serial computer require *thousands* of steps.

5. Parallel systems, in contrast, can be carrying out many steps simultaneously and would therefore be able to complete thousands of steps in 100 milliseconds.

6. Therefore, in order for the brain to carry out the complex cognitive processes that it does in such a short time, it seems that it must operate as a parallel system. (Cunningham, 2000, 211)

Taken by itself, the conclusion of the hundred-step argument can be accommodated by the classical approach to cognitive science. All that's required of the classicist is that she construct models of

multiple classical computers all operating in parallel. But this theoretical strategy would violate the requirement of neurophysiological
realism in another way: the units that run in parallel in the brain are
the neurons, and taken individually, neurons are quite simple and
stupid. They either fire, or they don't. The requirement of brain-like-
ness suggests that the parallel processors postulated by our cognitive
theories should also be simple and stupid. This is the essential idea
behind the most important postclassicist development in cognitive
science—the approach known as *connectionism*. Connectionists try to
explain complex cognitive activity in terms of the activity of multiple simple processors running in parallel. The idea is that, although
the individual processors are stupid, they can give rise to many interesting features when they're wired up into large and complicated
networks. Like pop stars and politicians, "The brain exemplifies the
fact that it is all right to be very stupid if you're well connected"
(Lloyd 1989, 92).

Although some of connectionism's central ideas had been
around for a while, the approach was transformed into a full-
fledged postclassical movement upon the 1986 publication of a
two-volume collection of research papers edited by David
Rumelhart and James McClelland. The articles in this collection
attempted to show how "neural networks" of very simple but
highly interconnected neuron-like processors could carry out a
vast array of cognitive activities. The reference to neural networks
illustrates the importance of neurophysiological realism to the new
paradigm. It should not, however, be thought that connectionism
is of interest solely for physiological reasons. As McClelland,
Rumelhart, and Hinton note:

> Though the appeal of PDP models is definitely enhanced by
> their physiological plausibility and neural inspiration, these
> are not the primary bases for their appeal to us. We are, after
> all, cognitive scientists, and PDP models appeal to us for psy-
> chological and computational reasons. They hold out the
> hope of offering computationally sufficient and psychologi-
> cally accurate mechanistic accounts of the phenomena of
> human cognition which have eluded successful explication in
> conventional computational formalisms. . . . (McClelland,
> Rumelhart, and Hinton 1986, 11)

(PDP—parallel distributed processing—is frequently used as a synonym for "connectionism." The P's of PDP are clear enough; the D will be explained shortly.) In the end, neurophysiological realism is just a heuristic that motivates us to explore certain volumes of theoretical space. Whether the theories discovered therein are worthy of adoption depends on the same factors that are used in evaluating any theoretical choices: do the theories have explanatory and predictive power? Let's look at a simple connectionist theory and see.

We need to begin by spelling out the typical architecture of connectionist systems in a little more detail. A connectionist model is usually built up out of a collection of units (rather like neurons in the brain) that are linked to one another by connections. In just the same way that neurons can fire at different rates, each unit in a connectionist model has a variable activity level. A unit's activity level corresponds to how "excited" the unit is at any given time. Strictly, a unit's activity level is a continuous variable between zero and one. In practice, however, most connectionist models are built so that the unit counts as "on" if its activity level is above a specified threshold, and as "off" if its activity level is below that threshold.

The connections between units can be either *excitatory or inhibitory*. When a connection between two units is excitatory, an increase in activity level in one unit will tend to increase the activity level in the other. By contrast, if the connection is inhibitory, activity in one unit will tend to *prevent* the second from becoming active. In addition, the connections between units can have different strengths or weights so that the degree to which one unit excites or inhibits another varies as a function of both the strength of the connection between them and their respective levels of activation. For example, suppose unit A is connected to unit B with an excitatory connection of weight +0.5. If unit A's excitation level is 0.7, then it will cause unit B to have an activation of $(0.7 \times +0.5) = 0.35$.

Connectionist systems are usually structured into layers. The input layer is built out of a collection of units that receive input from outside the system, and that may become active as a result. Similarly, the output layer is built out of a collection of units that generate behavior depending on their level of activity. In most connectionist models, there are also one or more hidden layers of units in between the input and output layers. The different layers are connected in such a way that activation can flow from input to output. Here is a typical sequence of events: (1) some input excites some of the units of the input layer; (2) the excitation travels from the input units through the connections to units in the hidden layer(s), which also become active; (3) the active hidden layer units convey their excitation via connections to units in the output layer; (4) the excited output units cause the system to produce a certain output behavior.

McClelland and colleagues (1986) give a nice example of a simple network constructed according to these principles. This network is able to recognize four-letter words based on the perceptual features of the letters that make up the words. The network consists of an input layer, an output layer, and one hidden layer. The units in the input layer increase their activity level in response to different features of individual letters (these features constitute the input). One unit responds to diagonal lines (like those in K and R and N), another unit responds to vertical lines (like those in L and E and P), and so on. The input layer units are connected to hidden units that correspond to letters of the alphabet. The connections are arranged so that, for example, the input unit that responds to diagonal lines has excitatory connections to the hidden units for letters like K and R and N, but inhibitory connections to the hidden units for letters like O and P and L. Finally, the hidden units are connected to output units that represent a small set of four-letter words. These connections are arranged so that, among other things, the hidden layer unit for E has an excitatory connection to the output unit for HIDE or MOVE, but an inhibitory connection to the output unit for WORK or PAIN. When the input units are presented with a collection of letters, say W, O, R, and K, they become active if the feature they detect is present. They consequently excite or inhibit the relevant hidden units (corresponding to the letters being "recognized") and, in turn, the hidden units excite or inhibit the output layer so that the most active output unit is the one representing the four-letter word WORK. This shows how simple units can be arranged to function as a network that can recognize four-letter words. It's also an example we will return to below, in our discussion of what happens if the input is faulty in some way.

McClelland and colleagues' word recognizer is admittedly a trivial cognitive mechanism. We discuss it at length because its simplicity makes it suitable for illustrating the main features of connectionist models. Note, however, that the last couple of decades have seen the publication of literally hundreds of connectionist models dealing with a wide variety of cognitive tasks. Another of McClelland and colleagues' networks was able to learn to form the past tenses of English verbs (Rumelhart and McClelland 1986). Plunkett, Sinha, Moller, and Strandsby (1992) built a network that replicated the rapid growth in vocabulary that children display at around the age of two. Gorman and Sejnowski (1988) constructed a network that could learn to distinguish between mines and rocks based on the characteristics of their respective sonar echoes. Hoffman and McGlashan (2001) even built a network that would produce "hallucinations" (understood as activity in the hidden layers despite the absence of any input), and used the model to develop a connectionist account of some of the positive symptoms of schizophrenia.

Each of these examples demonstrates the fact that, like classical cognitive science, connectionism subscribes to the notion that the mind works by creating, storing, and manipulating *representations*. The two approaches differ, however, on the precise nature of these representations. When we discussed RTM in section 7.3, we supposed that the mind contained many different boxes (for belief, desire, and so on) into which one could place representations. This kind of representation is sometimes known as "local" because one can imagine each representation being written on a postcard and stored in an exact unique location corresponding to the correct box. Such information storage systems are very familiar in everyday life—dictionaries, telephone directories, and filing cabinets all store pieces of information in a precise location given by a kind of address. In connectionist systems, however, representations are *distributed* (that's the D of PDP). This means that a given representation is, as it were, "spread out" over a number of the processing units. The idea of your lolling on a Hawaiian beach, in this case, is not found in a particular location in the system. Rather, it corresponds to a distinctive pattern of activation found in a *collection* of units.

To make this a bit more precise, consider a collection of ten units, each of which, for simplicity's sake, can either be a 1 or a 0—on or off. Suppose we want to use those units to represent your desire to loll on a Hawaiian beach. That desire might be 1001110110—the representation is encoded across multiple units in the network, rather than in any individual unit. Now suppose we wanted to represent your desire to loll on a *Caribbean* beach. Under the classical RTM picture, we would have to create an entirely new representation (by copying the [Lolling on a beach] part, and swapping [in Hawaii] for [in the Caribbean]). We could then store this new representation in the same box as the one concerning Hawaii. By contrast, in connectionist models the desire to loll on a Caribbean beach can be represented on the *same* set of units as the Hawaiian desire, with only a small change, say to 1001110101. Notice that there is only a very slight difference in the case of the second representation, and that this corresponds to the slightly different object of desire—the Caribbean as opposed to Hawaii. For the most part, the two representations are quite similar:

1001110110: Desire to loll on a Hawaiian beach

1001110101: Desire to loll on a Caribbean beach

We might further imagine that these representations constitute the *input* to some process for which the generation of behavior is the output. Because of the close similarity between the input representations, they will tend to give rise to similar kinds of output behavior—daydreaming of the sea and sand, making a call to the travel agent, and so on. The important point to note is that in connectionist models, it's the pattern of activity across *all* the input units that constitutes a representation.

The distributed nature of representations allows for some of the greatest strengths of connectionist models. Because the representations are distributed over many units, a network will not suffer if one or two units are damaged. This is particularly important when applied to the brain. Neurons themselves are pretty unreliable—they're prone to spontaneous random noise, they die off all the time, and their response is probabilistic rather than fixed. If this state of affairs were to be found in a traditional computer, the result would be disastrous. When a "local" representation is lost, the system simply cannot access the information that the representation encoded. Random data loss and unpredictable behavior would follow. An organism that failed in this way would likely be unable to survive. But when a representation is distributed over many units, it doesn't matter so much if one of the units is damaged. To use an analogy: everyone knows when you make a mistake if you're singing solo, but your mistake isn't so noticeable when you're in a choir.

The distributed nature of connectionist representations accounts for two important features of connectionist models: *fault tolerance* and *graceful degradation*. Fault tolerance refers to the ability of a network to cope with missing or "noisy" input data. Because input representations are distributed, the network is able to give reasonable outputs even if the input is slightly muddled. Continuing with McClelland, Rumelhart, and Hinton's example, suppose that the input is W, O, R, and the fourth letter is partially obscured so that it's ambiguous between R and K. McClelland and colleagues found that because the ambiguous input was *similar enough* to the input W, O, R, K, the network still generated the correct output WORK. Thus the network can read a word that's partially smudged or obscured, in just the same way humans can.

Graceful degradation refers to the gradual (rather than abrupt) decline in the network's performance following damage to the system or to the input data. In a large network that uses distributed representations, removing some of the units will lead to only a slightly impaired output. If one of the units in McClelland and colleagues' word-recognition network were removed, the output unit for the correct word would still be the most active, but its activity level might be slightly lower; the network still recognizes the correct word, but one might say that the network is marginally less confident about its judgment. By contrast, in a system employing local representations, the removal of a representation results in a total inability to perform: if someone has removed the S page of the phone book, you simply won't be able to find Smith's telephone number.

In addition to their capacity for overcoming obstacles that are put in their paths, connectionist systems also display some positive abilities. The most prominent of these is the ability to *learn*—i.e., to change their input-output relations. Recall that the influence of one unit on another is accounted for by the strength of the connection between them. Connectionist models are able to learn by *changing* the strengths of the connections between units. For example, one learning rule might be: if the connected units A and B are both active at the same time, increase the strength of the connection between them. This is reminiscent of the kind of conditioning we saw in behaviorist psychology, but transposed to the level of neurons. Pavlov's dogs came to associate two events that were presented simultaneously; in connectionist models, association can be between two simultaneously active units. This kind of learning is sometimes called Hebbian learning (after

Donald Hebb, who first proposed it). Proponents of the Hebbian learning rule put it this way: units that fire together, wire together.

There are many different ways in which learning can take place in a neural net. The example above is a case of unsupervised learning, because the connection strengths are not directly manipulated by an outside force. In other cases, learning is supervised by an experimenter who acts as a teacher by telling the network whether it got the association right or wrong. The network can thus learn from its experience by changing the weights of its connections so that the next time it receives that input, it will produce an output that is closer to being correct. In each case, learning is implemented by precise rules that determine *how much* the weights of the connections between units are to be changed in response to some stimulus. The teacher can help a connectionist network to home in on the right output, in a manner akin to the children's game where someone calls out "hotter" or "colder" depending on how close the players are to finding an object.

Because networks learn in this way, researchers have found that they can respond to new or unanticipated input in an appropriate fashion. Suppose the network knows the correct output when faced with the thought of lolling on a Hawaiian beach, but then receives some input about lolling on a Caribbean beach. Since these two inputs are similar, the outputs of the network will also be similar. Even if the network has never before received any information about the Caribbean, its existing set of weights and connections ensure that it is capable of an educated guess as to what the right output will be. Connectionists therefore claim that their models are capable of appropriate *generalizations.*

As a result of this ability to learn and generalize, the type of memory that one finds in connectionist models is quite different from that found in classical models. If you want to access a piece of information in a standard computer memory, you must locate the address before retrieving the information contained there. In a desktop computer, for example, the "address" is the name of the file, and the information stored there is the content of that file. You have to know what the file is called before you can open and read it. Similarly, in a telephone directory the address is the spelling of the person's name, and the information stored there is their telephone number. The only way to retrieve the number is with the correct spelling of the name—you have to know the "address" in order to get the information you want.

Connectionist models can, in effect, work the other way around;

they can use part of the content of a stored item as a kind of cue for accessing the rest of it. As we saw in the example of fault tolerance, the distributed representations used by connectionist models allow them to fill in missing pieces of information. In the case of connectionist memory, networks are often able to reconstruct a whole pattern if they are given only part of that pattern as input. Since memories can be accessed by their contents, connectionists call this *content-addressable memory.*

Content-addressable memory is also a prominent feature of the human mind. Consider the following question: what's the name of a cold-blooded vertebrate that has gills, lives in water, and is sometimes eaten by humans? It's not very easy to answer this sort of question with a dictionary. To find the place where the requisite information— the word "fish"—is stored, one would have to use either trial and error, or exhaustive search. Human beings, however, are exceptional in their ability to answer such questions, as you doubtless proved to yourself upon reading the question above. Similarly, connectionist models display content-addressable memory as a natural consequence of their use of distributed representations. Since both humans and connectionist systems are good at performing feats of content-addressable memory, advocates argue that connectionist models can provide a better insight into the nature and operations of the human mind.

The same kind of argument is often repeated with the other putative strengths of connectionist models. Graceful degradation following injury and fault tolerance are both prominent features of real human cognition. Connectionist systems naturally display these abilities, whereas classical systems generally don't. So, the argument goes, connectionism seems to be the better approach for explaining human performance. As we noted above, although it might seem that the strongest allure of connectionism is its neurophysiological realism, connectionist models are of *psychological* interest insofar as they do a good job of modeling various aspects of real cognition.

8.2. Criticisms of Connectionism

Section 8.1 summarized what was good about connectionism. We turn now to the negative side of the ledger. The most influential criticism of the connectionist approach comes from Jerry Fodor and

Zenon Pylyshyn (Fodor and Pylyshyn 1988). Recall that according to Fodor's language of thought hypothesis, our mental representations are structured in a language-like way. One language-like feature of thought that was barely mentioned in Chapter 7 is the fact that thoughts can be added together to form other thoughts in just the same way that letters are put together to form words, words are put together to form sentences, and so on. If you can form the ideas of "John," "Mary," and "love," then you can compose the thought "John loves Mary," or "Mary loves John." These more complex thoughts have what Fodor and Pylyshyn call *composite structure*.

The notion of composite structure can be made clear by an example from chemistry. Consider the difference between atoms and molecules. Atoms are the basic building blocks of ordinary matter, whereas molecules are complex structures that are built out of collections of atoms. For example, the water molecule is built out of two hydrogen atoms and one oxygen atom. The laws of chemistry specify which atoms can combine to form molecules. Fodor's language of thought hypothesis may be understood in similar terms. We can liken the sentence or the thought "John loves Mary" to a molecule composed of three atoms. The sentence or thought "Mary loves John" would be a *different* molecule composed of a different arrangement of the same atoms—like an isomer. The laws of grammar specify all the permissible ways that words can be joined to form sentences, and the laws of cognition specify how the corresponding atomic thoughts can be combined into molecular thoughts. The sentences and thoughts that have a composite structure are those that are akin to molecules.

It's clear that cognitive operations must be sensitive to the composite structure of the thoughts that they process; there's a world of difference between the thought "John loves Mary" and the thought "Mary loves John," even though the two molecules are composed of the same atoms. Classical symbol-crunching architectures are very good at portraying this sort of thing, since the rules they obey—their programs—can be set up so that their operations are sensitive to the structure of the symbolic representations that they manipulate. In the case of language, we could construct a rule that says, "If 'A loves B' is a grammatically correct sentence, then so is 'B loves A'." More generally, the rules could be written so that certain atoms are labelled as nouns and other atoms are labelled as verbs, and the computer's program (like the rules of grammar) specifies the ways in which it is permissible to combine them.

Fodor and Pylyshyn try to show that connectionist systems, in stark contrast to classical systems, cannot process representations in a way that is sensitive to their composite structures. As a result, they argue, connectionist systems cannot account for two important features of thinking: its *productivity* and its *systematicity*. What Fodor and Pylyshyn mean by the productivity of thought is the fact that, just as there are indefinitely many molecular sentences that can be composed from a language with only a finite set of atomic words, so can a person compose and entertain any of an indefinite number of molecular *thoughts* that are composed from a finite number of atomic mental representations. Fodor and Pylyshyn argue that we can do this because our "programs" allow us recursively to combine atomic thoughts in such a way as to *produce* a vast number of molecules. If we are in possession of a handful of atoms, such as "John," "Bob," "Mary," "Anne," "loves," "hates," "fears," we can specify rules of combination that enable us to produce a huge variety of molecular thoughts—"John loves Mary," "Bob loves Anne," "Anne fears Mary," "Mary hates Bob," "John fears Bob," and so on. With the addition of a sentential connective like "and," the number of constructible thoughts becomes strictly infinite—one available infinite series is "John loves Mary," the redundant but coherent "John loves Mary, and John loves Mary," "John loves Mary, and John loves Mary, and John loves Mary," and so on.

What Fodor and Pylyshyn mean by systematicity is that there is often an intrinsic and essential relationship between molecules composed of the same atoms: some thoughts are systematically related to other thoughts. So, for example, the molecular thoughts "John loves Mary" and "John loves pie" both contain the atomic representation "John." If you lack the atomic representation "John," you will be unable to form *either* molecular thought. Similarly, if you're capable of entertaining the thought "John loves Mary," you're also capable of forming the thought "Mary loves John" (even if you don't *believe* either one). Psychologists have never found a person who could think the thought "John loves Mary" but could *not* think the thought "Mary loves John." The two thoughts are part of a *system* of ideas that's possessed completely, or not at all. This is why we say thinking is systematic.

As we noted above, classical systems are very good at processing molecules in a way that is sensitive to their atomic structure; the rules that they follow when combining and manipulating representations can be set up to do so. Classical systems can therefore offer an explanation of why it is that human thought displays productivity and systematicity: humans can reason productively and systematically because our programs are set up that way. By contrast, Fodor and Pylyshyn argue, connectionist systems cannot process representations in a way that is sensitive to their structure because connectionist representations *do not have* a composite structure. Consider the two connectionist representations, mentioned above, of the desire to loll on a Hawaiian or Caribbean beach. Although we view the representations as being composed of 0s and 1s, the way a network *processes* these representations is by treating them as unique, indivisible *atomic* structures. For a connectionist model, the two representations are:

[lolling on a beach in Hawaii]

and

[lolling on a beach in the Caribbean].

A network can compare these different representations and calculate their relative similarity, but each representation is nonetheless regarded as an atom rather than as a molecule composed of atoms. A virtue of doing so, as we have seen, is that connectionist networks can display fault tolerance and graceful degradation: if part of the representation is faulty or damaged, then its similarity to a previously learned representation is enough to allow the network to give a sensible response. However, in some cases, very similar representations should give rise to very *different* responses. Although they differ only in terms of the location of the beach, the two desires we are considering should give rise to different behaviors—booking different flights, going to different airports, obtaining different travel visas, and so on.

Classical systems will allow for this difference because their representations have composite structure. The difference between the following two representations, both stored in the "desire" box,

[Lolling on a beach] + [in Hawaii]

and

[Lolling on a beach] + [in the Caribbean],

should be enough to generate different behaviors by virtue of the differences in one of their atoms. Classical systems also allow for systematicity because both representations contain one and the same lolling-on-a-beach atom; an essential relationship between the two representations is guaranteed. Finally, classical systems allow for productivity, because the "location" atom could be replaced with many alternatives (such as [in France] or [in Spain] or [on the moon]), so as to generate an enormous number of other possible desires.

Because connectionist models treat all representations as atoms rather than molecules with composite structure, Fodor and Pylyshyn conclude that they cannot display productivity and systematicity. Since productivity and systematicity are important features of human cognition, connectionism does not provide a good model of cognitive processes. The allure of connectionism, they argue, can only be that it provides one account of how computational processes are implemented by the brain. Contrary to the point made by McClelland, Rumelhart, and Hinton, connectionism according to Fodor and Pylyshyn is *only* of interest insofar as it explains the physiological mechanisms underlying a cognitive-level story that is better told by the classical approach. The ultimate conclusion of this argument isn't that connectionism is worthless. Even if Fodor and Pylyshyn are right that connectionism can only tell a story about how cognition is physiologically implemented, that would still be a significant accomplishment for cognitive science:

> If connectionism implements classicism, connectionism gets to be quantum mechanics, and classicism only gets to be chemistry. If there were a Nobel Prize in psychology, an account of how a connectionist network in the brain implements a classical cognitive architecture would surely win it. (McLaughlin 1992, 184)

The debate between classical cognitive scientists and advocates of connectionism has not yet been settled. There currently exists voluminous literature in which some authors have tried to show how connectionist systems *can* be constructed so as to display systematicity and productivity. Some researchers have even attempted to build models that contain *both* neural networks and classical structures. There have been successes and failures on both sides in various battles, but nobody has yet won the war.

8.3. The Dynamical Approach

In an attempt to avoid the seemingly intractable debate between connectionists and classical cognitive scientists, some researchers have tried
to find a "third contender" (this phrase is used by Eliasmith 1996). The
most prominent alternative is advanced by a loosely knit collection of
cognitive scientists who think that the mathematical framework of
dynamical systems theory (DST) is the most appropriate formalism for
describing cognition. DST is an area of mathematics concerned with
describing how complex systems change over time as a result of the
interaction of the different forces operating on them. Instead of com-
putations, representations, and algorithms, DST operates in terms of
forces and differential equations. When DST is applied to the mind,
the main emphasis is on the importance of timing in cognition; DST
is naturally suited to describing how systems change in time. Advocates
of the dynamical approach argue that, since the operations of the mind
are essentially temporal, DST should be used by cognitive scientists.
The dynamical approach is simply the willingness to acknowledge the
seemingly obvious, yet surprisingly neglected, fact that cognition is a
temporal phenomenon. Obvious or not, DST is often seen as a radical
alternative to its classical and connectionist predecessors.

But why must symbol-processing systems neglect issues having to
do with time? After all, in our characterization of Turing machines,
we specified how they function in terms of the different steps they
take; sometimes these are even referred to as time–steps, and numbered
t_1, t_2, and so on. To understand a Turing machine in temporal terms,
you could simply specify how long each step takes; you could then
work out how long the whole process would take by adding up the
steps. The point urged by advocates of the dynamical approach, however, is that in this case, the important thing about the operation of a
Turing machine is the (mere) *ordering* of the steps. The Turing machine
will compute the same function whether its time steps all take one
second or one hour; the actual issues of timing do not matter. What
advocates of the dynamical approach try to emphasize is that actual
quantities of time (not just mere orderings of steps) really are essential
for describing the cognitive activity of a system; in mathematical ter-
minology, they say that the temporal *geometry*, not just the *topology*, is
important. In slightly less technical terms, two of the dynamical
approach's founders, Tim van Gelder and Robert Port, write:

The heart of the problem is *time. Cognitive processes and their context unfold continuously and simultaneously in real time.* Computational models specify a discrete sequence of static internal states in arbitrary "step" time (t_1, t_2, etc.). Imposing the latter onto the former is like wearing shoes on your hands. You can do it, but gloves fit a whole lot better. (van Gelder and Port 1995, 2)

By way of example, consider the problem of making a decision about which stereo system to buy. Many variables must be taken into consideration in order to come up with a decision—price, power, size, aesthetic appearance, availability of service, and so on. In a classical account of such decision-making, the decision maker would assign relative "weights" to each factor (indicating an estimation of that factor's overall importance), as well as specific values for those variables, for each stereo system under consideration. She would come to a decision by representing all these factors symbolically, calculating the weighted sum for each stereo, and choosing the one with the highest score.

Such a view of decision-making is inadequate in the sense that it fails to take into account the phenomenology of the decision-making *process.* Decision-making in humans takes time. It involves deliberation, "changing one's mind," vacillation, inconsistency, and many other features. Some decisions take longer to make than others. Sometimes the mere *passage* of time is enough to make you change your mind (one stereo seemed like the best bargain yesterday, but today you prefer the one that's loudest). These elements don't seem to be included in classical models where issues of time are either ignored or subdued. A dynamical model of decision-making (such as that of Townsend and Busemeyer 1995) would, by contrast, attempt to model the phenomenon in terms of the way the different interacting forces compete and vary as a function of time.

The fundamental dynamical hypothesis is the claim that cognitive systems are dynamical systems. This claim, however, is ambiguous between two alternative readings, resulting in two hypotheses that need to be evaluated. The distinction between the two hypotheses is strongly reminiscent of the distinction in Chapter 6 between metaphysical and methodological behaviorism. Akin to metaphysical behaviorism is what van Gelder calls the *nature hypothesis.* This is the proposal that the mind *is* a dynamical system, and that cognitive performance is the activity of such a system. It's reminiscent of metaphysical behaviorism insofar as it attempts to specify what agents *are*. Akin to methodological behaviorism is what van Gelder calls the *knowledge hypothesis*. This is the proposal that psychology should use the resources of DST, such as differential equations, quantitative time, and talk of interacting forces. It's reminiscent of methodological behaviorism insofar as it attempts to specify how agents should be *studied*, rather than what they actually *are*.

Below, we'll look at one example of the knowledge hypothesis in action that seems to show how some cognitive phenomena can indeed be explained using the theoretical resources of DST. The nature hypothesis, however, has proven to be much more controversial; indeed, it's the target of one of the most prominent criticisms of the dynamical approach to cognition. The objection is that the nature hypothesis is *trivially true*. It's noted that everything in the universe is a dynamical system. Since cognitive agents are part of the universe, it's hardly surprising that they're dynamical systems too. Wielders of this objection point out that everything changes continuously in time: rivers flow, planets orbit around the sun, weather patterns change, and so on. In fact, even computers change continuously in time when you get down to the atoms of which they're composed. Moreover, all these temporal changes are causally determined by a set of interacting forces. It's therefore not surprising that cognitive agents—whether they be people introspecting and lying on psychoanalysts' couches, rats running around in mazes, or thinking supercomputers—also change continuously in time as a result of multiple interacting forces. In sum, the objection is that the nature hypothesis is true of cognitive agents because it's true of *everything*.

Whether or not this objection is taken to be damaging, the knowledge hypothesis doesn't seem to be subject to it—it's an open question whether or not psychology ought to be done using the mathematical framework of DST. The last decade or so has seen the knowledge hypothesis in action with the development of a number of relatively successful dynamical models of cognitive phenomena. One of the most famous examples is a dynamical model of the famous *A-not-B error*, which was first studied by Jean Piaget (1952, 1954). If you take an infant between seven and twelve months old and hide a toy she likes under one of two boxes in front of her, she will reach for the correct box in order to get the toy. However, if you hide the toy under box A a few times, and then switch to hiding the toy under box B, the infant makes the A-not-B error and reaches toward box A, even though she saw you hiding it under B.

Why does this happen? Piaget argued that it has something to do with the infant's understanding of object permanence. Some have contended that the error is due to the infant's impoverished concept of space. Others have suggested that the infant's memory is underdeveloped. Investigation of the matter is substantially complicated by the fact that the effect is enormously sensitive to slight changes in the experimental conditions, such as the delay between viewing and reaching, the way the scene is viewed, the number of trials, the presence of distracting stimuli, and so on. Given the right configuration of experimental conditions, even adults can succumb to the error!

Each of the hypotheses manages to explain a limited subset of the data, but fails to deliver an adequate account of the overall phenomenon. Psychologist Esther Thelen and her colleagues (Thelen, Schöner, Scheier, and Smith 2001) contend that this is because all of the competing hypotheses focus on the infant's *internal* machinery—the way she thinks about the world. Such accounts view the error as a *cognitive* one, which is to be explained in terms of the infant's grasp of concepts, her mental representation of objects, and her underdeveloped way of processing those representations. Thelen et al. suggest that, in explaining the error, we focus instead on the infant's *reaching activity*, where the important factors are looking, planning, reaching, and remembering. According to their dynamical view, the infant's reaching behavior is subject to many different competing forces—those of memory, visual input, planning, and even seemingly mundane features, such as the mass of the arm. These forces interact and evolve over time so as to generate the observed reaching behavior. The model proposed by Thelen et al. quantifies all these factors and relates them in a complicated differential equation that specifies how an infant's inclination to reach in a certain direction changes over time. Their model reproduces the classic A-not-B error, together with many of the contextual subtleties that caused problems for previous hypotheses. Moreover, it does so without making reference to inner representations or algorithms. Because of this, many commentators (including Thelen et al. themselves) have pointed out the strong contrast between this kind of dynamical model and the more familiar computational models favored by its classical and connectionist predecessors.

Thelen et al.'s model provides some evidence in favor of the knowledge hypothesis by showing that psychology *can* proceed using the tools and concepts of dynamical systems theory. Another theoretical implication of the model is that, by focusing on the *activity of reaching* instead of on internal representations and programs, Thelen et al. are concerned with what the infant is *doing* rather than what she is *thinking*. As a consequence, their model emphasizes the constraints of the body and of the environment on cognitive processes. We'll have a closer look at these bodily and environmental factors in the next section.

8.4. Situated Cognition

It's almost a truism that a cognitive agent's body and environment are pragmatically important for cognitive activity: we all rely on devices such as shopping lists and diaries, and even adults sometimes resort to counting on their fingers. What is relatively new is the growing realization that these "implementation details" are of *theoretical* significance. Thelen et al.'s model fits in with this growing movement toward theories of cognitive activity that emphasize the role of the body and the environment. These different aspects are sometimes called "embodiment" and "embeddedness" separately; taken together, they constitute what has been called the situated approach to cognition.

It's instructive to note the reasons why an agent's situatedness has traditionally been underemphasized. The historical roots of the kind of cognitive science that downplays situatedness can be traced back at least as far as Descartes. Of course, Descartes is (in)famous for his metaphysical doctrine of dualism; the chief feature of the Cartesian conception of mind is the fact that it need not be embodied. The methodological consequence of this metaphysical view is that, just as physiologists need not study the mind in order to understand the body, so psychologists need not study the body (or the environment) in order to study the mind. Classical (and, to a lesser extent, connectionist) cognitive science inherited the view that the mind is something to be studied apart from the body and the world. Of course, the mind-world interface—the mechanisms of sensory transduction and, to a lesser extent, muscular activity—*are* still studied by classical cognitive scientists, but only insofar as they are (mere) implementation details concerning how the self-sufficient mind is connected with the body and the world.

In Thelen et al.'s model, referring only to inner processes, would not be sufficient to account for the observed behavior, since such internal processes are only one part of a bigger explanatory story that includes aspects of the infant's body and environment. Dynamical systems theory has been touted as the ideal mathematical framework for understanding this situatedness: one can conceive of an agent's body and its environment as "coupled" dynamical systems, and then use the mathematical framework of DST for explaining their interaction.

This move toward including aspects of an agent's body and environment as essential parts of their cognitive capabilities is a growing trend. The examples we mentioned above—the use of diaries and shopping lists—are cases in which humans are capable of modifying the environment so as to increase their *storage* capacity. In other cases, there is some evidence that humans can use the environment to augment their *processing* capacity (or speed). One example, described by Lave, Murtaugh, and de la Rocha (1984), involves people who were asked to make three-quarters of a recipe that called for two-thirds of a cup of cottage cheese. They found that one participant, who was unable to do the calculation in her head, simply measured out the full two-thirds of a cup, flattened the cottage cheese out into a circle, and then cut away and discarded the unneeded quarter of that circle. One natural way of interpreting this example is to say that the person let the world do the processing, rather than shouldering the computational load internally. These kinds of examples shift focus away from the abstract and detached reasoning with which classical cognitive science (following Descartes) has traditionally been concerned, and toward the more concrete and engaged activity involved in making one's way through a "noisy" environment. As Brian Cantwell Smith puts it,

> The situated movement . . . views intelligent human behavior as engaged, socially and materially embodied activity, arising within the specific concrete details of particular (natural) settings, rather than as an abstract, detached, general-purpose process of logical or formal ratiocination. (Smith 1999, 769)

This insight has been employed with some success in the design of robots. Perhaps the most famous example is the robot "Herbert" designed by Rodney Brooks of the MIT AI lab (Brooks 1991). Herbert's task was relatively simple—to collect empty soda cans from around the laboratory—but accomplishing the task was made quite tricky by the complex, cluttered, and changing environment he would have to negotiate. A robot with a classical architecture might try to accomplish this task by using visual data to generate an internal map of the environment, identifying the locations of the cans on that internal map, and then computing the optimal route between all the locations thus identified. Such a solution would be computationally expensive (since it requires the map to be *stored* and the optimal route to be *computed*) as well as fragile (since the environment can change rapidly as the other inhabitants of the lab go about their business).

Brooks' alternative approach was to build a robot composed of several relatively independent subsystems, each of which responds directly to some feature of the local environment. Herbert's subsystems displays such low-level abilities as obstacle avoidance, and the abilities to follow a wall, recognize soda cans, and move the arm toward recognized objects. Each of the subsystems is structured so that once its job is complete, control is handed over to a different subsystem. For example, the recognition module locates a soda can, and then hands over control to Herbert's wheels; the wheels move toward the target, and then hand over control to Herbert's arm; the arm extends toward the target, and then hands over control to the "grasping" mechanism, and so on. Brooks' contention is that Herbert does not work, as classical systems would, by constructing an internal map on which the can's location is plotted. Rather, he argues, each of these behaviors is controlled directly by local environmental stimuli (such as the presence of a can or the presence of an obstacle).

Brooks explicitly cites the *lack* of internal representations as an advantage. Since Herbert doesn't have to construct or process representations, he avoids spending time doing so. Since he doesn't maintain an internal map, he can do without costly memory resources; moreover, he doesn't need to spend time updating the map when faced with environmental changes. Brooks suggests that rather than representing the world, the world itself is its own best model.

It's not clear, in fact, that Herbert is entirely devoid of internal representations. "Soda can recognition," it would seem, must make use of some representational abilities, even if Herbert doesn't plot the locations of soda cans on an internally represented map. Furthermore, it would be premature to conclude, on the evidence of Herbert alone, that *humans* don't need to use internal representations to navigate their way around the world. Indeed, one of the striking things about human cognition is that we can sometimes reason about things in the *absence* of interaction with the world—we can sit silently in an armchair with our eyes closed and entertain the idea of lounging on a Hawaiian beach. In contrast, systems like Herbert depend on the world to organize their actions.

Perhaps it's best to take the antirepresentational pronouncements of robotics enthusiasts with a grain of salt. Nonetheless, the central insight—that in many cases, cognitive tasks can be performed with *less* by way of internal resources than the classical approach suggests—is an important one, particularly from the viewpoint of evolution. If some cognitive tasks can be accomplished by making use of environmental "shortcuts," then it's likely that creatures would have evolved to capitalize on such a possibility. Andy Clark refers to this as the "007 principle":

> In general, evolved creatures will neither store nor process information in costly ways when they can use the structure of their environment and their operations upon it as a convenient stand-in for the information processing operations concerned. That is, know only as much as you need to know to get the job done. (Clark 1989, 64)

In short, there's no need to use costly internal processing and storage resources when you can use the environment to do the job instead.

A lot is hidden, however, in the final sentence of the 007 principle. For one thing, just how much is "as much as you need" will vary from case to case; perhaps in sufficiently complex cases, we *do* need representations as stand-ins for environmental features. If one has inner resources that are not in use (i.e., if it would *not* be costly to use them), then one is free to know *more* than one needs to. It may also be that the kinds of capacities that we class as paradigmatically *cognitive* are just those that require something more than low-level sensory-motor interaction with the world. Nobody contends that Herbert really does have a mind, and perhaps that's precisely because of his inability to reason about soda cans in the absence of environmental interaction. So it seems that a strong antirepresentationalism may not be warranted on the evidence of extant research in situated activity alone.

This complaint—that dynamical and situated approaches make too much of a generalization on the basis of insufficient evidence—forms the heart of what we take to be the most substantial criticism of the most recent developments in cognitive science. Many authors have alleged that these approaches are too new to permit an accurate judgment of whether they will prove to be successful in the long run. In particular, to assume that the low-level behaviors will "scale up" smoothly to the higher-level ones requires a leap that many cognitive scientists are unwilling to make. The charge is that what passes for dynamical or situated *cognitive* science is in fact kinesiology or mere ethology, and furthermore that it's not obvious that kinesiology and ethology are continuous with psychology.

The assumption implicitly relied on by proponents of DST and situatedness is one that Andy Clark calls *cognitive incrementalism*. This is the thesis that "you do indeed get full-blown, human cognition by gradually adding 'bells and whistles' to basic (embodied, embedded) strategies of relating to the present at hand" (Clark 2001, 135). The trouble is that nobody knows whether the thesis of cognitive incrementalism is true—it's too early to tell whether psychological capacities such as planning next year's vacation and thinking about philosophy can ultimately be understood in the same terms as the capacity to reach for an object or navigate an environment in search of soda cans. In fact, the thesis of cognitive incrementalism seems to be intuitively quite *im*plausible. To the extent that some psychological functions rely on abilities that are relatively *independent* of low-level sensory-motor skill, the incrementalist assumption will turn out to be unwarranted. At present, nobody has any idea which way it will go.

8.5. Conclusions

Where does this leave us? Although each approach in contemporary cognitive science seems to offer some insight into the nature of the mind, each also has its own distinctive shortcomings. Connectionism looks promising because it offers an explanation of features of cognitive performance such as fault tolerance and graceful degradation, which elude the explanatory scope of the classical approach. But connectionism has problems of its own. Despite its strength in areas where the classical approach is weak, connectionism proves to be *weak* where classical cognitive science is *strong:* it can't account for the productivity and systematicity of human thought. Finally, although both dynamical and situated approaches seem to succeed in accounting for the importance of timing and embodiment in cognition, they both rely on an assumption which at best looks to be as yet unwarranted by the evidence, and at worst looks to be intuitively implausible. Despite some relatively successful work in small areas of psychology, none of the most recent developments in cognitive science has been able to provide us with a theoretical framework for the whole of psychology.

The same conclusion can be arrived at via different and more fundamental considerations: all of the recent approaches to the study of mind that we've canvassed remain disturbingly quiet on the unresolved problem of qualia—how it is that our mental states and processes are imbued with qualitative or phenomenal content. Searle's Chinese room thought experiment is a variant of this problem, and as such, applies to the approaches discussed in this chapter as well as to the classical approach. In the vocabulary advanced in Chapter 6, we can imagine connectionist and dynamical/situated zombies who function just as these theoretical approaches stipulate, but who have no accompanying subjective experiences. Neither the classical nor the postclassical approaches have anything to say about qualia. The irony is that many nonpsychologists believe that qualia are what psychology is all about.

The grand conclusion of this section, of this book, and of a generation of cognitive-scientific research is quickly stated: *the mind is still a mystery.* There is no persuasive account of where and how it fits into our otherwise coherent and enormously successful scientific view of the world. One fascinating possibility is that the current scientific world-view will have to be drastically altered in order to make room for mind. Alternatively, it's been suggested by respectable cognitive scientists that the mystery of mind is irremediable (e.g., McGinn 1989, 1996). After all, there's no a priori reason to suppose that the human mind possesses the cognitive capacity to answer every question that it's able to frame. Our inability to get clear on the nature of mind may be due to the special reflexivity involved in the mind's trying to understand itself. Perhaps close analysis will show that this enterprise is akin to trying to lift oneself by one's own bootstraps.

Suggestions for
Further Reading

Cartesianism

For a brief but precise discussion of Descartes' philosophy, J. Cottingham's *Descartes* (New York: Blackwell, 1986) is widely regarded as authoritative, and its discussion of Descartes' philosophy of mind in Chapters 5 and 6 is particularly good. M. Rozemond's *Descartes' Dualism* Cambridge, MA: MIT Press, 1998) is a more thorough treatment of Descartes' view, situating it in its historical and philosophical context. A modern reinterpretation and defense of the Cartesian theory of the mind is given in J. Foster *The Immaterial Self: A Defence of the Cartesian Dualist Conception of the Mind* (London: Routledge, 1991).

The quintessential statement of materialism is given in P. M. Churchland *Matter and Consciousness* (Cambridge, MA: MIT Press, 1988). A more technical discussion can be found in J. Kim, *Mind in a Physical World* (Cambridge, MA: MIT Press, 1998). Attempts to find some middle ground between the extremes of materialism and dualism include D. C. Dennett *Consciousness Explained* (Boston: Little, Brown & Co., 1991); D. Chalmers *The Conscious Mind: In Search of a Fundamental Theory* (New York: Oxford University Press, 1996); and C. McGinn *The Mysterious Flame* (New York: Basic Books, 1999), all of which offer widely divergent viewpoints on the mind-body problem and the nature of consciousness.

Introspective Psychology

Most of the important works in the introspective tradition are out of print. The interested reader will have to visit the local university library. W. Wundt *Principles of Physiological Psychology* (New York:

MacMillan, 1904) was translated by Titchener, and provides a nice overview of the former's take on scientific psychology. Alternatively, W. Wundt *Lectures on Human and Animal Psychology* (New York: Macmillan, 1896) gives a more compressed introduction. Titchener's psychological system can be found in his *A Textbook of Psychology* (New York: Macmillan, 1910). O. Külpe's *Outlines of Psychology* (New York: Macmillan, 1895), again translated by Titchener, provides the other side of the terminal imageless-thought debate. W. Köhler's *Gestalt Psychology* (New York: Liveright, 1930) and K. Koffka's *Principles of Gestalt Psychology* (London: K. Paul, Trench, Trubner, 1935) are classic statements of the gestalt alternative. More recently, some theorists have resurrected the introspectionists' issues in a modern light. Of these, W. Lyons *The Disappearance of Introspection* (Cambridge, MA: MIT Press, 1986), and T. H. Leahey "The Mistaken Mirror: On Wundt and Titchener's Psychologies," *Journal of the History of Behavioral Sciences* 17 (1981): 273–82, are particularly interesting.

Psychoanalysis

S. Freud's *The Complete Introductory Lectures on Psychoanalysis* (New York: Norton, 1917/1966) was intended by Freud as an introduction to his major ideas that's accessible to the nonspecialist. A more comprehensive selection of Freud's writings can be found in A. A. Brill (ed. and trans.) *The Basic Writings of Sigmund Freud* (New York: Modern Library, 1938). This book contains many of Freud's classic works, such as *The Psychopathology of Everyday Life, The Interpretation of Dreams,* and *The History of the Psychoanalytic Movement.* P. Roazen *Freud and His Followers* (New York: Knopf, 1975) is a collection of biographies of all the main psychoanalytic players. A key player was Heinz Hartmann, whose *Ego Psychology and the Problem of Adaptation* (trans. D. Rapaport) (New York: International Universities Press, 1958) introduced the most important amendment to orthodox psychoanalytic theory.

Behavioral Psychology

B. F. Skinner's *Science and Human Behavior* (New York: Macmillan, 1953) is an introduction to the science of behavioral psychology by the prototypical behavioral psychologist. B. F. Skinner's *About Behaviorism* (New York: Knopf, 1976) is an introduction to the philosophy of behaviorism by the prototypical behaviorist. It's also still valuable to read the words of the founder—J. B. Watson *Behaviorism* (New York: W. W. Norton & Co, 1930/1970). The works of Clark Hull are indigestible to the modern reader, but the seminal critique by R. W. White "Motivation Reconsidered: The Concept of Competence," *Psychological Review* 66 (1959): 297-333 contains everything that the nonspecialist needs to know about drive theory. The most influential critique of the behavioral approach was undoubtedly N. Chomksy "A Review of B. F. Skinner's *Verbal Behavior,*" *Language* 35 (1959): 26-58, which was far broader in its import than its title might suggest. For an extended treatment of behaviorism by a philosopher, the classic work is G. Ryle *The Concept of Mind* (London: Hutchinson, 1949).

Classical Cognitive Science

J. Fodor's *The Language of Thought* (New York: Thomas Crowell, 1975) is pivotal in the development of cognitive science, as is J. Fodor *The Modularity of Mind* (Cambridge, MA: MIT Press, 1983). J. Fodor's *The Mind Doesn't Work That Way* (Cambridge, MA: MIT Press, 2000) provides a relatively recent overview of some of the key tenets (and resulting problems) of the classical approach. Hilary Putnam's *Mind, Language and Reality* (New York: Cambridge University Press, 1975) contains many of his classic papers on the functionalist foundations of early cognitive science. The contribution of Noam Chomsky—the third founding father—is probably best represented by his *Rules and Representations* (New York: Columbia University Press, 1980). An accessible introduction to the entire field is A. Clark *Mindware* (New York: Oxford University Press, 2001). Another is P. Thagard *Mind: Introduction to Cognitive Science* (Cambridge, MA: MIT Press, 1996). Thagard has also edited a collection of important papers in cognitive science: P. Thagard (ed.) *Mind Readings* (Cambridge, MA: MIT Press, 1998). On the question of artificial intelligence, one need look no further than J. Haugeland (ed.) *Mind Design II: Philosophy, Psychology and Artificial Intelligence* (Cambridge, MA: MIT Press, 1997).

Connectionism

For the seminal and technical introduction to connectionism and its applications, one must look to D. E. Rumelhart, J. L. McClelland, and the PDP Research Group *Parallel Distributed Processing: Explorations in the Microstructure of Cognition* (Cambridge, MA: MIT Press, 1986). A more accessible introduction to the theory and practice of connectionism is P. McLeod, K. Plunket, and E. T. Rolls *Introduction to Connectionist Modelling of Cognitive Processes* (Oxford: Oxford University Press, 1998). Philosophical investigations of connectionism's impact and scope can be found in both T. Horgan and J. Tienson *Connectionism and the Philosophy of Psychology* (Cambridge, MA: MIT Press, 1996), and A. Clark *Microcognition* (Cambridge, MA: MIT Press, 1989). T. Horgan and J. Tienson (eds.) *Connectionism and the Philosophy of Mind* (Boston: Kluwer, 1991) provide an excellent selection of papers that explore the philosophical consequences of connectionism. On the debate between classical and connectionist cognitive science, see S. Pinker and J. Mehler (eds.) *Connections and Symbols* (Cambridge, MA: MIT Press, 1988); this book contains the famous Fodor and Pylyshyn paper, together with a number of connectionist responses.

Dynamical and Situated Cognitive Science

On the dynamical approach to cognitive science, many of van Gelder's papers are especially illuminating—see his "What Might Cognition Be, if Not Computation," *Journal of Philosophy* 92 (1995): 345-81, and his "The Dynamical Hypothesis in Cognitive Science," *Behavioral and Brain Sciences* 21 (1998): 615-28. For a look at the variety of dynamical models, see R. Port and T. van Gelder (eds.) *Mind as Motion* (Cambridge, MA: MIT Press, 1995). M. Giunti's *Computation, Dynamics and Cognition* (New York: Oxford University Press, 1997) provides some interesting insights into issues relating to the philosophy of science. E. Thelen and L. Smith *A Dynamic Systems Approach to the Development of Cognition and Action* (Cambridge, MA: MIT Press, 1994) apply the dynamical approach to developmental psychology. The antidynamicist viewpoint is presented in C. Eliasmith "The Third Contender: A Critical Examination of the Dynamicist Theory of Cognition," *Philosophical Psychology* 9 (1996): 441-

63, and in R. Grush "Review of Port and van Gelder's *Mind as Motion*," *Philosophical Psychology* 10 (1997): 233-42. Finally, A. Clark *Being There* (Cambridge, MA: MIT Press, 2001) provides us with a philosophical treatment of embodied and embedded cognition.

Overviews

An introduction to more or less the same subject matter as the present volume—the competition—is O. Flanagan *The Science of The Mind* (2nd ed.) (Cambridge, MA: MIT Press, 1991). The topics discussed in S. Cunningham's *What Is a Mind?* (Indianapolis: Hackett Publishing Company, 2001) also have a substantial amount of overlap with ours. G. Miller *Psychology: The Science of Mental Life* (New York: Harper & Row, 1973) is an engaging survey of various topics and famous figures in psychology. For a more historical take (going right back to Plato) on some of the big theoretical debates in psychology, see the witty and comprehensive survey by J. Macnamara *Through the Rearview Mirror* (Cambridge, MA: MIT Press, 1999).

Collections of Primary Source Materials

There are many excellent anthologies in which the interested reader can find the primary sources for the positions discussed in this book. D. C. Chalmers (ed.) *Philosophy of Mind: Classical and Contemporary Readings* (Oxford: Oxford University Press, 2002) is a wide-ranging and nicely organized collection of many of the foundational papers in the discussion of dualism, behaviorism, identity theory, and functionalism. It also contains many articles on specific problems, such as consciousness and the problem of mental content. A shorter but nonetheless useful paperback collection of articles in a similar vein is W. Lyons (ed.) *Modern Philosophy of Mind* (London: Dent, 1995). For a collection of many of the papers to which we refer in this volume, see A. Kukla (ed.) *Personality Theory: A Book of Readings* (Toronto: Canadian Scholars' Press, 1996). For primary sources in the history of psychology more generally, Chris Green has developed an excellent online collection available at http://psychclassics.yorku.ca/.

Bibliography

Bandura, A., and Walters, R. H. *Social Learning and Personality Development.* New York: Holt, Rinehart & Winston, 1963.

Bannister, D. "A New Theory of Personality." In *New Horizons in Psychology,* edited by B. M. Foss. Harmondswoth: Penguin, 1966.

Brooks, R. "Intelligence Without Representation." *Artificial Intelligence* 47 (1991): 139–59.

Bruce, V., and Young, A. W. "Understanding Face Recognition." *British Journal of Psychology* 77 (1986): 305-27.

Campbell, R., Landis, T., and Regard, M. "Face Recognition and Lipreading: A Neurological Dissociation." *Brain* 109 (1986): 509–21.

Chalmers, D. *The Conscious Mind: In Search of a Fundamental Theory.* New York: Oxford University Press, 1996.

Chomsky, N. "On Cognitive Capacity." In *Readings in Philosophy of Psychology Vol. 2,* edited by N. Block. Cambridge, MA: Harvard University Press, 1980.

———. *Knowledge of Language: Its Nature, Origins, and Use.* New York: Praeger, 1986.

Clark, A. *Microcognition.* Cambridge, MA: MIT Press, 1989.

———. *Mindware: An Introduction to the Philosophy of Cognitive Science.* Oxford: Oxford University Press, 2001.

Cottingham, J., Stoothoff, R., Murdoch, D., and Kenny, A., eds. *The Philosophical Writings of Descartes: The Correspondence.* Cambridge: Cambridge University Press, 1991.

Cunningham, S. *What Is a Mind: An Integrative Introduction to the Philosophy of Mind.* Indianapolis: Hackett Publishing Company, 2000.

Davidson, D. "Mental Events." In *Experience and Theory,* edited by L. Foster and J. W. Swanson. Amherst: University of Massachusetts Press, 1970.

Dennett, D. C. "Cognitive Wheels: The Frame Problem of AI." In *Brainchildren,* edited by D. C. Dennett. Cambridge, MA: MIT Press, 1998.

De Renzi, E. "Current Issues in Prosopagnosia." In *Aspects of Face Processing,* edited by H. D. Ellis, M. A. Jeeves, F. Newcombe, and A. Young. Dordrecht: Martinus Nijhoff, 1986.

Descartes, R. *Meditations on First Philosophy.* In *The Philosophical Writings of Descartes, Vols. I & II,* edited by J. Cottingham, R. Stoothoff, and D. Murdoch, Cambridge: Cambridge University Press, 1984.

Dreyfus, H. L. *What Computers* Still *Can't Do: A Critique of Artificial Reason.* Cambridge, MA: MIT Press, 1992.

Eliasmith, C. "The Third Contender: A Critical Examination of the Dynamicist Theory of Cognition." *Philosophical Psychology* 9 (1996): 441–63.

Ellis, A. W., and Young, A. W. *Human Cognitive Neuropsychology.* London: Lawrence Erlbaum Associates, 1988.

Festinger, L. *A Theory of Cognitive Dissonance.* Stanford: Stanford University Press, 1957.

Fodor, J. A. *The Language of Thought.* New York: Thomas Y. Crowell, 1975.

———. "The Mind-Body Problem." *Scientific American* 244 (1981): 114–23.

Fodor, J., and Pylyshyn, Z. "Connectionism and Cognitive Architecture: A Critical Analysis." *Cognition* 28 (1988): 3–71.

Foster, J. *The Immaterial Self: A Defence of the Cartesian Dualist Conception of the Mind.* London: Routledge, 1991.

Franklin, S. *Artificial Minds.* Cambridge, MA: MIT Press, 1998.

Freud, S. *The Complete Introductory Lectures on Psychoanalysis.* New York: Norton, 1917/1966.

———. "Beyond the Pleasure Principle." In *On Metapsychology: The Theory of Psychoanalysis,* edited by S. Freud. London: Penguin, 1920/1984.

Gorman, R.P., and Sejnowksi, T. J. "Learned Classification of Sonar Targets Using a Massively Parallel Network." *IEEE Transactions: Acoustics, Speech and Signal Processing* 36 (1988): 1135-140.

Hartmann, H. *Ego Psychology and the Problem of Adaptation,* translated by D. Rapaport. New York: International Universities Press, 1958.

Hoffman, R. E., and McGlashan, T. H. "Neural Network Models of Schizophrenia." *The Neuroscientist* 7 (2001): 441-54.

Hull, C. L. *Principles of Behavior: An Introduction to Behavior Theory.* New York: Appleton-Century-Crofts, 1943.

James, W. *Principles of Psychology* (2 Vols.). New York: Dover, 1890/1950.

Kimble, G. A., and Garmezy, N. *Principles of General Psychology* (2nd ed.). New York: Ronald Press Co., 1968.

Koffka, K. *Principles of Gestalt Psychology.* London: K. Paul, Trench, Trubner, 1935.

Köhler, W. *Gestalt Psychology.* New York: Liveright, 1930.

Kukla, A. "Toward a Science of Experience." *Journal of Mind and Behavior* 4 (1983): 231–45.

Kurucz, J., and Feldmar, G. "Prosopo-affective Agnosia as a Symptom of Cerebral Organic Disease." *Journal of the American Geriatrics Society* 27 (1979): 225-30.

Kurucz, J., Feldmar, G., and Werner, W. "Prosopo-affective Agnosia Associated with Chronic Organic Brain Syndrome." *Journal of the American Geriatrics Society* 27 (1979): 91–5.

Lackner, J. R., and Garrett, M. "Resolving Ambiguity: Effects of Biasing Context on the Unattended Ear." *Cognition* 1 (1972): 359–72.

Lashley, K. S. "The Problem of Serial Order in Behavior." In *Cerebral Mechanisms in Behavior,* edited by L. A. Jefress. New York: John Wiley, 1951.

Lave, J., Murtaugh, M., and de la Rocha, O. "The Dialectic of Arithmetic in Grocery Shopping." In *Everyday Cognition: Its Development in Social Context,* edited by B. Rogoff and J. Lave. Cambridge, MA: Harvard University Press, 1984.

Lloyd, D. *Simple Minds.* Cambridge, MA: MIT Press, 1989.

Locke, J. *An Essay Concerning Human Understanding,* edited by P. H. Nidditch, Clarendon edition. Oxford: Oxford University Press, 1690/1975.

Macfarlane, D. A. "The Role of Kinesthesis in Maze Learning." *University of California Publications in Psychology* 4 (1930): 277–305.

Malinowski, B. *Sex and Repression in Savage Society.* London: Routledge and Kegan Paul, 1927.

Malone, D. R., Morris, H. H., Kay, M. C., and Levin, H. S. "Prosopagnosia: A Double Dissociation between the Recognition of Familiar and Unfamiliar Faces." *Journal of Neurology, Neurosurgery and Psychiatry* 45 (1982): 820–22.

Maslow, A. *Toward a Psychology of Being* (2nd ed.). Princeton, NJ: Van Nostrand, 1968.

McClelland, D. C., and Atkinson, J. W. "The Projective Expression of

Needs: I. The Effect of Different Intensities of the Hunger Drive on Perception." *Journal of Psychology* 25 (1948): 205–22.

McClelland, J. L., Rumelhart, D. E., and Hinton, G. E. "The Appeal of Parallel Distributed Processing." In *Parallel Distributed Processing: Explorations in the Microstructure of Cognition. Volume 1: Foundations,* edited by D. E. Rumelhart, J. L. McClelland, and the PDP Research Group. Cambridge, MA: MIT Press, 1986.

McGinn, C. "Can We Solve the Mind-Body Problem?" *Mind* 98 (1989): 349–66.

———. *The Character of Mind* (2nd ed.). Oxford: Oxford University Press, 1996.

McLaughlin, B. "The Connectionism/Classicism Battle to Win Souls." *Philosophical Studies* 71 (1992): 163–90.

Mead, M. *Coming of Age in Samoa: A Psychological Study of Primitive Youth for Western Civilisation.* New York: Blue Ribbon Books, 1928.

Montgomery, K. C. "Exploratory Behavior as a Function of 'Similarity' of Stimulation Situations." *Journal of Comparative and Physiological Psychology* 46 (1953): 129–33.

Olds, J. "Physiological Mechanisms of Reward." In *Nebraska Symposium on Motivation* (Vol. 3.), edited by M. R. Jones. Lincoln: University of Nebraska Press, 1955.

Olds, J., and Milner, P. "Positive Reinforcement Produced by Electrical Stimulation of Septal Area and Other Regions of Rat Brain." *Journal of Comparative and Physiological Psychology* 47 (1954): 419–27.

Pavlov, I. P. *Conditioned Reflexes: An Investigation of the Physiological Activity of the Cerebral Cortex,* translated and edited by G. V. Anrep. New York: Dover, 1927/1960.

Piaget, J. *The Origins of Intelligence in Children.* New York: International Universities Press, 1952.

———. *The Construction of Reality in the Child.* New York: Basic Books, 1954.

Plunkett, K., Sinha, C., Moller, M. F., and Strandsby, O. "Symbol Grounding or the Emergence of Symbols? Vocabulary Growth in Children and in a Connectionist Net." *Connection Science* 4 (1992): 293–312.

Preston, J., and Bishop, M. *Views into the Chinese Room: New Essays on Searle and Artificial Intelligence.* Oxford: Oxford University Press, 2002.

Putnam, H. "The Nature of Mental States." In *Mind, Language and Reality,* edited by H. Putnam. Cambridge: Cambridge University Press, 1975.

Rogers, C. *Client Centered Therapy.* Boston: Houghton Mifflin, 1951.

Rumelhart, D. E., and McClelland, J. L. "On Learning the Past Tenses of English Verbs." In *Parallel Distributed Processing* (Vol. 2), edited by D. E. Rumelhart, J. L. McClelland, and the PDP Research Group. Cambridge, MA: MIT Press, 1986.

Rumelhart, D. E., McClelland, J. L., and the PDP Research Group. *Parallel Distributed Processing: Explorations in the Microstructure of Cognition. Volume 1: Foundations.* Cambridge, MA: MIT Press, 1986.

Searle, J. "Minds, Brains and Programs." *Behavioral and Brain Sciences* 3 (1980): 417–57.

Skinner, B. F. *Science and Human Behavior.* New York: Macmillan, 1953.

———. "Paraphrase of Discussion of 'Behaviorism at Fifty'." In *Behaviorism and Phenomenology,* edited by T. W. Wann. Chicago: University of Chicago Press, 1964.

———. *Beyond Freedom and Dignity.* New York: Bantam Books, 1971.

———. *About Behaviorism.* New York: Knopf, 1976.

Smith, B. C. "Situatedness/Embeddedness." In *The MIT Encyclopedia of Cognitive Sciences,* edited by R. A. Wilson, and F. C. Keil. Cambridge, MA: MIT Press, 1999.

Thelen, E., Schöner, G., Scheier, C., and Smith, L. B. "The Dynamics of Embodiment: A Field Theory of Infant Perseverative Reaching." *Behavioral and Brain Sciences* 24 (2001): 1–86.

Thorndike, E. L. *Animal Intelligence: Experimental Studies.* New York: Macmillan, 1911.

Tolman, E. C., and Honzik, C. H. "Introduction and Removal of Reward and Maze Performance in Rats." *University of California Publications in Psychology* 4 (1930): 257–75.

Townsend, J. T., and Busemeyer, J. "Dynamic Representation of Decision Making." In *Mind as Motion,* edited by R. Port and T. van Gelder. Cambridge, MA: MIT Press, 1995.

Turing, A. "Computing Machinery and Intelligence." *Mind* 59 (1950): 433–60.

Tversky, A., and Kahneman, D. "Judgement Under Uncertainty: Heuristics and Biases." *Science* 185 (1974): 1124–131.

van Gelder, T., and Port, R. "It's About Time: An Overview of the

Dynamical Approach to Cognition." In *Mind as Motion,* edited by R. Port and T. van Gelder. Cambridge, MA: MIT Press, 1995.

Watson, J. B. "Psychology as the Behaviorist Views It." *Psychological Review* 20 (1913): 158–76.

———. *Behaviorism.* New York: W. W. Norton & Co, 1930/1970.

Watson, J. B., and Rayner, R. "Conditioned Emotional Responses." *Journal of Experimental Psychology* 3 (1920): 1–14.

Wertheimer, M. *Gestalt Theory.* In *A Sourcebook of Gestalt Psychology,* edited by W. D. Ellis. London: Routledge & Kegan Paul, 1925/1938.

White, R. W. "Motivation Reconsidered: The Concept of Competence." *Psychological Review* 66 (1959): 297–333.

Wundt, W. *Grundzüge der Physiologischen Psychologie (Principles of Physiological Psychology).* Leipzig: Wilhelm Engelmann, 1874.

———. *Lectures on Human and Animal Psychology.* New York: Macmillan, 1896.

Index

ad hoc adjustment, 98, 99
affective discharge, 55
algorithm, 149
anxiety, 73–77
artificial intelligence (AI), 63,
    122–23, 149–51; weak AI,
    151–52, 154; strong AI, 155–56,
    158–59
attribution theory, 132

Bandura and Walters, 103, 104,
    107–8
behavioral psychology, 14, 79–82,
    90, 101, 104–5, 109, 129
behaviorism, 21–3, 28, 35, 36, 37,
    54, 62, 79–81, 84–5, 90, 109,
    129; methodological, 29, 110–13;
    metaphysical, 29, 113–14; radical,
    114, 118; logical, 114–19, 125–26
Berkeley, G., 6
bias, 77–8
Brooks, R., 180
Bruce and Young, 147, 148

Cartesianism, 1–2, 4–5, 46, 60
causation, 10–12
chemistry, 24
Chinese Room argument, 156–59,
    183
Chomsky, N., 105, 141–44
cognitive incrementalism, 182
cognitive science, 36–7, 44–5, 51,
    109, 129, 148
compatibilism, 16
computers, 36, 139

conditioning: classical, 81, 83–5, 89;
    operant, 89. See also law of effect.
connectionism, 162–73, 182
conscious, in the Freudian sense, 30,
    50–51, 57–8, 62–3, 66
content-addressable memory, 169
Copernicus, 14

Dalton, J., 24
Davidson, D., 123
decision theory, 132
defense mechanisms, 72, 75–6
Descartes, R., 1, 4–6, 7–9, 21, 39,
    81–2, 178
determinism, 4–6, 15–20
displacement, 72
dispositions, 116
double dissociation, 146–47
dreams, 30, 56
drive theory, 91–7
dualism, 1–8, 11–13, 15, 21, 29, 114,
    121, 128
dynamical: approach to cognition,
    174–76, 182–83; systems theory,
    (DST), 174, 176, 179

ego, 50–51, 59–60, 64–9, 71–2, 74,
    148; ego psychology, 64
Electra conflict, 67, 68
empirical equivalence, 43
empiricism, viii, 144–45
epiphenomenalism, 9–11, 13
exploratory behavior, 97–9, 100
extinction (in classical conditioning),
    84

197